SELDEN F. COOPER
P.O. Box 36
HERSHEY, PA 17033
HOME: (717) 534-1295
WORK: (908) 775-8953
DECEMBER, 1992

D1559491

NARRATIVE PSYCHOLOGY

The Storied Nature of Human Conduct

Edited by
Theodore R. Sarbin

New York
Westport, Connecticut
London

Library of Congress Cataloging-in-Publication Data

Narrative psychology.

   "Praeger special studies."
   Bibliography: p.
   Includes index.
   1. Discourse analysis, narrative—psychological
aspects. I. Sarbin, Theodore R.
P302.7.N37 1986   401'.41   86-8130
ISBN 0-275-92103-4 (alk. paper)

Library of Congress Catalog Card Number: 86-8130
ISBN: 0-275-92103-4 (alk. paper)

First published in 1986

Praeger Publishers, One Madison Avenue, New York, NY 10010
An imprint of Greenwood Publishing Group, Inc.

Printed in the United States of America

The paper used in this book complies with the Permanent
Paper Standard issued by the National Information Standards
Organization (Z39.48-1984).

10 9 8 7 6 5 4 3

Contents

Preface

The epistemological crisis in social psychology has created a readiness to set aside positivist assumptions and to replace them with other ways of conceptualizing the human condition. The essays collected in this book exemplify the use of the narrative as a root metaphor. Long before there was a science of psychology, men and women created and told stories about the efforts of human beings to make sense of their problematic worlds. Novelists, dramatists, poets, essayists, and film makers – storytellers all – have continued to provide insights about human motives and actions, even during the hundred years that human conduct has been examined by scientific psychology.

The essays make clear that story making, storytelling and story comprehension are fundamental conceptions for a revived psychology. Each makes a case for the storied nature of human action. When taken together, the essays support my claim that narrative psychology is a viable alternative to the positivist paradigm.

Each of the essayists is an established contributor to the corpus of knowledge for which I use the shorthand term "narrative psychology." To each, I convey my heartfelt gratitude for participating in this adventure.

Many colleagues, students, and friends encouraged me in this enterprise and I am grateful for their support and advice. I single out for special thanks Ralph M. Carney, James B. Hall, John I. Kitsuse, James C. Mancuso, and Karl E. Scheibe. I am grateful also to Lorelei Cotovsky for bibliographical assistance and for preparing the index.

No brief acknowledgement can adequately tell a story the central theme of which is my gratitude for the warm encouragement, interest, and understanding of my wife, Genevieve. Her companionship provided the background for what otherwise would have been a lonely occupation – the authorial and editorial work required to bring this project to completion.

Theodore R. Sarbin

Introduction and Overview

Like many of my contemporaries, I became disillusioned with the outcomes of social psychological research and theorizing carried out under the guiding postulates of positivism. In the mid-seventies, the disillusionment was described as a "crisis" (Elms, 1975), and some behavior scientists talked about a malaise, the cause of which was the low predictability and lack of generality of conclusions drawn from traditional research. The influence of the positivist ethos on the discipline was reflected in the entrenched belief that social behavior could be dissected into its elements in the laboratory.

In a time of "blurred genres," to use Geertz's felicitous phrase, I extended my search for metaphors that would attenuate the crisis and enliven the discipline. Clearly, mechanical, spatial, and energy metaphors – the customary sources of dimensions for those who were committed to making social psychology a science – were worn out, no longer capable of generating interesting concepts. I had already raided humanistic studies for metaphors to guide my work. The drama was the source of metaphors for my earlier proposals that social behavior could be more meaningfully described and explained as role enactment (Sarbin, 1943; Sarbin, 1954; Sarbin & Allen, 1968).

From the drama as a basic metaphor to the narrative was but a short step. Since the drama is embedded in narrative, the transition to the study of narrative required no great revision of my study program. To look upon human conduct from the perspective of narrative was facilitated by my encounter with Hayden White's *Metahistory* (1973), which is cited by several contributors to this volume. His demonstration that history writing was a form of storytelling convinced me that the narrative process could be applied to psychological analysis.

Having been influenced by Stephen Pepper's root metaphor method, I entertained the hypothesis that the narrative functioned as a root metaphor (Pepper, 1942). Without identifying it as such, I had been using the "narratory principle" for many years. In my teaching of abnormal psychology, I had found it more useful to report on and analyze life histories, that is, stories about concrete individuals, than to review the experiments done on nameless, faceless subjects, the results of which were expressed as probabilities. Further, in my role as clinician, I could not carry out my work unless I located the clients and their significant others in a narrative plot.

The plan for this volume first came to life during one of my visits to the Center for the Humanities at Wesleyan University in the mid-1970s. Hayden White and the late Louis Mink had each written about the role of narrative in historiography, and Stephen Crites had written about the narrative quality of experience. [These scholars are represented in this book, either as author (Stephen Crites) or as authoritative source.] Leaning on their writings in the philosophy of history and religion, I used narratory ideas in my lectures and occasional papers. In recent years, I have read the books and papers of a score of social scientists and humanists who found the narrative indispensable for reconstructing history or persons.

In the summer of 1983, I prepared a paper for a symposium arranged by Brian Sutton-Smith on psychology and the narrative. Shortly thereafter, I put the plan for this volume into action. *Narratology and Psychology* was the original working title. I invited 14 scholars to write original chapters dealing with one or more aspects of narrative as employed in psychology and related sciences. With but one exception, all agreed to participate.

The chapters are arranged according to the emphasis given different features of the narrative process. The first group centers on the use of the narrative as an integral feature in the scientific enterprise. My chapter, "The Narrative as a Root Metaphor for Psychology," takes Pepper's root metaphor method as a point of departure. I argue that adopting the world view of contextualism for understanding human conduct is likely to lead to better understanding than continuing in the traditions of mechanistic science. The root metaphor of contextualism is the historical act, in all its complexity. I make the claim that the historical act and the narrative are cut from the same cloth. In the body of my chapter, I point to the universality of the story as a guide to living and as a vehicle for understanding the conduct of others.

In "Narrative Form and the Construction of Psychological Science" Kenneth and Mary Gergen address the storied nature of psychological theories of development. They begin their chapter with a reasoned rejection of the empiricist assumption that traditional science provides theories that serve as objective mirrors of the world. Scientific theories are "underdetermined" by events in the world. They are written from preconceptions or world views. They are linguistic products. The authors hold that the form of theoretical description is to a great extent determined by the conventions of discourse, that is, narrative.

Employing a taxonomy for classifying narrative – stability, progression, and regression – they trace the evolution and current status of stimulus-response theories, Piagetian stage theories, and Freudian theories of human development from birth to maturity. The claim that scientific theories are constructed from a scaffold of narrative plots is convincingly argued.

Misia Landau's chapter extends the argument with a concrete example of the implicit use of the hero narrative in forming a theory of evolution. She uses as her text the writings of one of the important early twentieth century authorities on archeology. In "Trespassing in Scientific Narrative: Grafton Elliot Smith and the Temple of Doom" Landau shows how Elliot Smith's hero story influenced his theories of the role of the brain in directing the course of human destiny. The scientist as storyteller trespassed on the scientist as discoverer of fact and creator of theory. The analysis exemplifies Landau's theme: that the ordering and explaining of events are not necessarily separate steps in the rendering of a scientific story.

The three papers included in Part II, Studies of Narratory Competence, address various problems connected with the acquisition of story making and story comprehension. This section may be regarded as the link between traditional psychology and the hermeneutic approach that characterizes much of this book. Appropriately, Brian Sutton-Smith begins his chapter with the recognition of two emerging perspectives for narrative analysis: textual (structural) and hermeneutic (contextual). He points to the parallel dichotomy suggested by Bruner (1984) and employed by Spence in his chapter. Textual analysis follows the paradigmatic mode, and contextual analysis follows the narrative mode. In the first, emphasis is on correlations of competence with age, gender, and so on. In the second, emphasis is on the "meanings" derived from observing the child in the context of storytelling and story comprehension. Sutton-Smith's chapter reflects an alternation between the two perspectives.

He reviews the phase development of story making by children from age two to 12. The youngest children reflect in their stories the interactive play with parents: they produce prosodic patterns when asked to tell a story. No hints are forthcoming of the later story making that is characterized by plot structures.

It is interesting to note that during the period when parents tell stories from picture books, the forms of the stories told by parents and children are different. Parents are plot oriented, young children emphasize melodic patterns. As they mature, children tell more plot-oriented stories. Sutton-Smith introduces us to a useful scheme for sorting the plots. By age ten, the stories are characterized by plots that are familiar to storytellers of the Western world: the hero encounters obstacles in his pursuit of a goal, and undertakes to neutralize or transform the obstacles.

A large body of research is accumulating in the literature of cognitive science that is labelled discourse processing or text comprehension. The research is in the tradition of experimental psychology and is influenced by the textual orientation in which the search for structure is the primary goal. The results of some of the important research investigations are reviewed by James Mancuso in his chapter, "The Acquisition and Use of Narrative Grammar Structure." He interprets the research from his constructivist orientation. He formulates an argument to demonstrate that narrative grammar develops epigenetically and, further, that the development is directed by an intrinsic motivational system based on the discrepancy notion.

Mancuso reviews some studies the findings of which are congenial with the hypothesis that the narrative is an assimilating structure. The studies support the belief that textual input from written or spoken sources is assimilated to an acquired narrative grammar. The categories of the grammar have been identified by a number of investigators. The study of children's implicit use of narrative grammar supports Sutton-Smith's conclusion that the concept of story is acquired early in life.

The final section of the chapter incorporates a creative approach to the self-as-narrator, thus broadening the meaning of the research carried out under the structuralist banner. Especially thought provoking is Mancuso's narratory view of the concept of the unconscious.

John Robinson and Linda Hawpe explore the narrative as a cognitive instrument in their chapter "Narrative Thinking as a Heuristic Process." They approach the topic from the orientation of cognitive science. Making a story out of bits and pieces of action requires skill, judgment, and experience. Narrative thinking makes possible the interpretation of events by putting together a causal pattern which makes possible the blending of what is known about a situation (facts) with relevant conjectures (imagination).

The authors make use of one of the studies reviewed by Mancuso (Stein and Policastro, 1984) to support the notion that no rigid formula can be established as to what constitutes a story, although there is some commonality in judging the relative "goodness" of a story. Thus, there are good stories and poor stories. The orientation of the chapter is that narrative thinking involves efforts to move from a poor or unconvincing story to one that would be judged good and convincing.

It is refreshing that Robinson and Hawpe require that the cognitive analysis of the actions of self and others be carried out in a social context. Narratives are solutions to problems-in-living in that they have the potential for creating order in human affairs. Like several other contributors to this volume, the authors contrast narrative thinking to scientific thinking, using descriptions that overlap, but do not duplicate, the descriptions considered by Spence and by Sutton-Smith. They emphasize the context-free requirement of scientific thought, and the centrality of context in narrative thought.

Robinson and Hawpe devote considerable space to a presentation of original ideas about narrative thinking being motivated by the search for causes of conduct. They also discuss the need for narrative "repair" under conditions where the narrative causal model does not satisfy tests of relevance or coherence. The arguments are similar to those offered by Mordechai Rotenberg under the rubric "biographical rehabilitation" (1983) and by practitioners of psychotherapy who assist the client in reconstructing a life story.

The chapters in the section entitled "The Emplotment of Self-Narratives," each describe themes that give body to stories in which self is protagonist. In "Self-Narratives and Adventure" Karl Scheibe addresses a problem to which little attention has been paid: the meaning of the quest for thrills and excitement. Scheibe portrays adventure as an important feature of the construction and development of self-narratives, and he indicates how self-narratives support human identities.

Scheibe delves into two common forms of adventure, sport and gambling, and elaborates their role in the construction of identities that become the centers of life stories. Adventure and its opposite, repose, are essentially unstable states, and it is the recursive sequencing of these states from which come the actions that create and sustain the self-narrative. The theme of adventure and return is found in numerous guises. The trials, risks, and uncertainties of sport and gambling take turns with the security, rest, and preparation for the next adventure. The hypothesis is entertained that without adventure, there would be little movement in one's life story. Scheibe employs a wide variety of source materials: the tales of Arthurian knights, professional boxing, track, arcade video games, Don Quixote, and even Chaucerian tales.

The creative leap of defining participation in the sporting life or in the gambling casino as adventure provides Scheibe with a model for interpreting certain styles of world politics as adventure seeking. The participants enact their roles dramaturgically: in making a story, they make history.

In "Storytime: Recollecting the Past and Projecting the Future" Stephen Crites enlightens us about the temporal dimension in story making. As a point of departure, he begins his chapter with a discussion of one of Kierkegaard's short pieces entitled "The Unhappiest." Crites' quotation from Kierkegaard delivers the message that the unhappiest person is one who is outside himself. And one can be absent from self only in time past or time future. Time past is achieved through recollections, time future through the experience of hope.

In the body of the chapter, Crites argues that appropriating the past and anticipating the future require different narrative strategies. When these strategies are mixed, the resulting self-narrative is confused, inconsistent, and even chaotic. Recollections of a personal past give rise to a sense of continuity, an identity. From his phenomenological stance, Crites illustrates how one's personal past is situated in relation to the present in which the past is reconstructed. In this respect, Crites' theory of memory is consonant with current theories of memory derived from the work in experimental psychology.

The chapter explores territory that has been bypassed by less adventurous explorers: the relation between the self (I) as the one who engages in the act of remembering and the self (me) that is the actor in the remembered stories. The relation is clarified when one considers it to be connected linguistically to the point of tension between present and past. The grammar of tense helps convey the point of tension.

What wé call the present is always edging into the unknown – the future. The images of the past can be reconstructed with reasonable clarity, but the images of the future are necessarily vague in outline, they are only possibilities. Here Crites' analysis makes contact with one of the features of Scheibe's chapter. We seek adventure to test the possibilities that exist in the uncertain, risky future. All new things come out of the future.

In "Paranoia and Cataclysmic Narratives," Ernest Keen has undertaken a task that has challenged many other writers: the analysis of that puzzling phenomenon that has come to be called paranoia. His analysis is far removed from the descriptions offered in standard textbooks of abnormal psychology. He takes the perspective of the phenomenologist: experience is "languaged," and the language of experience is narratory.

Keen proposes three polarities that are constitutive of experience and of narrative. The first polarity is past and future. Keen's temporal polarity is remarkably similar to that provided in the chapter by Crites. The person is ever on the edge between the past and the future. The paranoid's self-narrative is tightly packed with episodes from the past. No room is left for the new, for the possibilities of the future to influence the plot of the story. The paranoid resists entry into the future. The successful resistance against entering future time is the condition for cataclysm. That is to say, the life story contains no "after." In place of the new, there is nothingness.

The second polarity is good and evil. The paranoid story locates evil outside the self and good inside. Self-righteous, the paranoid defends good against evil. Paranoid stories cannot readily serve as models for cultural myths because social beings, to survive, must negotiate good and evil. Paranoids typically emplot the self-narrative so that the good – an attribute of the self – is destroyed by the forces of evil that are alien to the self.

The third polarity, self and other, helps to account for the loneliness of the paranoid. Unlike the temporary loneliness that is a universal experience, the loneliness of the paranoid is permanent. Loneliness may be defined as the inability or refusal to share stories with others.

Keen illustrates the use of the polarities with a reanalysis of the celebrated Schreber case. In the development of the paranoid emplotment, Schreber located his past and future into a story the end of which was experienced as a forthcoming cataclysm.

I have grouped five chapters under the heading "Constructing and Deconstructing Self-Narratives." Frederick Wyatt's chapter, "The Narrative in Psychoanalysis," brings to the foreground the observation that psychoanalysis deals *with* and *in* stories. He considers the implications of the narrative metaphor in fashioning an active listening attitude on the part of the clinician. Among other things, Wyatt makes us aware of the commonality of the aims of the historian and the psychoanalyst. Both are deeply involved in the hermeneutic enterprise. The data provided by the client or from the archives do not come with ready-made meanings. Meanings are constructed only when the context is taken into account. Wyatt takes issue with those psychoanalysts and other therapists who claim to work on materials provided by the client. In the therapeutic context, the interpreter is not a member of the genus *homo faber* but is a member of the genus *homo narrens*. In common with current theories of remembering, Wyatt makes a convincing argument that the stories told by clients in therapy are reconstructions, not videotape images. Underlying the chapter is the theme of Pirandello's *Six Characters in Search of an Author*.

In "Narrative Smoothing and Clinical Wisdom" Donald Spence carries the argument further. Using Freud's Dora as a starting point, Spence raises the issue of the validity of case reports. He identifies two levels of narrative smoothing that distort "what really happened." One level is exemplified by the typical case report in which some details are omitted and others are enlarged so that the final product fits a pattern required by theory. The other kind of narrative smoothing takes place in the consulting room, in the kinds of story lines solicited by the analyst. The discussion of interpretation as a hermeneutic exercise is further developed with the aid of a distinction made by Jerome Bruner (1984). The interpreter can adopt a paradigmatic posture or a narrative posture. The former is the method usually associated with scientific reporting, with replicability as a desideratum. The focus is on concepts, such as gravity, force, id, or anxiety, which are denotatively encoded. The aim is to find the *one* truth and to show the inadequacy of competing claims to truth. The narrative posture sacrifices denotation to connotation. A coherent story is the goal. The dramatic story may have a moral force that cannot be matched by the objective, detached, formulaic account created by adopting the paradigmatic mode. Narrative truths contain the implication that they can be displaced by other narratives created in another place or another time. Spence offers some concrete suggestions to interpreters of life stories to sensitize them to the potential mischief created by the two levels of narrative smoothing.

The content of Elliot Mishler's chapter carries further the concerns expressed in the chapters by Wyatt and Spence. In "The Analysis of Interview Narratives" Mishler addresses the interview as a central procedure in the behavioral sciences. Whether engaged in therapy or in information gathering for social policy decisions, the interview serves as an instrument for story making and storytelling. In his chapter, Mishler reproduces portions of a long interview. This material may be regarded as *text* which may be taken apart for literary analysis, that is, "deconstructed." The deconstruction serves the goal of sense making, of discovering meaning in the context of the interview setting. He demonstrates how the interpreter, also a storyteller, makes sense of the respondent's answers to questions posed by the interviewer in the dialogue. The respondent's contribution, however, is more than a response. It is part of a self-narrative.

Mishler's chapter opens new vistas for social scientists who have uncritically accepted the interviewer's question and the subject's answer as stimulus and response. The narrative as a replacement for the stimulus-response model broadens the scope and the utility of interviews.

In a dramatic coda, Mishler demonstrates how the respondent's life story as told by a significant other reveals the ubiquity of narrative smoothing. In this case, the plot of the self-narrative and the plot of the other-narrative are radically different. (There is raw material in the two texts for the study of self-deception.) Mishler removes interviewing from its traditional niche as a research technique and gives it a new home in the world of narrative construction.

In "Deconstructing Histories: Toward a Systematic Criticism of Psychological Narratives," Robert Steele offers some profound ideas on the interpretation of life narratives that are taken as historical truths. He takes a fresh look at the problems identified in the chapters contributed by Wyatt, Spence, and Mishler. Like Wyatt, he treats the writing of history and the writing of life stories as two forms of the same genre. The uttered or written statements about self are to be interpreted not as true or false, but as evidence to be sorted and re-sorted into different stories. The case material in Steele's chapter – the life stories of Freud and Jung – lend themselves to hermeneutic decoding in much the same manner as Mishler's deconstruction of an interview protocol.

Steele has created a guide to identifying textual distortions. Five signs of distortion are described and illustrated with texts from the life stories of Freud and Jung. Inconsistency is one of the signs. Both Freud and Jung persisted in the claim that they were rejected by their contemporaries and alienated from professional peers. Both present the self as the lonely hero struggling against great odds, in the end providing the world with some valued talisman. These autobiographical themes are inconsistent with other evidence, such as that provided by concurrent reviews of their work, public recognition, and so on. Both of these great men were practitioners of all five types of textual distortion. Steele relates the manifold distortions to the self-narrative that each had created and attempted to ratify.

Steele takes several perspectives to deconstruct the texts, among them, feminist criticism. He supplies evidence from the writings of Freud and Jung to show how the masculist bias permeated their theories and colored the histories they wrote about their female clients.

In his chapter, "Literary Pathfinding: The Work of Popular Life Constructors," Kevin Murray focuses on the narrative structure of popular life manuals. In analyzing the rhetorical content of the popular writings of Gail Sheehy, Murray identifies the underlying narrative structure as romance, where the hero engages in adventures of self-discovery filled with hope. He compares the underlying themes of other life constructors, including that of the Victorian moralist, Samuel Smiles. Murray makes use of illustrative life stories written by both Sheehy and Smiles to tease out the methods employed by these popular life constructors. When the life histories are subjected to scrutiny as texts, it becomes clear that rhetorical language, aesthetic and moral interests guide the writers' narrative development.

Murray's textual materials differ from those analyzed in the other chapters in this section. The conclusions, however, are like those of the other writers: lives are presented as narratives, and the form and content of the narratives are fashioned not only by "facts" but by the purposes, biases, interests, and moral posture of the storyteller.

REFERENCES

Bruner, J. (1984). *Narrative and paradigmatic modes of thought.* Invited address, American Psychological Association, Toronto, August 1984.

Elms, A. C. (1975). The crisis of confidence in social psychology. *American Psychologist,* 30, 967-976.

Kermode, F. (1967). *The sense of an ending.* Oxford: Oxford University Press.

Pepper, S. (1942) *World hypotheses.* Berkeley: University of California Press.

Rotenberg, M., The Midrash and Biographical Rehabilitation, unpublished, 1983.

Sarbin, T. R. (1943). The concept of role-taking. *Sociometry,* 6, 273-284.

Sarbin, T. R. (1954). Role theory. In G. Lindzey (Ed.), *Handbook of social psychology.* Reading, MA: Addison-Wesley.

Sarbin, T. R. and Allen, V. L. (1968). Role theory. In G. Lindzey and E. Aronson (Eds.), *Handbook of social psychology* (rev. ed.). Reading, MA: Addison-Wesley.

Stein, N. L. and Policastro, M. (1984). The concept of story: A comparison between children's and teacher's viewpoints. In H. Mandl, N. L. Stein, and T. Trabasso (Eds.), *Learning and comprehension of text.* Hillsdale, NJ: Lawrence Erlbaum Associates.

White, H. (1973). *Metahistory.* Baltimore, MD: Johns Hopkins University Press.

PART I

The Narrative in Scientific Theories

1

The Narrative as a Root Metaphor for Psychology

Theodore R. Sarbin

INTRODUCTION

To validate the title of this essay, it is necessary to spell out its terms. For our present heuristic purposes, *narrative* is coterminous with *story* as used by ordinary speakers of English. A story is a symbolized account of actions of human beings that has a temporal dimension. The story has a beginning, a middle, and an ending [or, as Kermode (1967) suggests, the sense of an ending]. The story is held together by recognizable patterns of events called plots. Central to the plot structure are human predicaments and attempted resolutions. (Other essays in this volume deal more fully with definitional problems. See especially the essays by Mancuso, Sutton-Smith, Robinson and Hawpe, and Gergen and Gergen.)

The concept of root metaphor requires more extensive elaboration. The root metaphor method was central to the creation of Stephen Pepper's seminal work, *World Hypotheses* (1942). A recognized authority on aesthetics, values, and metaphysics, Pepper traced the history of metaphysics and concluded that any metaphysical posture, or

3

world hypothesis, is derived from a basic or root metaphor. He demonstrated how the root metaphor provides the framework for the construing of occurrences in the natural and man-made worlds. The root metaphor constrains the kinds of philosophical or scientific models to be applied either to the task of observing and classifying or to the task of interpreting and explaining. The categories of analysis and the sorts of questions asked are similarly constrained by the choice of root metaphor.

To create and use root metaphors is a special case of metaphor making, a common achievement of human beings. When a person confronts a novel occurrence for which no ready-made category or class is available, the occurrence remains uninstantiated, unclassified, or unassimilated until a class or category is located or invented. The recognition of partial similarity on some dimension or construct provides the basis for analogy, and if linguistic translation is necessary, the partial similarity is expressed as metaphor. The novel occurrence is named with the metaphor.

Once the metaphor is expressed by the speaker and decoded by the listener, actions and properties related to the chosen metaphor serve as the source of auxiliary and supporting metaphors. To identify a political figure as a puppet, for example, leads to the use of related metaphors, such as pulling strings, manipulating characters, the puppet stage, scriptwriting, and so on.

As preliminary to establishing the proposition that the narrative is potentially a useful root metaphor for psychology and other human sciences, I point to some observations that help clarify how contemporary science has been guided by well-entrenched, and usually unrecognized, root metaphors.

When a metaphor is marked by clear context, emphasis, or by forms that clearly identify the expression as a figure of speech, the interpreter is free to construct and use other figures. "It is as if the mind is a telephone system" is a clearly marked figure – the *as if* construction makes clear to both the speaker and the listener that identity is not intended. The speaker or the listener may notice partial similarities between the occurrence of interest and familiar events other than those that supplied the vehicle for the expressed metaphor. The metaphor maker is not bound to the telephone figure and is free to entertain alternate constructions, among them, the mind (itself a metaphor-turned-myth) is a many-layered geological system, or a tree with roots, trunk, and branches, or a multistranded rope, or a blank tablet, or a computer, and so on.

For reasons that can be identified (Chun, 1970; Chun & Sarbin, 1970; Lewis, 1939; Sarbin, 1968), once a metaphor has done its job of sense making, the metaphoric quality tends to become submerged. Unless constantly reminded of the *as if* quality of the expression, users of the term may treat the figure as a literal expression. The once tentative poetic expression may then become reified, literalized. The reification provides the foundation for belief systems that guide action.

The root metaphors of metaphysical systems were constructed to answer cosmological questions, such as, What is the substance of the world? or What is the essence of creation? or What is humanity? Finding answers to such abstract questions encourages the construction and use of metaphors. At first, the metaphors are poetic creations. Once the metaphors are reified, frozen into tight belief patterns, metaphysical systems come into being.

Pepper (1942) summarized the root metaphor method as follows:

> A man desiring to understand the world looks about for a clue to its comprehension. He pitches upon some area of commonsense fact and tries to understand other areas in terms of this one. This original idea becomes his basic analogy or root metaphor. He describes as best he can the characteristics of this area, or ... discriminates its structure. A list of its structural characteristics [categories] becomes his basic conceptions of explanation and description.... In terms of these categories he proceeds to study all other areas of fact.... He undertakes to interpret all facts in terms of these categories.... (P. 91)

As background for my argument that the narrative is a candidate for the status of basic or root metaphor, I provide a brief sketch of Pepper's classification of root metaphors from which he derived six types of world views: animism, mysticism, formism, mechanism, organicism, and contextualism. Pepper rejected animism and mysticism as inadequate for modern purposes because they lacked sufficient scope and communicable categories.

Formism is the term Pepper applied to world views that stress the organization of the world on the basis of similarities and differences among entities. Plato, Aristotle, and the Scholastics are exemplars of formist thought. The common sense root metaphor of formism is found in the activities of an artisan fashioning products on the same plan, and in the observation of objects in nature the appearance of which satisfies criteria of similarity. The plan or form is not fully revealed in particular instances, it transcends them. Forms exist in nature. Psychological models flowing from the root metaphor of formism would include turn-of-the-century structuralism, contemporary personality trait theories, and the official doctrine of schizophrenia.

Mechanism is the dominant world view in Western civilization. The root metaphor is the machine. The kind of machine employed to provide imagery may be a clock, a dynamo, a computer, an internal combustion engine, or a municipal water system. The mechanist world view sees events in nature as the products of the transmittal of forces. Modern science has taken this world view as its metaphysical foundation – a view that supports the scientist's search for causes. Efficient causality description is the goal for scientists working with one or another paradigm within the mechanist world view. Behaviorism and radical empiricism exemplify psychological and philosophical movements committed to this world view.

Organicism views the world as an organism rather than a machine or a set of forms. The organicist tries to locate parts within wholes. Every actual event is more or less concealed organic process. The organicist examines an event to determine its organic structure. An ideal structure is there to be discovered at the end of progressive steps or stages. This world view is associated in philosophy with Hegel, among others. In psychology, organicists would include Maslow (self-actualization), Rogers (personal growth), and developmentalists who depend upon the notion of stages of maturation.

Contextualism is reflected in the work of such scholars as C. S. Pierce, William James, John Dewey, and G. H. Mead. The root metaphor for contextualism is the historical event. Not necessarily an event in the past, the event is alive and in the present. In this sense history is an attempt to re-present events, to revive them, to breathe life into them. Pepper writes of the historic event as the event in actuality – the dynamic dramatic act.

The imagery called out by the historical event metaphor is that of an ongoing texture of multiply elaborated events, each leading to others, each being influenced by collateral episodes, and by the efforts of multiple agents who engage in actions to satisfy their needs and meet their obligations. Contained in the metaphor is the idea of constant change in the structure of situations and in positions occupied by actors. The texture of events does not require linearity (Sarbin, 1977).

To those steeped in the traditions of mechanistic science, traditions that emphasize order, predictability, and causality, contextualism at first appears chaotic. The categorical statements of contextualism assert change and novelty. Events are in constant flux, the very integration of the conditions of an event alters the context for a future event.

CONTEXTUALISM AND THE HISTORICAL ACT

Novelists and historians are not strangers to contextualism. Social psychologists, however, having their roots in efforts to establish a science of behavior on mechanistic principles, have been slow to adopt concepts and methods that depart from the objective of uncovering context-free laws of behavior. Exceptions to this conservatism in social psychology include Goffman's development of the dramaturgical interpretation of public conduct (1959, 1961, 1974), the more recent ethogenic view of social behavior associated with Harré and Secord (1972), and my work in role theory (1943, 1954, 1968). Role is a central category for these theoretical achievements. Borrowed from dramatic arts, role directs attention to public performances and to the inferred or claimed reasons for action. In drama, the original home for role, we find a clear example of the application of the historic act metaphor. The actors' performances, the setting, the time and place, the nature of the audience, the script, the props, and so on, must all be taken into account to make sense of an episode or scene. The actors and the audiences play out their parts according to their individual and collective emplotments. Sense making in the drama is openly contextual. The meanings to be assigned to any actor's performance are a function of the context.

Drama, the vehicle for dramaturgical and dramatistic accounts of conduct, is a subordinate concept to the superordinate narrative. Other subordinate concepts are novels, epic poems, fairy tales, parables, myths, fables, morality plays, folktales, and autobiographies. In considering narrative as representing the contextual requirements of Pepper's historical act, I examined the semantic structure of both terms. The argument can be made that the narrative and the historical act have approximately the same semantic structure. Contained in the adjective historical are the meanings of the noun history. We have learned that history is more than a collection of records of past or present events. Annals and chronicles are used by lay and professional historians as raw materials for the construction of narratives. Both the novelist and the historian are narrativists, but their emphases are different. The novelist writes about fictive characters in a context of real world settings; the historian writes about presumably actual events, populated by reconstructed people, the reconstruction being carried out through the use of imagination. Both kinds of narrativists make use of so-called "facts" and "fictions." The historian aims at historical truth, the novelist at narrative truth (Mink, 1978; Spence, 1982; see also essays in this volume by Wyatt, Steele, and Mishler).

To strengthen my redefinition of the historical act as narrative, I refer to Gergen's influential paper, "Social Psychology as History" (1973). Gergen advances a convincing argument that theories of social behavior are primarily reflections of contemporary history. The scientific examination of the authoritarian personality in the 1950s, for example, was a response to historically generated interest in the personality characteristics of fascists. Once research findings are publicized, people react to the results. Because they are agents, not passive machines, people may choose to engage in conduct that would contradict, confirm, or ignore the published findings. Making public the results of psychological research thus introduces change and novelty, conditions that cannot be assimilated by subscribers to world views other than contextualism. Gergen's conclusions are powerful: social psychology is history, and the use of the root metaphor of the historical act is likely to lead to a more profound understanding of the human condition than the prevailing mechanistic perspective. If we treat Gergen's conclusion, *social psychology is history,* as the major premise in a syllogism, and conjoin it with *history is narrative,* a minor premise developed in the preceding paragraphs, then the conclusion follows: *social psychology is narrative.* (Parenthetically, save for that part of human psychology that deals with sensory physiology, psychology and social psychology may be regarded as equivalent. So, psychology is narrative.)

NARRATIVE AS ORGANIZING PRINCIPLE

More needs to be said about narrative. I propose the narratory principle: that human beings think, perceive, imagine, and make moral choices according to narrative structures. Present two or three pictures, or descriptive phrases, to a person and he or she will connect them to form a story, an account that relates the pictures or the meanings of the phrases in some patterned way. On reflection, we discover that the pictures COHERENCY or meanings are held together by the implicit or explicit use of plot. When the stimulus material depicts people, the story will reflect recognizable human sentiments, goals, purposes, valuations, and judgments. The plot will influence the flow of action of the constructed narrative figures.

I defer discussion of the problem of classifying plots for another time, save to mention that the problem has been addressed by a number of writers. White (1973) has suggested tragedy, comedy, romance, and satire. Gergen and Gergen (1983) have proposed the use of three dimensions: stability, progression, and regression. Polti (1916) classified 1,200 literary works into 36 classes that he labeled "emotions." Professional folklorists have introduced categories based on the special roles of narrative figures. However the classification problem is ultimately resolved, it seems clear that the taxonomist of plots must begin not with the acts of narrative figures per se but with the structure of the context that determines whether a reader or spectator will be saddened, amused, inspired, or enlightened by the actions of the constructed narrative figures.

The narrative is a way of organizing episodes, actions, and accounts of actions; it is an achievement that brings together mundane facts and fantastic creations; time and place are incorporated. The narrative allows for the inclusion of actors' reasons for their acts, as well as the causes of happening.   GOOD REASONS

I am treating the narrative as an organizing principle for human action. As such, it may be compared with other, more conventional, organizing principles. The widely cited studies of Kahneman and Tversky (1972), for example, make use of heuristics as the organizing principle in their version of decision theory. Rosenberg (1971) employs implicit personality theory as an organizing principle to account for the systematic ways that people convert cues into personality descriptions. The burgeoning field of discourse processing has introduced macrostructure as the organizing principle that gives form to discourse (Kintsch, 1977; see essay by Mancuso in this volume).

Organizing principles are invoked, then, to help account for the observation that human beings impose structure on the flow of experience. Unlike organizing principles drawn from humanistic sources such as dramaturgy, rhetoric, game playing, and storytelling, most of the extant organizing principles are expressed in abstract or schematic language, as, for example, heuristics, integrating hypotheses, macrostructures, and so on. The use of such dead metaphors is guided by the objective of mechanistic science to discover forces (like gravity, energy, photosynthesis) that could be used in a causality equation.

The power of root metaphors to direct behavior is nowhere better illustrated than in psychological theorists' choice of descriptive categories. The world view of mechanism, the root metaphor of which is the transmittal of force, insisted upon discovering and eventually controlling the forces that were to be found in nature. The standard lexicon of psychology – dead metaphors that no longer have the power to stimulate imagery – is comprised of terms that represent such forces: drive, instinct, libido, cognitions, reinforcement, mental states, and so on. It is as if there is a moral imperative to reduce the drama of humanity to the play of impersonal forces. Thus, if one were to "emperson" a thing in order to tell a story, the charge of anthropomorphism, or worse, animism, might be made. The commitment to discovering context-free forces as the source of conduct has served to separate psychological theorists from common sense wisdom as seen in the concreteness of Aesopic fables and the imaginativeness of mythic tales.

Freud was a notable exception. Although he, too, was caught up in the mechanistic world view, he was apparently unconcerned with being charged with the misdemeanor of anthropomorphism. He wrote of the struggles, battle, and maneuvers of the allegorical figures – id, ego, and superego – as if they had become empersoned, had become narrative figures in life histories.

These allegorical figures have recently been unmasked. A number of scholars have made the case that Freud was primarily a narrativist, but, in common with other nineteenth century scientists, he was constrained by the categories of the world view of mechanism. Schafer (1980), Spence (1982), and Wyatt (this volume) have examined the practice of psychoanalysis from a narrativist viewpoint. One conclusion is that the analyst helps the client repudiate a self-narrative that is inconsistent, contradictory, or unconvincing and replace it with a more satisfying self-narrative. Such an interpretation is a far cry from the search for unconscious forces in a reified psyche.

The employment of the narrative metaphor to illuminate human actions is consistent with the current refiguration of social science. Geertz (1980) has identified a movement in recent times in which students of human conduct are retreating from their reliance on energy, spatial, and mechanical metaphors and embracing metaphors drawn from the humanities: drama, game playing, ritual, rhetoric, and text.

More than a half century ago, John Dewey (1922) remarked on the implications of adopting humanistic over scientific (mechanistic) metaphors.

The novelist and the dramatist are so much more illuminating as well as more interesting commentators on conduct than the schematizing psychologist. The artist makes perceptible individual responses and thus displays a new phase of human nature evoked in new situations. In putting the case visibly and dramatically he reveals vital actualities. The scientific systematizer treats each act as merely another sample of some old principle, or as a mechanical combination of elements drawn from a ready-made inventory. (Pp. 145-46)

Unlike the cold abstractions contained in conventional mechanistic or formistic theories, the narrative metaphor calls up images of storytellers and storytelling, heroes, villains, and plots, and in the narrative that is dramatized, images of actors performing and engaging in dialogue with other actors.

To entertain seriously the proposal that the narratory principle guides thought and action, we can reflect on any slice of life. Our dreams, for example, are experienced as stories, as dramatic encounters, often with mythic shadings. It is a commonplace that our fantasies and our daydreams are unvoiced stories. The rituals of daily life are organized to tell stories. The pageantry of rites of passage and rites of intensification are storied actions. Our plannings, our rememberings, even our loving and hating, are guided by narrative plots. The claim that the narratory principle facilitates survival must be taken seriously. Survival in a world of meanings is problematic without the talent to make up and to interpret stories about interweaving lives.

MacIntyre (1981) makes a strong case for considering the narrative as central to an understanding of human conduct.

In successfully identifying and understanding what someone else is doing we always move towards placing a particular episode in the context of a set of narrative histories, histories both of the individuals concerned and of the settings in which they act and suffer. It is now becoming clear that we render the actions of others intelligible in this way because action itself has a *PRAXIS* basically historical character. It is because we all live out narratives in our lives and because we understand our own lives in terms of the narratives that we live out that the form of narrative is appropriate for understanding the actions of others. Stories are lived before they are told – except in the case of fiction. (P. 197)

Because storytelling is commonly associated with fiction, fantasy, and pretending, some critics are skeptical about the use of the narrative as a model for thought and action. For the serious scientist, storytelling is related to immaturity and playfulness. To regard storytelling as the exclusive property of childhood is consistent with a world view that places a high value on positivism, technology, and realism and a low value on imagining and ludic behavior.

To the potential criticism that the narratory principle is suspect because it embraces imaginative constructions, one may reply with a defense of the imagination. The semantic structure of the word storytelling includes such elements as making up reasons to account for actions, inferring the silent problem solving of the actors, creating images the better to deal with the meanings of abstract or opaque words, and so on. In short, a lot of fictive activity takes place in addition to constructing meanings for everyday perceptible objects and events. No less a figure than Bentham sensitized us to the proposition that fictions are a part of the reality in which we live our lives.

The discussion of fact and fiction is not idle. I want to accent that all stories, whether in the lively, transparent idiom of fairy tales or in the dull, opaque idiom of psychological theories, are compounds of happenings and imaginings. It matters not whether historian, novelist, or student: a person tries to make sense of the world with limited epistemic and linguistic skills. Where there are no firm connections between empirical events, the individual organizes them into an imaginative formulation that meets one or more tests of coherence.

SUPPORT FOR THE NARRATORY PRINCIPLE

To show the narratory principle at work, I retrieved from the dusty shelves of the library some old reports of laboratory exercises. The experiments were designed primarily to throw light on the perception of causality. Serendipitously, they illuminate the narratory principle. For one study, Michotte (1946/1963) constructed an apparatus that allowed an observer to see two or more small colored rectangles in motion. The experimenter controlled the speed, direction, and distance travelled of the figures. For certain patterns the observers were found to attribute causality to the movements of the rectangles. For example, if rectangle A stopped after moving toward B, and if rectangle B then began to move, the observers would say that B "got out of the way" of A. In one set of experiments, rectangle A "triggers" an action from B. Michotte comments:

Some very amusing descriptions are given: "It is as if A's approach frightened B and B ran away." "It is as if A, in touching B induced an electric current which set B going." "The arrival of A by the side of B acts as a sort of signal to B...." "It is as if A touched off a mechanism inside B and thus set it going" and so on. Also this experiment often produces a comical effect and makes the observers laugh.

From the description of the experiments it is clear that the meaningless movements of the rectangles were assigned meaning and described in the idiom of the narrative. Each of the illustrative reports is a miniature plot. Could laughter have been a response unless the observer emplotted the actions of the rectangles as narrative figures in a comedy?

Another experiment supports the notion that people are ready to describe nonhuman actions by making up a story. Heider and Simmel (1944) made a short motion picture film of three geometrical figures that moved in various directions and at various speeds. A large triangle, a small triangle and a circle moved in the circumscribed field that also contained a rectangle, a part of which was sometimes open. Observers reported the movements of the geometrical shapes as human action. The three geometrical figures in action became narrative figures. The reports were not about physical movements of geometric forms, but about people, and the reports made use of sequences in the forms of plots and subplots.

One subject reported (in part):

A man has planned to meet a girl and the girl comes along with another man. The first man tells the second to go; the second tells the first, and he shakes his head. Then the two men have a fight and the girl starts to go into the room.... She apparently does not want to be with the first man. The first man follows her into the room after having left the second in a rather weakened condition leaning on the wall outside the room. The girl gets worried and races from one corner to the other in the far part of the room.... The girl gets out of the room in a sudden dash just as man number two gets the door open. The two chase around the outside of the room together, followed by man number one, but they finally elude him and get away. The first man goes back and tries to open his door, but he is so blinded by rage and frustration that he cannot open it.... (Heider & Simmel, 1944)

Some of the observers were instructed merely to report what they saw; others were instructed to regard the geometric figures as human. The results were similar whether the set for human action was explicitly given or not. It is also of interest that there was considerable agreement on the qualities of the "characters" and on the plots and subplots in the created stories. These studies point up the phenomenon of emplotment, and that human beings are ready to make use of plots to give meaning to meaningless movements. I have already alluded to this readiness as the narratory principle.

Another source of support for the operation of such a principle is in the history and prehistory of humanity. In *The Roots of Civilization*, Marshack (1972) sought to establish the meaning of a bone fragment from the Mesolithic period upon which appeared single line markings in irregular clusters. Taking into account known geological and climatic information, he deciphered the marks as notations that denoted a lunar calendar. Further, the calendar appeared to be consistent with the seasonal timing of such agricultural activities as tilling, planting, harvesting, and so on. The more far-reaching conclusion is that prehistoric man, in order to be an agriculturist, had to take *time* into account. The pursuit of agriculture cannot proceed without considering temporality. The notations on the bone, and on other archeological finds, such as the cave art of France and Spain, tell stories. Marshack refers to the notations as storied.

To generalize from this detailed work, one could say that notational systems came into being as a means of telling a story to help prehistoric man employ the abstract concept of time. The construction of such a concept grew out of the creation of symbolic systems – first bone markings, later, oral stories. The familiar criteria of story – beginning, middle, and ending – could not be formed until there was a way of symbolizing the time factor in human activities. The concept of time and the narratory principle are interdependent notions.

We know that storytelling is a pervasive activity. It is supported by the oral tradition and in historical times goes back at least to the Homeric epics. The pervasiveness of storytelling is seen in the ancient and still extant practice of guiding moral behavior through the reciting of parables and fables. Shortened fables, that is, traditional proverbs, are widely used to give counsel and to urge wisdom. The pervasiveness is further witnessed by the universality of the use of the story to entertain and to enlighten, and by the omnipresence of special kinds of stories – myths – to answer recurring cosmological questions.

It is not necessary to posit a deep structure within the nervous system to account for the universality of story making and storytelling. Rather the readiness to construct narratives can be tied to the acquisition of skill in using symbols, learning to talk about absent things as if they were present (that is, imagining), making use of the concept of time, and, of course, participation in social life.

The inclusion of the narratory principle in psychological theory gives added emphasis to theories that recognize that human beings are constantly confronted with the problem of choosing roles. G. H. Mead took the first step in his recognition of the importance of taking-the-role-of-the-other. The special features of any "other" can be identified only if it is known in what drama, in what story, the actor is participating. The appropriateness, propriety, and convincingness of the actor's performance depends upon the degree of overlap of the stories imagined or enacted by other actors. I mentioned before that the sources of such stories are to be found in enculturation and socialization programs.

Although his objective was the development of a theory about how we are educated in the virtues, MacIntyre's description of the narratory basis of experience applies to social interaction generally:

> It is through hearing stories about wicked stepmothers, lost children, good but misguided kings, wolves that suckle twin boys, youngest sons who receive no inheritance but must make their own way in the world and eldest sons who waste their inheritance on riotous living and go into exile to live with the swine, that children learn or mislearn both what a child and what a parent is, what the cast of characters may be in the drama into which they have been born and what the ways of the world are. Deprive children of stories and you leave them unscripted, anxious stutterers in their actions as in their words. Hence there is no way to give us an understanding of any society, including our own, except through the stock of stories which constitute its initial dramatic resources. Mythology, in its original sense, is at the heart of things. . . . (1981, p. 201)

THE NARRATORY PRINCIPLE AT WORK

In the preceding pages, I have argued that the narrative is a fruitful metaphor for psychology. Because twentieth century psychology has for the most part adopted the root metaphor of mechanism together with an uncritical acceptance of the authority of facts, my proposal of a patently humanistic formulation might prompt the query: how does one *do* psychology from the narratory perspective?

In the remainder of this essay, I illustrate the use of the narratory principle in understanding a phenomenon that continues to puzzle contemporary psychologists: self-deception.

Self-deception is frequently observed in everyday life. A person makes claims about self that are contrary to evidence. To an observer, it appears that the self-deceiver believes his or her story, even in the face of overwhelming contrary evidence. In practice, it is frequently the case that a person will say "I don't know" when the evidentiary context would lead one to expect that the person would say "I know." Self-deception is a fairly common event; its most florid examples would include classical hysteria, hypnotic amnesia, and delusions. Until recently, the explanations for the self-contradictory action of claiming truth for that which is contrafactual have been couched in the language of repression and dissociation. These metaphors have their origins in the causality requirement of the mechanistic world view. Repression is a force that operates to reduce psychic (read: metaphoric) pain. Dissociation is a mechanism that presumably provides barriers that keep psychic contents separated. Neither of these mechanistically inspired concepts has proven useful. Although at first posited as hypothetical constructs, they have become reified and they continue to be used even though they have no explanatory power.

In recent years, several writers have described self-deception from the narrative perspective (Crites, 1979; Fingarette, 1971; Sarbin, 1981, 1984). The underlying assumption is that the self-deceiver, like the rest of us, lives according to an ongoing plot structure. The self-deceiver tells stories both to self and to audiences. In order to maintain or enhance self-identity, people will reconstruct their life histories through the employment of two identifiable skills: the skill in spelling out engagements in the world, and the skill in not spelling out engagements. These skills are not arcane – they are the stock-in-trade of novelists, historians, journalists, poets, raconteurs, in fact, any person who goes beyond chronicles to render an account of human interaction. The same skills are employed whether the vehicle is a historical account, a biography, or an autobiography. To spell out one's engagements means articulating, elaborating, sharpening, focusing, finding reasons for actions of the narrative figures, and providing all the contextual markers that help the reader or the observer to follow the story. Not to spell out one's engagements means the studied avoidance of those contextual features that would render the story inconsistent, unconvincing, or absurd. In self-narratives that assign truth value to the contrafactual, the narrator constructs the text so that the self as narrative figure is protected, defended, or enhanced. The narrative smoothing (see Spence, this volume) is carried out in the service of maintaining an acceptable identity.

To understand the process of self-deception, then, requires that the observer inquire into the person's self-narrative and identify the features of the self as narrative figure or protagonist (as distinguished from the self as narrator or story maker). The observer must be ready to recognize the inconsistency or absurdity of the story if the narrator were to spell out engagements that appeared to violate the integrity of the self as narrative figure. (See Steele, this volume, for an account of how Freud and Jung each constructed their self-narratives by spelling out certain of their engagements and not spelling out other engagements that would deform the image of the hero.)

The relevance of the self-narrative for understanding the actions of human beings is clearly demonstrated in critical studies of biographical and autobiographical accounts (Runyan, 1982). Such accounts mention with great frequency the influence of stories upon the development of a self-narrative. One of the most illuminating models for the formation of the self-narrative is the protagonist of Cervantes' novel, *Don Quixote*. From the reading of adventure tales about chivalric characters, Don Quixote constructed an identity for himself and a corresponding narrative plot in which to act out his role. Levin (1970) has assigned the label, the Quixotic Principle, to the frequently observed practice of a reader building an identity and a self-narrative from reading books. It appears indubitable that human beings construct identities not only out of their reading, like Don Quixote, but also out of imaginings stirred by orally told tales or by the direct or vicarious witnessing of the actions of role models. Lord Byron, for example, depended less on his reading and more on his fertile imagination to create a self-narrative and then proceeded to live out his few years in seeking ratification of his identity through romantic and heroic exploits (Sarbin, 1983). (See Scheibe, this volume, for a discussion of adventure in the self-narrative.) Once the story is begun, the actor sets out to validate the constructed narrative figure, the hero, in the self-narrative. The self-narratives of co-actors impose constraints on the actor's efforts to satisfy the requirements of his or her own narrative role. Because the stories of the co-actors may not be compatible with the hero's story, the text – the actual living of the narrative role – is usually a negotiated story. To be sure, Thurber's unforgettable daydreamer, Walter Mitty, was not required to negotiate his self-narrative inasmuch as Mitty's dreamed-up narrative figure performed his heroic feats only in his active imagination.

The self-narrative need not appear as a remote hypothetical construct. It can be seen as an emergent from our grammatical rule for using first person singular pronouns. The pronouns, I and me (and their equivalents in other European languages), were accented by James, Mead, Freud, and others in the effort to give meaning to that vague but indispensable construct, the self. Their strategy was to uncover the references for I and me. They substantiated the pronouns by adding the definite article, thus rendering it possible to speak of *the I* and *the me*. In substantiating the pronouns in the context of the grammatical rules that govern the use of I as subject and me as object, these writers (perhaps unwittingly) introduced a narrative metaphor. The uttered pronoun, *I*, stands for the author, *me* stands for the actor, the character in the drama, the narrative figure. The self as author, *the I*, imaginatively constructs a story in which the narrative figure, *the me*, is the protagonist. Such narrative construction is possible because the self as author can imagine the future and reconstruct the past (see Mancuso & Sarbin, 1983, and Crites, this volume). In the same way that a person may become overinvolved in a narrative figure portrayed in a novel, play, biography, folktale, or film, so may that person become overinvolved in the narrative figure (*the me*) created by the self as author (*the I*). Cyrano de Bergerac is a good example of the overinvolvement in the self-created role. Such involvement would set the stage for a person to make liberal use of his or her skills in spelling out engagements that were congruent with the goals of the narrative figure and not spelling out engagements that were inconsistent with the goals.

The self-narrative, as discussed in the foregoing paragraphs, is a necessary construct for understanding self-deception. It can be argued that the self-narrative is also central to the study of virtue (moral judgment and conduct), such study beginning with the proposition that the actor holds the status of agent. Such a study provides a more meaningful approach to the dilemmas of moral action than the popular templatic theories that depend upon stages of maturation. That the self-narrative is central to understanding moral choice is convincingly argued by Crites (1975), Fingarette (1971), Hauerwas (1977), and MacIntyre (1981). (I defer a discussion of the relative utility of narrative and organismic approaches to the study of moral choice until another time.)

RECAPITULATION

I have not dwelt on the current dissatisfaction with the positivist framework, although this has been amply documented. The positivist perspective flows from the mechanistic world view, one of the basic metaphysical positions identified by Pepper (1942). An alternate world view, contextualism, includes change and novelty as central categories, categories that are applicable to the human condition. The root metaphor of contextualism is the historical act, a metaphor that corresponds to the description of the narrative. I argue that the narrative is a fruitful metaphor for examining and interpreting human action.

The body of the essay deals with the narrative as an organizing principle. I illustrate the principle by referring to studies on causality that show how random nonhuman stimulus events are interpreted as human actors performing in familiar stories. That is to say, a narratory principle operates to provide meaning to the often nonsystematic encounters and interactions experienced in everyday life.

Definitions of narrative are only touched upon in this essay. The perception and experience of time appears to be a central feature of any definition. The concepts of time and of narrative are closely related concepts.

To illustrate how the narrative root metaphor may be employed in understanding nontrivial psychological problems, I discuss the phenomenon of self-deception. From the observation that human beings are authors *of* self-narratives and actors *in* self-narratives, I show how self-deceivers make use of epistemic skills to maintain or enhance their narrative identities. Unlike mechanistic interpretations of self-deception rendered in the opaque language of repression and dissociation, I interpret self-deception as a narrative reconstruction in which the person is the agent of the reconstruction.

Self-deception is only one of a number of concepts that can be illuminated by invoking the self-narrative. Moral choice is another. I suggest that the study of virtue would be more rewarding if scientists replaced the popular templatic conceptions with the more humanistic conceptions embraced by the narrative root metaphor.

REFERENCES

Chun, K. T. (1970). *A psychological study of mythmaking: A three-factor theory of metaphor to myth transformation.* Unpublished doctoral dissertation, University of California, Berkeley.

Chun, K. T. and Sarbin, T. R. (1970). An empirical study of metaphor to myth transformation. *Philosophical Psychologist,* 4, 16-20.

Crites, S. (1979). The aesthetics of self deception. *Soundings,* 42, 197-229.

Crites, S. (1975). Angels we have heard. In J. Wiggins (Ed.), *Religion as story.* New York: Harper.

Dewey, J. (1922). *Human nature and conduct.* New York: Holt.

Fingarette, H. (1971). *Self deception.* New York: Routledge & Kegan Paul.

Geertz, C. (1980). Blurred genres: The refiguration of social thought. *American Scholar,* 80, 165-179.

Gergen, K. J. (1973). Social psychology as history. *Journal of Personality and Social Psychology,* 26, 309-320.

Gergen, K. J. and Gergen, M. (1983). Narratives of the self. In T. R. Sarbin and K. E. Scheibe (Eds.), *Studies in social identity.* New York: Praeger.

Goffman, E. (1974). *Frame analysis.* New York: Harper & Row.

Goffman, E. (1961). *Encounters: Two studies in the sociology of interaction.* Indianapolis: Bobbs-Merrill.

Goffman, E. (1959). *The presentation of self in everyday life.* Garden City, NY: Doubleday.

Harré, R. and Secord, P. (1972). *The explanation of social behavior.* Oxford: Blackwell.

Hauerwas, S. (1977). *Truthfulness and tragedy.* Notre Dame, IN: University of Notre Dame Press.

Heider, F. and Simmel, E. (1944). A study of apparent behavior. *American Journal of Psychology,* 57, 243-259.

Kahneman, D. and Tversky, A. (1973). Subjective probability: A judgment of representativeness. *Cognitive Psychology,* 3, 430-454.

Kintsch, W. (1977). On comprehending stories. In M. A. Just and P. A. Carpenter (Eds.), *Cognitive processes in comprehension.* Hillsdale, NJ: Laurence Erlbaum Associates.

Levin, H. (1970). The Quixotic principle. In M. W. Bloomfield (Ed.), *Harvard English Studies I, The Interpretation of Narrative: Theory and practice.* Cambridge, MA: Harvard University Press.

Lewis, C. S. (1939). Bluspels and Flalansferes, in *Rehabilitations and other essays.* London: Oxford University Press.

MacIntyre, A. (1981). *After virtue.* Notre Dame, IN: University of Notre Dame Press.

Mancuso, J. C. and Sarbin, T. R. (1983). The self narrative in the enactment of roles. In T. R. Sarbin and K. E. Scheibe (Eds.), *Studies in social identity.* New York: Praeger.

Marshack, A. (1972). *Roots of civilization: The cognitive beginnings of man's first art, symbol and notation.* New York: McGraw-Hill.

Michotte, A. E. (1963). *The perception of causality.* London: Methuen. Trans. Miles, T. R. and Miles, E. from *La Perception de la causalité,* Louvain, France, 1946.

Mink, L. O. (1978). Narrative form as a cognitive instrument. In R. H. Canary and H. Kozicki (Eds.), *The writing of history: Literary form and historical understanding.* Madison, WI: University of Wisconsin Press.

Pepper, S. (1942). *World hypotheses.* Berkeley: University of California Press.

Polti, G. (1916). *The thirty-six dramatic situations* (L. Ray, Trans.). Boston: Writer, Inc.

Runyan, W. M. (1982). *Life histories and psychobiography.* New York: Oxford Unviersity Press.

Rosenberg, S. (1977). New approaches to the analysis of personal constructs. In A. W. Landfield (Ed.), *1976 Nebraska symposium on motivation.* Lincoln, NE: University of Nebraska Press.

Sarbin, T. R. (1943). The concept of role taking. *Sociometry,* 6, 273-284.

Sarbin, T. R. (1954). Role theory. In G. Lindzey (Ed.), *Handbook of Social Psychology.* Cambridge: Addison-Wesley.

Sarbin, T. R. (1968). Ontology recapitulates philology: The mythic nature of anxiety. *American Psychologist,* 23, 411-418.

Sarbin, T. R. (1977). Contextualism: A world view for modern psychology. In A. W. Landfield (Ed.), *1976 Nebraska symposium on motivation.* Lincoln, NE: University of Nebraska Press.

Sarbin, T. R. (1981). On self deception. In T. A. Sebeok and R. Rosenthal (Eds.), *The clever Hans phenomenon: Communication in horses, whales, apes, and people. Annals of New York Academy of Sciences,* 364, 220-235.

Sarbin, T. R. (1982). The Quixotic principle: A belletristic approach to the psychological study of imaginings and believings. In V. L. Allen and K. E. Scheibe (Eds.), *The social context of conduct: Psychological writings of Theodore Sarbin.* New York: Praeger.

Sarbin, T. R. (1983). Role transitions as social drama. In V. L. Allen and E. Van de Vliert (Eds.), *Role transitions.* New York: Plenum.

Sarbin, T. R. (1984). Nonvolition in hypnosis: A semiotic analysis. *Psychological Record,* 34, 537-552.

Sarbin, T. R. and Allen, V. L. (1968). Role theory. In G. Lindzey and E. Aronson (Eds.), *Handbook of Social Psychology* (Rev. Ed.), Volume I. Reading, MA: Addison-Wesley.

Schafer, R. (1980). Narration in the psychoanalytic dialogue. *Critical Inquiry,* 7, 29-53.

Spence, D. P. (1982). *Narrative truth and historical truth: Meaning and interpretation in psychoanalysis.* New York: Norton

White, H. (1973). *Metahistory.* Baltimore: Johns Hopkins University Press.

2

Narrative Form and the Construction of Psychological Science

Kenneth J. Gergen and
Mary M. Gergen

THE VANISHING OBJECT IN
THEORETICAL ACCOUNTS

The present chapter is concerned with the ways in which scientific understanding is governed by nonobjective factors. In particular we wish to explore the ways in which literary conventions serve to fashion the theories of science. Of focal interest is the importance of narrative form in theoretical constructions. To appreciate the argument more fully let us begin with an overview of the present status of scientific metatheory. For many years empiricist metatheory has served as the major rationale for scientific procedure. This metatheory holds that theories about the world can be formulated and constrained on the basis of systematic observation. By rigorously employing systematic empirical procedures, it was believed, one could emerge with theoretical maps to successfully guide one's actions in the world. However, this compelling promise of early empiricism depended on the justification of several major premises. As this attempt at justification has proceeded, it has been found that at least one of these critical premises, rather than garnering the necessary support, has been subjected to a continuing series of critical blows. At this juncture, the status of this premise is sufficiently deteriorated that many philosophers (for this and other reasons) consider the philosophy of science to be in a post-empiricist phase (Thomas, 1979).

The critical premise in this case is that theoretical terms within a science can refer to real world events with sufficient precision that the propositions in which such terms are featured can be subjected to empirical assessment. If unambiguous reference cannot be established, then objectivity is beyond the capacity of scientific theory. If one cannot determine the referents for theoretical terms, it is impossible to falsify such theories by objective means.

This simple but key assumption has fallen prey to a series of debilitating attacks over the past several decades. First, the relationship between word and referent has been critically explored. For example, to what does such a homely and seemingly unambiguous term as "desk" refer? Does it refer to any particular configuration of wood, metal, or glass, to the uses these or other materials are put, to the designer's plans for the construction, or something else? Further, when the attempt is made at closer specification, we find the terms of definition equally ambiguous (for example, precisely what is a "configuration of wood"?). Most trenchant in this case was Quine's (1960) demonstration that two users of the same descriptive term could fully agree on the way in which the term should be used but hold entirely different conceptions of the object itself. For example, we might both use the term "rabbit" on the same occasions but you might be referring to the wholistic form of the animal while I might be referring to individual rabbit parts in their attached form.

To this problem of word-object ambiguity Wittgenstein (1963) and others added a second: the limitations placed on the way a term is used depend substantially on the linguistic context in which the term is embedded. What color is the desk before us? One is permitted to say that it is blue in a poetic context, brown to a visiting friend, and without color (but merely reflecting light) to the psychophysiologist. Thus, whether the desk is blue, brown, or colorless depends not so much on the actual properties of the desk itself but the linguistic context one employs. Finally, there is the argument made by Hanson (1958) and others to the effect that objects or events of the world cannot be identified independently of the concepts of understanding with which one approaches them. The concepts must precede, rather than be derived from, observation. Desks are not objects to be discovered in the world.

Rather, one possesses a concept of desk that is used to select certain features of the world and avoid others. In effect, theoretical language so acts as to determine what are taken to be entities in the world. Together these various lines of argument pose severe difficulties for the assumption of unambiguous empirical reference.

Although such arguments have greatly weakened the empiricist assumption that scientific theories can serve as objective maps or mirrors of the world, they have simultaneously opened a new and exciting realm of inquiry. Quine (1960) concluded his attack on the theory of reference by stating that scientific theories are grossly underdetermined by the nature of the world. Wittgenstein's arguments further suggest that attention should be turned from the constraints over theory engendered by the world itself to those imposed by linguistic context. And, to extend the implications of Hanson's (1958) views, if it is preconception that largely determines what counts as fact, then serious attention must be given to the process of preconception. In effect, each of these critiques invites concern with the process of theory construction. If scientific theories are principally linguistic implements, then rules of linguistic practice may largely govern their potential for elaboration. This is not to say that the scientist must simply adopt proper grammatical rules in communicating about the world. Rather, it is to suggest that the form of depiction, the "objective" characterization itself, may be importantly determined by conventions of discourse.

This latter possibility has become amplified in recent years in theories of literary criticism – most particularly within deconstructionist theory (Culler, 1982). Here it is reasoned that what a reader brings to a text in terms of expectations, skills, and affective dispositions are major determinants of the text's meaning. In this sense the text in itself (including the author's intentions) are deconstructed. That is, it is not the text that determines the reader's reaction, but the reader who determines what the text is saying. Theorists such as Derrida (1972) and DeMan (1978) further propose that as the literary critic constructs an interpretive account of a passage, this construction will be governed largely by the convention of proper interpretation. In particular, most descriptive accounts revolve around a guiding metaphor. Once one has selected the central metaphor, it will largely determine the subsequent account of the work one is ostensibly attempting to depict. By analogy, when psychologists attempt to account for people's actions their theories will be importantly guided by the root metaphors they select. For example, after one chooses to view human cognition as computer-like, the metaphor of the computer dictates how the mind may be subsequently described. The theorist is virtually bound to carry out research on such processes as information processing, storage, retrieval, heuristics, and so on. Such processes do not lie there to be discovered in nature, but are the necessary outcome of adopting the organizing metaphor.

As we see, contemporary thinking about the nature of reference greatly weakens the link between theory and object, and opens consideration of the ways in which the construction of scientific theories is governed by conventions of discourse. The present chapter attempts to extend this line of thinking to the realm of knowledge making in psychology. Specifically, our concern is with the literary device of the narrative. After proposing a particular view of narrative construction, we shall explore the guiding effects of narrative form on the scientific attempt to understand the development of the child. Finally we shall consider the implications of our analysis for future efforts in developmental theory. The present analysis is not without important predecessors. The attempts of Mink (1969), Gallie (1968) and Danto (1965) to demonstrate the dependency of historical accounts on narrative explanation have been groundbreaking. More recently Landau (1984) has demonstrated how the various scientific accounts of human evolution represent variations on the folk myth of the hero. McClosky (1983) has also attempted to show how contemporary economic theory is governed by rhetorical necessities. The present chapter extends such concerns in new directions.

ELEMENTS AND FORM IN NARRATIVE CONSTRUCTION

Perhaps the most essential ingredient of narrative accounting (or storytelling) is its capability to structure events in such a way that they demonstrate, first, a connectedness or coherence, and second, a sense of movement or direction through time ("selectivity" and "movement" are the terms of Scholes and Kellogg, 1966). Yet, it may be asked, how is the narrative able to achieve these ends? Or to put it another way, what is it about a story that enables it to convey the sense of orderly movement? An earlier discussion of literary narratives (Gergen & Gergen, 1984) suggests two related ingredients, which together foster such ends. To succeed as a narrative the account must first *establish a goal state or valued endpoint*. For example, it must succeed in establishing the value of a protagonist's well-being, the destruction of an evil condition, the victory of a favored group, the discovery of something precious, or the like. With the creation of a goal condition, the successful narrative must then *select and arrange events in such a way that the goal state is rendered more or less probable.* A description of events unrelated to the goal state detracts or dissolves the sense of narrative. In effect, all events in a successful narrative are related by virtue of their containment within a given evaluative space. Therein lies the coherence of the narrative. As one moves from one event to another, one also approaches or moves away from the desired goal state. Through this latter means one achieves a sense of directionality.

Although these components seem essential to the narrative there may be others that improve on its sophistication or efficacy. One ancillary component of particular significance is the availability of causal linkages between the various elements making up the story. Each event furnishes the grounds for understanding why the next event occurs. For example, a story in which someone suddenly wins a lottery and becomes wealthy is less satisfying than one in which the protagonist has planned and plotted for months to develop a way of improving on the lottery chances and then wins. The scorn reserved for dramatic endings employing a deus ex machina can be traced to the criterion of causal linkage; it is unsatisfactory by present standards to resolve a tense story situation by an event (such as the sudden intervention of a god or the appearance of a long lost relative out of the blue) with no causal relation to the preceding tale.

Other components of narrative form may be located, and the present analysis could prove more or less accurate across history. The conception of the proper narrative has undergone change over time, and its future alteration is to be anticipated. As Genette (1980) has described, for example, writers such as Proust and Joyce have had a major impact on the contemporary conception of proper fictional narrative. The demand for arranging events in a temporal order relevant to goal attainment is far less powerful in this century than the last.

It is our view that the rules for narrative construction guide our attempt to account for human actions across time. They do so both in informal relationships, where we attempt to make ourselves intelligible to each other (Mancuso & Sarbin, 1983; Bertaux & Kohli, 1984), and in the scientific attempts to describe and explain human behavior. Given such constraints over our attempts to "make sense," how are we to understand the various forms that narrative can take? What are the constraints on our means of explaining life through narrative explanation? An answer to this question is furnished by elaborating the logic of our preceding account.

That is, if the successful narrative is one that arranges a sequence of events as they pertain to the achievement of a particular goal state, then there are only three prototypical or primitive narrative forms: those in which progress toward the goal is enhanced, those in which it is impeded, and those in which no change occurs. When events are linked in such a way that one steadily progresses toward a goal we may speak of *progressive* narrative; if one is continuously moving away from the valued state it may be called a *regressive* narrative (see Figure 2.1). For example, the individual might be engaged in a progressive narrative with the surmise, "She is really learning to overcome her shyness and be more open and friendly with people," or a regressive narrative with the thought, "He can't seem to control the events of his life anymore." Directionality is also implied in each of these narratives with the former anticipating further increments and the latter further decrements. The last of these prototypical forms may be termed the *stability narrative*, that is, a narrative that links incidents, images or concepts in such a way that the protagonist remains essentially unchanged with respect to evaluative position.

As indicated, these three narrative forms, stability, progressive, and regressive, exhaust the fundamental options for the direction of movement in evaluative space. As such they may be considered rudimentary bases for other more complex variants. Theoretically one may envision a potential infinity of variations on these rudimentary forms. However, for reasons of social utility, aesthetic desirability, and cognitive capability, the culture may limit itself to a truncated repertoire of possibilities. For example, of prime interest within this limited set is the tragic narrative. In the present framework such a narrative would possess the structure depicted in Figure 2.2. The tragedy, in this sense, would tell the story of the rapid downfall of one who had achieved high position. A

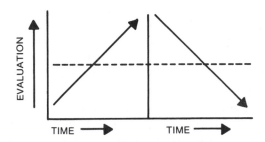

FIGURE 2.1 Progressive and regressive narratives

progressive narrative is thus followed by a rapid regressive narrative. This common narrative form may be contrasted with that of the happy-ending or comedy, as it was termed by Aristotle. The comedy is the reverse of the tragedy: a regressive narrative is followed by a progressive narrative. Life events become increasingly problematic until the denouement, whereupon happiness is rapidly restored to the major protagonists (see Figure 2.2). Further, if a progressive narrative is followed by a stability narrative (see Figure 2.3), we have what is commonly known as the "happily ever after" myth widely adopted in traditional courtship. And we also recognize the romantic saga as a series of progressive-regressive phases. In this case, for example, the individual may see life as a continuous array of battles against the powers of darkness.

DRAMATIC ENGAGEMENT IN NARRATIVE FORM

We have said nothing so far about one of the most phenomenologically salient aspects of narrative form: the capacity to create feelings of drama or emotion. We may refer to this aspect of narrative form with the term *dramatic engagement*. In the same way that theatrical productions vary in their capacity to arouse and compel an audience, so may the narrative forms of daily life and of science vary in their dramatic impact. How are we to understand the elements giving rise to these variations? Of course, dramatic engagement cannot be separated entirely from the content of a given narrative. Yet, segmented events in themselves appear limited in their capacity to sustain engagement. For example, a film depicting the continuous, random juxtaposition of startling events (an auto crash, circus acrobats, a passionate embrace, a dog fight) would soon produce tedium. It is the *relationship* among events, not the events themselves, that seems chiefly responsible for sustaining dramatic engagement, and a theory of narrative form is essentially concerned with such relationships. What characteristics of narrative form are necessary, then, to generate dramatic engagement?

At this preliminary juncture, one must consider the dramatic arts as a source of insight. In this case, it is of initial interest that one can scarcely locate a theatrical exemplar of the three rudimentary narratives proposed above. A drama in which all events were evaluatively equivalent (stability narrative) would scarcely be considered drama. Further, a steady but moderate enhancement (progressive) or decrement (regressive narrative) in a protagonist's life conditions would also seem to produce ennui. At

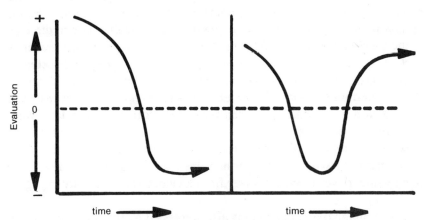
FIGURE 2.2 Tragedy and comedy-melodrama narratives

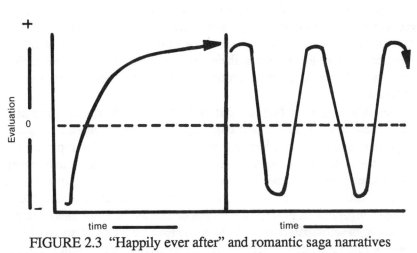
FIGURE 2.3 "Happily ever after" and romantic saga narratives

the same time, it is also interesting to observe that the tragic narrative depicted in Figure 2.2 bears a strong resemblance to the simpler, but unarousing regressive narrative (Figure 2.1). How does the tragic narrative, with its consistently powerful dramatic impact, differ from the more rudimentary regressive narrative? Two characteristics seem particularly significant. First, we note that the relative decline in events is far less rapid in the prototypical regressive narrative than it is in the case of the tragic narrative. Whereas the former is characterized by moderate decline over time, the latter organizes events in such a way that decline is precipitous. In this light one may conjecture that the rapidity with which events deteriorate in such classic tragedies as *Antigone, Oedipus Rex* and *Romeo and Juliet* may be essential to their dramatic impact. More generally, it may be suggested that the rate of change, or more formally *the acceleration of the narrative slope*, constitutes one of the chief components of what is here termed dramatic engagement. The more rapidly one moves toward or away from a valued state the more engaging the story.

A second major component is also suggested by the contrast between the regressive and the tragic narratives. In the former and less dramatic case (Figure 2.1) there is unidirectionality in the slope line; by contrast, in the tragic narrative (Figure 2.2) we find a progressive narrative followed by a regressive narrative. It would appear to be this turn of events, or more precisely, the change in the evaluative relationship among events, that contributes to a high degree of dramatic engagement. It is when the individual who has attained high goals, has reached the apex of ecstasy, or has at last discovered life's guiding principle is brought low that drama is created. In more formal terms, the *alteration in the direction of narrative slope* may be considered a second major component of dramatic engagement.

Yet, there is one further and more subtle aspect of dramatic engagement to consider. In particular, one of the most engaging aspects of drama is often captured by the term "suspense." A goal is apparent, the protagonist is moving toward it, but at any moment a setback may occur – the secret agent may be discovered, a wild beast may leap from an overhead branch, or the lover's seamy past may be revealed. In effect, dramatic engagement in this case is created not by the story itself, but by a potential or anticipated series of events. How are we to understand this aspect of dramatic engagement in present terms? It appears that suspense is a derivative of the two components discussed so far. In particular, when the narrative slope can undergo sudden acceleration and/or shift in the opposite direction from its present course, dramatic engagement is accelerated. Thus, any indication that the story line could change rapidly and/or in a different direction adds substantially to the drama.

NARRATIVE STRUCTURE IN DEVELOPMENTAL THEORY

Given these various forms of narrative, so typical to theater, literature, and to daily life, what is to be said of developmental theory within psychology? At the outset it should be realized that observation itself places only minimal constraints upon the shape of such theorizing. There is, after all, no logical means by which accounts of development may be derived from the observation of infants moving through space and time. Such observation may furnish the opportunity for theoretical accounts; it does not, however, furnish the conceptual categories nor their particular forms of relationship. If observation plays only a delimited role in the determination of developmental theory, one's attentions turn to other sources. Among the most salient are the cultural forms relevant to discourse about events across time. As we have seen, such discourse is primarily narrative in structure. The developmental theorist can scarcely describe simple, disconnected events – the child's smile, then the movement of his forearm, then the utterance of a guttural sound, then the movement of the left forefinger; to do so would be considered pointless. If our analysis is correct, maximal intelligibility is achieved when the theorist includes in the analysis those events, and only those events, related to some evaluative endpoint. Ideally, these events should also be causally linked. In effect, to adhere to the characteristics of the well-formed narrative, the theoretical account must give unity, direction, and coherence to the life course. Further, this narrative is likely to draw from the pool of commonly accepted narratives within the culture. To do less would fail to participate in the communal practices of making sensible accounts.

Let us briefly consider three major developmental orientations with an eye toward their dominant narrative forms: Learning theory, Piagetian theory, and psychoanalytic theory. leanring theories, ranging from the Watsonian through the Skinnerian to more recent social modeling accounts, pose an immediate challenge to our analysis. As many would argue, they furnish no elaborated account of the developmental process. Both theoretical and empirical analyses are generally confined to temporally delimited and disembedded events (for example, the stimulus-response unit, the reinforcement trial, the immediate effects of the stimulus). Theorists seem most concerned with the immediate effects of the stimulus conditions, regardless of either the past history or the future trajectory of the individual. In effect one might contend that learning theories in general have no developmental story to tell.

Yet, on closer inspection, we find that there is an implicit story, and it approximates one of the more common narrative frames of the culture. If one examines the intellectual ethos in which learning theory sprang to life, one finds that it is strongly Darwinian in character. One of the major quests of evolutionary theory was that of understanding survival. In particular, how are we to understand the superiority of the human species and how can its continued survival be secured? Learning theory was a major attempt to furnish positive answers to these questions: processes of learning are the key to survival. For example, after discussing Darwin's work, Clark Hull (1943) proposed that "It is the primary task of a molar science . . . to understand why behavior is so generally adaptive, i.e., successful in the sense of reducing needs and facilitating survival" (p. 19). Survival is secured through the learning mechanisms by which humans acquire those habits or dispositions of adaptive value. Optimally functioning processes of learning should ensure the maintenance of the species.

Thus, learning theories typically embody a view of development with a positive endpoint. The individual who knows nothing at birth (the tabula rasa) learns to adapt. The implicit narrative is therefore a progressive one. However, it may also be ventured that in most cases such theories suggest a progressive narrative with a negatively accelerated slope. That is, attempts to master a changing environment become increasingly dependent on reinforcement history and less sensitive to environmental inputs. As explained more fully elsewhere (Gergen & Benack, 1984), most learning theory is committed to the view that any reinforcement or learning trial contributes to a given response disposition. On subsequent trials the organism will thus be disposed to react in a predetermined manner. With sufficient training of a given kind the organism may indeed be rendered insensitive to variations in subsequent environmental conditions. This is indeed the logic of underlying traditional research on both the strength of conditioning and extinction. It is also the logic underlying Seligman's (1975) more recent theory of learned helplessness; in this theory exposure to conditions of helplessness renders one incapable of action (or, unmotivated) on subsequent occasions when problems could otherwise be effectively solved. In effect, other things being equal, early experiences will be more potent in their effects than will later experiences. Any new stimulus is encountered within the context of a steadily increasing pool of predispositions.

In terms of narrative form we see, then, that the organism may demonstrate rapid acceleration in the acquisition of adaptive habits; however, as maturation is reached, the accretion of knowledge becomes less dramatic. The result is that in major respects learning theory accounts of development are generally committed to a narrative form of the "happily ever after" variety (Figure 2.2). The normal life should be one in which childhood and adolescence furnish the major habits, skills, or knowledge to ensure a positive life course thereafter. Perhaps it is not so surprising that learning theories came to flourish on U.S. soil. It should also be noted that in addition to furnishing an evaluative endpoint, and at least theoretically, being able to determine the critical events in the learning history, learning theory furnishes a means of meeting the third criterion of narrative construction – that of causal connection among events. In particular, to the extent that preceding learning trials establish parameters for subsequent environmental effects, learning experiences can be causally related across time.

Although for many purposes Piagetian theory (Piaget, 1952, 1968) of development can be usefully contrasted with learning theory, there is one major way in which they are similar. Both theories constitute variations on the progressive narrative. Piaget's genetic epistemology is first an attempt to account for the superior adaptability of the human (in this way forming parallel to the behaviorist mission), and second to account for what appears to be the outstanding knowledge-generating capacities of the advanced sciences. As Piaget proposes, "intelligence . . . is the most highly developed form of mental adaptation, that is to say, the indispensable instrument for interaction between the subject and the universe" (1968, p. 7). With the positive valuation endpoint thus established, normal development across time is characterized in terms of movement of the individual toward the endpoint.

Each stage of cognitive development (see Figure 2.4) represents a progressive step in the direction of mature or fully adaptive thought. Thus, in the sensorimotor stage of early childhood the child achieves the capacity to identify objects, and develops rudimentary concepts of time, space, and causality. In the subsequent, preoperational stage, the child moves ahead to form images of objects that are absent, to represent these

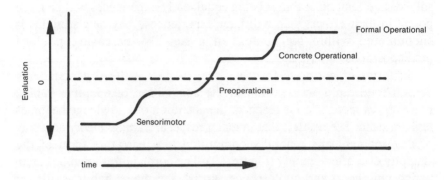

FIGURE 2.4 Piagetian theory as progressive narrative

images as words, and to take others' perspectives. These stages are essential prerequisites to the stage of concrete operations, in which the child gains the capacity for logical thought, including simple arithmetic. The crowning achievement is the subsequent stage of formal operations in which the child achieves the capacity to think in abstract terms, perform experiments, develop a belief system, and think reflexively about self.

As we see, Piagetian theory effectively employs the two major components of narrative: the establishment of a valuational endpoint and the ordering of relevant events. However, the criterion of causal dependency of events proves more problematic. Piaget's theory is essentially organismic (Overton & Reese, 1973); it likens the development of the child's intelligence to the maturing of a flower. One's genetic proclivities are sufficient to orient orderly intellectual growth. Much of the interest in Piagetian theory can be traced to the contrast that it provided with the mechanistic theories within the learning tradition. Yet, pure organismic approaches fall short of the third criterion of proper narrative: causal dependency. Interestingly enough, as Piaget continued to elaborate his theory he increasingly turned his attention to just such causal linkages. As he proposed, maturation is but one of several factors responsible for movement from one stage to the next. Direct experience with objects, logicomathematical experience, and social transmission (including explanation, instruction, and modeling) all play roles. The effects of each of these, in turn, would depend on the child's level of cognitive growth at the time. The result is that movement across stages is the result of an equilibration between external and internal influences (Piaget, 1968). One must have achieved a given stage of cognitive growth, and have employed it within the objective and social world in order to advance to the next stage. Although less fully articulated than other aspects of the theory, causal dependency among narrative events is thus approximated.

Freud's (1905, 1916) theorizing on the nature of psychosexual development stands in sharp contrast to both the learning and Piagetian accounts. In the preceding cases theorists have emphasized the capacity of the normal adult to adapt to environmental exigencies. Such capacities are taken to be given, and the theoretical problem is then to explain how they came about. Freud is in essential agreement with environmental adaptation as a proper endpoint for development. However, he fails to agree that the goal is frequently reached. Rather, proposes Freud, most people only appear to be congenially related to their surroundings. In fact, this apparent adaptation is achieved only at the cost of psychic disturbance and the adoption of neurotic mechanisms of defense. In effect, Freud thus offers not one, but two competing narratives: the one largely ideal and the other actual; the one progressive and the other regressive in character.

Let us briefly consider the opposing tales. The infant is essentially free of neurosis at birth, but not yet adapted to the social and physical environment (see Figure 2.5). With the oral stage of development the infant begins to develop ego capacities – the capability to take account of environmental contingencies and thus to fulfill psychic (Id) demands. However, while gaining an important positive capability, the infant simultaneously acquires tendencies (either incorporative or biting) that may unrealistically potentiate behavior for the remainder of its life. Additional tendencies toward expulsiveness and retentiveness are developed in the subsequent anal stage of development. With the phallic stage the repression of undesirable impulses (also present in earlier stages) becomes maximal. Libidinal desires for the parent of the opposite sex must be blocked from consciousness, and at least in the case of the male, buttressed by the development of the superego. In effect, the superego (or individual's set of goals, values, or morals) becomes an added form of neurotic defense in the regressive tale, but a necessary part of social adaptation in the progressive narrative. The latency stage of development offers no new developments (at least in Freud's own account), and the genital stage in which mature adaption should run – remains largely an ideal. The normal eprson is, by this time, carying the heavy psychic burden deposited by the past.

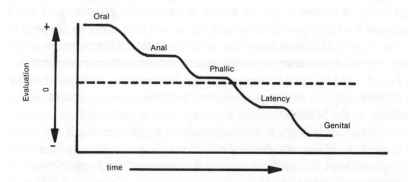

FIGURE 2.5 Psychosexual development as regressive narrative

ON THEORETICAL DEVELOPMENT AND EVALUATION

As we have proposed, the commonly available narrative structures in the society furnish important means by which the behavioral theorist makes intelligible comments. Without relying on such forms the theorist risks seeming incoherent, disorganized, or even absurd. To employ the forms with skill is to tell an agreeable story about human actions. Yet, it may be countered, although theorists may be pleased to tell good stories, they have traditionally been more concerned with telling true ones. What place does the concern with truth have in the present context? Is there not some sense in which the theorist's narrative is either suggested or corrected by what is the case? And if the importance of observation for theory development is reduced, what criteria are to replace them? How are theories to be evaluated?

These are indeed complex issues, and there is no way they can be exhausted in the present context. However, it will be useful to consider the degree of latitude that the developmentalist does have in generating theoretical accounts, and several alternative criteria of evaluation suggested by such considerations.

Narrative Formation and Objectivity

Regarding the objective anchoring of theory, we have already touched on a number of reasons why philosophers of science now consider scientific theories to be underdetermined by facts, and why many have turned their attention to the literary figuration of such theory. At this point, however, it is useful to consider the possibilities for objectively anchoring the narrative construction. For this purpose let us return to the three criteria of narrative construction offered earlier. As described, the initial task of a narrator is to develop an evaluative endpoint or goal of the story. As is readily apparent in this case, there is no means by which observation itself can determine what pursuits should count as valuable in human affairs. As has been maintained since Poincaré's time, there is no means of deriving "ought" from "is" (Kohlberg's theory notwithstanding). Of course, research can be useful in suggesting what people hold to be reasonable values or goals at a given time. Further, armed with such insights, scientists might develop theories of more broadly compelling means. For example, it is now common to view child development as a period of increasing maturity (a progressive narrative), middle adulthood as the stage of full maturity, and old age as decline (a regressive narrative). Indeed much developmental theory is based on just such a view. Yet, it must also be realized that such narratives are only sensible if one considers adult characteristics as more valuable, on one or more criteria, than the attributes of either the very young or very old. Common conceptions of development could be radically altered if societal values (or the values of the adult scientists constructing the theories) were different. Indeed, by selecting spontaneity as a major value or goal one might see child development as regressive; by middle adulthood we have virtually completed our downward course. Or, by counting wisdom or perspective as a major goal, the aging process could be reframed as ascendent. It is the very old who have finally reached developmental maturity. Public opinion can only suggest what people believe to be goals; it cannot furnish insight as to whether these goals are worthy or not. And, at least in the case of the aging process, one may well question the choice of many behavioral scientists to frame it as a decline.

If one abandons the possibility of objectively grounding narrative goals, what can be said about the second major component of the narrative, namely the temporal arrangement of events relevant to the goal? We find the objectively oriented theorist here faces additional difficulties. The observation of a person in motion over time furnishes the scientist with an immense array of potential facts. Each movement of every limb, each syllable, secretion, or silence could be recorded as a fact. Or, one may blend these microelements in a variety of ways – into gestures, phrases, sentences, speech acts, perseverance toward goals, and so on.

In effect, observation itself furnishes an immense array of opportunities for fact making. However, it does not furnish any directives as to how one is to go about selecting from the array. It is this task which is largely accomplished in developmental study by the narrative goal. Once one has selected the valuation endpoint of development it is possible to scan the array for relevant exemplars. By determining that adult rationality is a developmental goal, one can then turn to the array of preceding events to search out and construct events in such a way that they move toward this apex. The end of the story, in this sense, furnishes the major device by which the observer scans the world for relevant and related content. As Hayden White (1978) has characterized historical writing,

> The process of fusing events . . . into a totality capable of serving as the object of representation is a poetic one. . . . These fragments have to be put together to make a whole . . . and they are put together in the same way that novelists put together figments of their imaginations to display an ordered world, a cosmos, where only disorder or chaos might appear. (P. 124)

Once the endpoint has been established, can the observer then let the relevant facts speak for themselves? Can the scientist simply observe in such a way that the developmental story tells itself? It would not appear so. Again, to quote White's (1978) analysis of historical reporting, "The facts do not speak for themselves, but . . . the historian speaks on their behalf, and fashions the fragments of the past into a whole whose integrity is in its representation – a purely discursive one" (p. 124). For the behavioral scientist it is not the precise movements of the body through time and space that are critical. Each movement of concern must be given an interpretive label referring to the motive, disposition, or process underlying it. We don't understand action in terms of precise body movements but in such terms as intelligent, friendly, helpful, angry, aggressive, and so on, all of which refer to internal states. In effect, the behavioral scientist must continuously make interpretive (hermeneutic) judgments for which the criteria are conventional rather than objective (Gergen, 1982).

Further, as the present analysis indicates, not just any arrangement of facts will tell a proper or acceptable story. We would not accept a developmental account in which the child showed continuous decline until the age of six and then demonstrated miraculous recovery at the age of seven. Or, a developmental story in which odd years of development were progressive while even years were regressive would be equally untenable – not because such accounts are manifestly false, but because the narrative forms are not constituents of current intelligibility norms.

Toward Alternative Criteria for Theory Assessment

This analysis essentially contends that scientific theory is governed in substantial degree by what are essentially aesthetic forms (see also Kelly-Byrne & Sutton-Smith, 1983; Sutton-Smith, 1983). In this case the familiar forms of storytelling furnish the literary figures for establishing theories of child development. Yet, the present analysis furnishes the behavioral theorist an immense latitude for theoretical development. Observation need furnish only minimal constraints over the range of developmental stories that may be told. It is the selection of narrative form that largely determines what is to count as fact, and not fact which determines the developmental story. Narrative form is critical; observational grounding thereafter operates most importantly as a rhetorical device. Much as a news story often gains in vividness, credibility, and emotional impact as details are discussed, so may systematic observations aid the theorist in fashioning compelling theory. If this argument can be sustained, one is moved to reconsider the criteria typically employed in evaluating behavioral theory. Thus far we have found that the case for objective warrant is a tenuous one; the traditionally honored criterion of verisimilitude must be considered secondary in relevance. Other traditional criteria such as logical consistency, agreement with accepted theory, parsimony, and so on must also be reassessed (compare Feyerabend, 1975). Rather than viewing these as absolute or superordinate criteria, one may regard them in their rhetorical capacity. In what degree, it may be asked, do they aid the theorist in formulating a powerful and compelling account of human functioning? There is more to be said on this matter, but this must be postponed for another occasion.

We must finally ask about the particular criteria for theoretical evaluation implied by the present analysis. As we find, developmental theories in the sciences seem to approximate and to derive their sense-making capacity largely from existing narrative structures. To the extent that this is so, it is legitimate to evaluate such theories in the degree to which they fulfill the demands, or extend the possibilities, for good narrative form. In what degree does a theory approximate the mature or sophisticated narrative, and in what degree does it open new frontiers for human accounting? Let us briefly consider our earlier criteria in this light along with exemplary theory.

Establishment of Developmental Goal

At the most basic level, the narrative theorist must specify or imply an evaluative endpoint for the account. Without this initial step, indeed, the concept of development is rendered meaningless. To the extent that there is no point to the account it may thus be considered a decomposed form of narrative. In this sense, Piagetian theory is to be highly regarded. Piaget clearly articulates his beliefs about higher mental processes, and their place in both science and human adaptation more generally. Freud is somewhat less clear in this respect, and largely relies on an implicit, but unarticulated concept of the fully developed human being. This reluctance should largely be attributed to Freud's belief that the viability of society largely depends on the repression of its members. Thus, a person lacking all neurosis would constitute a social threat. Of the three theories considered, learning theory is perhaps the least mature in its narrative form. The implicit (and only occasionally explicit) assumption is that humans become increasingly adaptive. However, precisely what constitutes adaptation in the culture is left open. In this sense, learning theories are thus the least mature of the available orientations.

In another place (Gergen, 1982) an *aleatory* view of the life course has been proposed. From this perspective, development depends on the particular confluence of sociohistorical circumstances. Life trajectories may thus be of many different varieties, and there is little reason to suspect strong transhistorical or cross-cultural generality in developmental pattern. While this view does not saddle the individual with a necessary and predetermined life pattern, it fails to provide a functioning endpoint or developmental goal. In this sense it possesses little narrative structure and fails as a compelling story.

Organization of Events Relevant to Endpoints

A valuational endpoint without events leading toward or away is a conclusion without a story. The greater the number of salient points demonstrating how one proceeded from beginning to end, the more mature or well-developed the story. In this sense, a theory such as Piaget's is formidable. The theory accounts for virtually all periods preceding mental maturity. Even within developmental phases Piaget provides elaborate accounts of the particular mental accomplishments (for example, conservation) and the order of their development (for example, decalage). Freudian theory is less well-developed in this regard. The first six years of development are richly described, but between this period and young adulthood, the person enters a sparsely detailed period of latency. It is as if the story's end is simply postponed for a period of years – an awkward hiatus for which several theorists have since attempted to compensate (including Anna Freud and Erik Erikson). Learning theory is the least developed narrative in terms of its articulation of relevant events. This problem stems in important degree from the above-noted lack of an elaborated endpoint. Adaptation in itself furnishes an insufficient goal against which to assess progress or its lack. Without articulating the story's end, there is little way of selecting preceding events of relevance. Further, the theory is constructed in such a way that, in principle, a learning experience at any given point may cancel the effect of previous reinforcement. A child who is making increasing strides toward social adaptiveness may be set back at any point through a traumatic learning experience. In effect, the learning theorist offers no continuous or orderly trajectory but the potential for a chaotic juxtaposition of events across time.

Logical Connection of Developmental Events

The third criterion of a mature narrative form is its capacity to tie events together in a dependent or causal fashion. As we have seen, both learning theory and Piagetian theory do make strides in this direction. Neither is entirely successful. Learning theory does posit an interdependency among learned dispositions across time. However, there is no account given of why one particular experience should follow another. Thus the child may learn to be aggressive in one hour, altruistic in the next, and fearful in the next, with no connective tissue relating these separate experiences. Piaget does offer an account of stage shifts largely in terms of equilibration. However, equilibration itself appears to be an organismic-centered form of explanation. At certain points the child simply begins the process by which mental development progresses. Humans are genetically programmed to do so. Freudian theory is similarly organismic in its explanation for the shift in zones of id gratification (that is, oral, anal, and phallic) and thus the sequences of stages. Further, little is said about how experiences at one stage modify or influence events at the next. The one important way in which the theory makes use of causal links is in its account of the etiology of nervous disorders. In all cases, the explanation of adult neuroses is traced back to some preceding event(s), typically in the first six years of development. Early dynamics cause later disorder.

Dramatic Impact

Although sense of drama is a derivative rather than a component of narrative composition, it is useful to consider its relevance to behavioral theory. Such theory need not possess dramatic potential in order to make sense of the world. However, dramatic appeal generates interest or concern in the story, it invites the audience into one's theoretical edifice, and thereby increases understanding and the ultimate utility of the theory. In this respect one must view Freudian theory as far superior to either the Piagetian or learning frameworks. In the case of Piagetian theory, the slope line is steadily (with the exception of stage shifts) in the ascending direction. Years are also required to reach maturity, and thus neither alternation nor acceleration in the narrative slope can be achieved. Further, because the theory offers no means of cognitive regression, one never confronts the possibility of a sudden shift in the downward direction. Because of its lack of content, learning theory offers no definitive story line; in its abstract form it thus lacks any inherent drama. A specific life history could, in a learning theorist's hands, be rendered dramatic by the present criteria. However, the general model itself offers little in this regard.

Freudian theory does share with the Piagetian perspective a relatively steady developmental trajectory, and the amount of time required to the story's end is approximately two decades. Yet, the theory also possesses three special moments of dramatic impact. The first is derived from the possibility of a reversal in the slope line, and particularly a reversal that would shift the story's end from the dismal to the happy ending. This possibility is furnished through the vehicle of psychoanalytic treatment. This treatment is the only means provided by the theory through which the individual can alleviate repressed energy and thus the need for mechanisms of defense. The second moment of potential drama derives from the fact that, unlike Piagetian theory, regression to earlier stages of development is always possible. Momentary stress at any point may, within the Freudian perspective, catapult one into the past, seeking means of renewed psychic defense. Yet, the negative effects of development can be alleviated. Psychoanalytic treatment does furnish a means of reversing the slope line. Finally, the theory itself stands as a marked contrast to the popular conception of development – namely, the view that it is a progressive narrative. Thus, as the slope line steadily descends within the Freudian perspective, it increasingly deviates from normative expectations. "When," the reader might ask, "does the reversal occur; development is continuously unfolding, and we only move further away from the goals we know we seem to have achieved." Thus, the theory gains dramatic impact through its catalytic relationship with existing expectations. One can scarcely locate a more dramatic device in the annals of developmental theory.

This is not to conclude that scientific theories should only be evaluated with regard to their rhetorical power. Elsewhere a case has been made for assessing the generative potential (Gergen, 1982) of behavioral theories, that is, their potential to throw into question the acceptable or sedimented mores of the culture and to offer fresh alternatives for action. And too, one can no longer afford to construct theory without regard for its ideological, political, and social implications (compare Sampson, 1977; Gilligan, 1982; Wexler, 1983). However, it does seem apparent from the present analysis that critical attention must be given to the literary qualities of theoretical renderings, and in this case to their narrative components.

REFERENCES

Bertaux, D. and Kohli, M. (1984). The life story approach: A continental view. *American Sociological Review*, 10, 215-237.

Culler, J. (1982). *On deconstruction*. Ithaca, NY: Cornell University Press.

Danto, A. (1965). *Analytical philosophy of history*. Cambridge: Cambridge University Press.

DeMan, P. (1978). The epistemology of metaphor. *Critical Inquiry*, 5, 13-30.

Derrida, J. (1972). *Marges de la philosophe*. Paris: Minuit.

Feyerabend, P. K. (1975). *Against method*. Atlantic Highlands, NJ: Humanities Press.

Freud, S. (1943). *A general introduction to psychoanalysis*. Garden City, NJ: Garden City Publishing Co. (Original work published in 1916).

Freud, S. (1953). Three essays on sexuality. In *Standard edition*, Vol. VII. London: Hogarth Press (Original work published in 1905).

Gallie, T. (1968). *Philosophy and historical understanding*. London: Chatto and Windus.

Genette, G. (1980). *Narrative discourse*. Ithaca, NY: Cornell University Press.

Gergen, K. J. (1982). *Toward transformation in social knowledge*. New York: Springer Verlag.

Gergen, K. J. and Benack, S. (1984). Metatheoretical influences on conceptions of human development. In N. M. Lewin (Ed.), *In the shadow of the past: Psychology portrays the sexes*. New York: Columbia University Press.

Gergen, K. J. and Gergen, M. M. (1983). Narratives of the self. In T. R.Sarbin and K. E. Scheibe (Eds.), *Studies in social identity*. New York: Praeger.

Gergen, M. M. and Gergen, K. J. (1984). The social construction of narrative accounts. In K. J. Gergen and M. M. Gergen (Eds.) (in press, b) *Historical social psychology*. Hillsdale, NJ: Erlbaum.

Gilligan, C. (1982). *In a different voice*. Cambridge, MA: Harvard University Press.

Hanson, N. R. (1958). *Patterns of discovery*. London: Cambridge University Press.

Hull, C. L. (1943). *Principles of behavior*. New York: Appleton Century Crofts.

Kelly-Byrne, D. and Sutton-Smith, B. (1983). Narrative as social science: A case study. Unpublished paper. University of Pennsylvania.

Landau, M. (1984). Human evolution as narrative. *American Scientist*, 72, 262-267.

Mancuso, J. C. and Sarbin, T. R. (1983). The self-narrative in the enactment of roles. In T. R. Sarbin and K. E. Scheibe (Eds.), *Studies in social identity*. New York: Praeger.

McClosky, D. N. (1983). The rhetoric of economics. *Journal of Economic Literature*, XXI, 482-516.

Mink, L. A. (1969). History and fiction as modes of comprehension. *New Literary History*, I, 556-569.

Overton, W. R. and Reese, H. W. (1973). Models of development: Methodological implications. In J. R. Nesselroade and H. W. Reese (Eds.), *Life-span developmental psychology: Methodological issues*. New York: Academic Press.

Piaget, J. (1954). *The construction of reality in the child*. New York: Basic Books.

Piaget, J. (1952). *The origins of intelligence*. New York: International Universities Press.

Piaget, J. (1968). *Psychology of intelligence*. Totowa, NJ: Littlefield Adams.

Quine, W. V. O. (1960). *Word and object*. Cambridge, MA: M.I.T. Press.

Sampson, E. (1977). Psychology and the American ideal. *Journal of Personality and Social Psychology*, 35, 767-782.

Scholes, R. and Kellogg, R. (1966). *The nature of narrative*. New York: Oxford University Press.

Seligman, M. (1975). *Helplessness*. San Francisco: W. H. Freeman.

Sutton-Smith, B. (1983). The origins of fiction and the fiction of origins. Unpublished paper. University of Pennsylvania.

Thomas, D. (1979). *Naturalism and social science, A post-empiricist philosophy of science*. Cambridge: Cambridge University Press.

Wexler, P. (1983). *Critical social psychology*. Boston: Routledge & Kegan Paul.

White, H. (1978). *Tropics of discourse*. Baltimore: Johns Hopkins University Press.

Wittgenstein, L. (1963). *Philosophical investigations* (G. Anscombe, Trans.). New York: Macmillan.

3

Trespassing in
Scientific Narrative:
Grafton Elliot Smith
and the Temple of Doom

Misia Landau

I arrived at the Temple of Doom through a passage in Freud. Nudged by his frequent allusions to archeology, I discovered it in that famous footnote in which Freud elevates not psychoanalysis but our ape-like ancestors.

> The fateful process of civilization would thus have set in with man's adoption of an erect posture. From that point the chain of events would have proceeded through the devaluation of olfactory stimuli and isolation of the menstrual period to the time when visual stimuli were paramount and the genitals became visible, and thence to the continuity of sexual excitation, the founding of the family and so to the threshold of human civilization. (1961, pp. 46-47)

Ironically, *Civilization and Its Discontents* could be said to take its first steps in a footnote. And maybe its last, for, as Freud ventures, even human virtues merely follow the perverted path of the upright posture. Consider hygiene:

> The incitement to cleanliness originates in an urge to get rid of the excreta, which have become disagreeable to the sense perceptions. We know that in the nursery things are different. The excreta arouse no disgust in children. They seem valuable to them as being a part of their own body which has come away from it. Here upbringing insists with special energy on hastening the course of development which lies ahead, and which should make the excreta worthless, disgusting, abhorrent and abominable. Such a reversal of values would scarcely be possible if the substances that are expelled from the body were not doomed by their strong smells to share the fate which overtook olfactory stimuli after man adopted the erect posture. (P. 47)

The suggestion that the human body is a temple of doom follows from the fact that Freud refers here less to the body than to its products. It is common practice among paleoanthropologists to trace human destiny in human anatomy.

Not that it is an unusual habit. According to Grafton Elliot Smith, a British comparative anatomist and a contemporary of Freud, "civilisation itself evolved out of man's endeavours to understand the constitution of his own body and to preserve the life that animated it." An Egyptologist, Elliot Smith traces this practice back to the art of embalming.

> Hence around the mummy were created, not only many of the essential arts and crafts (architecture, stone and wood-working, sculpture and painting, the drama, dancing and music) that represent the scaffolding of civilisation, but also the deepest aspirations of the human spirit, the motives which have influenced the thoughts and actions of countless millions of human beings throughout the whole history of civilisation. (1929, pp. xv-xvi)

Mummies, not nurserymaids, were for Elliot Smith the epitome of civilization. Still, reading this passage Freud might have been in sympathy, for it was Elliot Smith who first explained human origins according to the fall of the olfactory sense and the rise of vision.

Whether or not Freud actually read Elliot Smith, and vice versa, interesting parallels can be drawn between them, and not just between the way Freud depicts the rise of the superego and Elliot Smith describes the ascent of vision. For both of these storylines rest on a common belief: that only by knowing *what* happened in the past can we understand *why* it happened; that is, that the ordering and the explanation of events are separate steps in the construction of a history. Thus, by uncovering individual case histories, Freud believed that he would discover the laws by which other lives could be unveiled. Similarly, Elliot Smith pieced together genealogies in order to derive general principles. For

> Without some definite scheme of the position in time and the relationship one to the other of the members of the Order Primates, to which Man belongs, it is impossible to form any idea as to the nature of the factors that determined the emergence of the qualities of mind and body that are distinctive of the Human Family. (1924, p. 1)

As if to emphasize the logical priority of genealogy, Elliot Smith immediately presents two diagrams, one showing the relationships of the primates and one of the human family, in the foreword to his 1924 classic, *The Evolution of Man*. But the history of the book contradicts this logic. For though they appear first, these two genealogies were added last. Indeed, they are the only new contributions to *The Evolution of Man*, which otherwise consists of previously published essays, one written ten years earlier.

It is true, of course, that what is placed first in a text is often the last thing to be written. Nor is this procedure illogical or unscientific. As Elliot Smith explains,

> In the days when only a very few fragments of bone and chipped flint provided all the information available for the study of Primitive Man, a scaffolding of hypothesis was necessary in order to make any sort of edifice of such broken and scanty debris. But now that so much more material is available it is possible to build up a structure capable of standing by itself. Hence this scaffolding is not only no longer necessary, but it interferes with the view of the building. (P. 55)

Placed at the front of his book like two sentinels, Elliot Smith's genealogies would thus seem to indicate that *The Evolution of Man* was firmly established on inductivist principles. Yet a close inspection would show otherwise. For Elliot Smith's 1924 genealogies are constructed according to a "scaffolding of hypothesis" that was established long before the fossil discoveries that appear as their cornerstones.

I have suggested elsewhere that early twentieth century theories of human evolution can be treated as variations on a basic narrative structure, and that such a model "can provide a useful method for the more ambitious exploration of the different ways in which people tell stories" (1984, p. 263). Now, in proposing to analyze Elliot Smith, it will appear that I have ulterior motives; that notwithstanding the connection to Freud, I present my subject primarily to exemplify my method (Figure 3.1). Still, I do not feel entirely selfish. For the point of my analysis will be to expose the fallacy in thinking that the ordering and explaining of events are necessarily separate steps in the construction of a history. Contrary to this rationale, Elliot Smith's general principles cannot be separated from his genealogy, for these principles consist of interrelated events or "trends" which depend on and define his genealogical sequence. One principle found in Elliot Smith's account that might have more general application is the retention of primitive traits, and yet it is used to explain how humans have escaped natural selection by virtue of a narrative sequence. For, according to Elliot Smith, it is

> The steady and uniform development of the brain along a well-defined course throughout the Primates right up to Man – which must give us the fundamental reason for "Man's emergence and ascent," whatever other factors may contribute toward that consummation. (P. 20)

It is not in the nursery but in narrative that humans begin and end for it is there that the ordering and explanation of events marry.

ENCEPHALIZATION: IN WHICH
(1) THE SCENE IS SET,
(2) THE HERO IS INTRODUCED, AND
(3) THE SITUATION CHANGES

And so we find "the first glimmerings of human characteristics amidst even the remotest of his ancestors" in the newly acquired neopallium of a primitive Therapsid (a mammal-like reptile).

> The possession of this higher type of brain enormously widened the scope for the conscious and intelligent adaptation of the animal to varying surroundings. In the exercise of this newly acquired power of discrimination and ability to learn from individual experience, and so appreciate the possibilities of fresh sources of food supply and new modes of life, the way was opened for an infinite series of adaptations to varying environments, entailing the structural modifications in which the enhanced plasticity of the new type of animal found expression. (1924, p. 27)

Transformed by their brains into creatures of infinite possibility, the first mammals similarly transform their surroundings.

The new breed of intelligent creatures rapidly spread throughout the whole world and exploited every mode of livelihood. The power of adaptation to the particular kind of life each group chose to pursue soon came to be expressed in a bewildering variety of specializations in structure, some for living on the earth or burrowing in it, others for living in trees or even for flight; others, again, for an aquatic existence. Some mammals became fleet of foot and developed limbs specially adapted to enhance their powers of rapid movement. They attained an early pre-eminence and were able to grow to large dimensions in the slow-moving world of the dawn of the Age of Mammals. (Pp. 27-28)

But danger lurks, as it often does in Eden. So the "inevitable penalty" is levied on all who succumb to the temptation to specialize. "They became definitely committed to one particular kind of life, and in so doing they sacrificed their primitive simplicity and plasticity of structure, and in great measure also their adaptability to new conditions" (p. 28). Clearly there is little value in the purely material for, as Elliot Smith warns, impressive specializations are actually "confessions of weakness," while primitive traits, thought by some biologists to be degraded, are signs of virtue.

It is important to keep in mind . . . that the retention of primitive characters is often to be looked upon as a token that their possessor has not been compelled to turn aside from the straight path and adopt protective specializations, but has been able to preserve some of the plasticity associated with his primitiveness, precisely because he has not succumbed or fallen away in the struggle for supremacy. It is the wider triumph of the individual who specializes late after benefitting from the many-sided experience of early life, over him who in youth becomes tied to one narrow calling. (Pp. 34-35)

Truly a golden mean, the road to evolutionary success is paved with the nonmaterial. But without a brain to compensate for physical simplicity, such an evolutionary path would lead nowhere. It is the brain, then, that is the key to the retention of primitive traits and to the plasticity signified by the "wider triumph." But perhaps I am giving away the story.

Like many mythical heroes, then, it is precisely because of its humble origins that a primitive mammal can become something better. It is only because it "took advantage of its insignificance to develop its powers evenly and gradually without sacrificing in narrow specialization any of its possibilities of future achievement" (p. 28) that, eventually, it turns into a human. For Elliot Smith, as for Darwin (Landau et al. 1982, p. 507), it was an "immense advantage" to have sprung from a creature of such small significance. Measuring it at about the size of a squirrel, Elliot

FIGURE 3.1 Early twentieth century accounts of human evolution usually feature four important episodes: terrestriality, or a shift from the trees to the ground; bipedalism, or the acquisition of upright posture; encephalization, or the development of the brain, intelligence, and language; and civilization, the emergence of technology, morals, and society. Although the order of these events may vary among accounts,

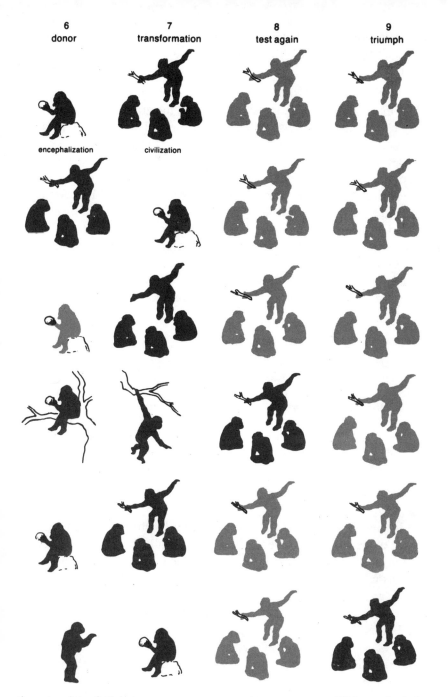

they tend to fall into a common narrative structure. This underlying structure can be represented by nine basic actions or "functions," each of which can be filled in several ways. (Events that are latent or continuing from a previous stage are shaded in light gray.) The views of Elliot Smith are represented below Darwin and Keith.

Smith models this ancestral creature very closely along the lines of the modern tree shrew: moving in the trees and on the ground, occasionally it sits back on its haunches, using its forepaws to feed on fruits and insects. Of "lively disposition and great agility" (Smith, 1924, p. 29), nevertheless this creature is not a primate. Not until it forsakes completely its mammalian birthplace does it give birth to the new order.

The move up into the trees is thus a pivotal episode in Elliot Smith's narrative, even more momentous, as we shall see, than the subsequent shift back down. Again, it is by the power of "intelligent adaptation" that Elliot Smith's hero enters the arboreal realm. There, new selective pressures act on the neopallium and in particular the areas devoted to the sense of sight. Though well-developed even in primitive mammals, until now vision had been subservient to the more ancient reptilian sense of olfaction.

> This was due not only to the fact that the sense of smell had already installed its instruments in and taken possession, so to speak, of the cerebral hemisphere long before the advent in this dominant part of the brain of any adequate representation of the other senses, but also, and chiefly, because to a small land-grubbing animal the guidance of smell impressions, whether in the search for food or as a means of recognition of friends or enemies, sexual mates or rivals, was much more serviceable than all the other senses. Thus the small creature's mental life was lived essentially in an atmosphere of odours; and every object in the outside world was judged primarily and predominantly by smell. The senses of touch, vision, and hearing were merely auxiliary to the compelling influence of smell. (P. 29-30)

Once in the trees, however, all this changes. Unable to respond to the arboreal demand for improved agility, smell "calls to its help the senses of vision and touch and what may be called the labyrinth sense" (1927, p. 13). Thus a "more equable balance" is brought about in the structure of the brain as large portions of the brain are "given up" to other senses.

It is this shift of power from smell to vision which signifies "the birth of the Primates and the definite branching off from the other mammals of the line of Man's ancestry" (1924, p. 31). Depicted as a struggle, the relationship between the olfactory region and other parts of the primate brain was the focus of one of Elliot Smith's earliest scientific papers, "On the morphology of the brain in the Mammalia" (1903). Though he claims, in this paper, to be concerned only with demonstrating the affinities between the brains of lemurs and anthropoids (monkeys, apes, and humans), Elliot Smith does not restrict himself merely to problems of taxonomy (1903, p. 425):

> After seeking for some explanation for all the apparently conflicting features of the Prosimian brain, the following tentative working hypothesis as to the ancestry of the Lemurs shaped itself in my mind, and I insert it here merely as a slender bond connecting certain facts scattered through these notes.
>
> The brain of the Primates was derived from some Insectivore-like type, the cerebral hemispheres of which attained a precocious development and, as one of the expressions of their greatness, bulged backward over the cerebellum. In consequence of this great extension of the "physical organ of the associative memory of visual, auditory, and tactile sensations," the sense of smell lost the predominance which it exercised in the primitive mammal (and in all the Orders of recent mammals), and the olfactory parts of the brain rapidly dwindled. . . .
>
> In the keen struggle for existence, the Lemurs ceased to keep pace with the other Primates so far as the increase in the size of the brain is concerned. They became more specialized, and their brain probably shrunk, thus leading to a retraction of the occipital pole of the hemispheres.
>
> With the diminution of the size of the neopallium the sense of smell comes to play a more important part, and a secondary re-enlargement of the olfactory region occurs. The blotting out of the rhinal fissure may be an indication of this phenomenon.

By following the rise and fall of the olfactory organs in relation to the neopallium, Elliot Smith sketches his storyline.

But it is by emphasizing the role of vision that Elliot Smith raises our interest.

> The high specialization of the sense of sight awakened in the creature the curiosity to examine the objects around it with closer minuteness and supplied guidance to the hands in executing more precise and more skilled movements than any that the Tree Shrew attempts. Such habits not only tended to develop the motor cortex itself, trained the tactile and kinaesthetic senses, and linked up their cortical areas in bonds of more intimate associations with the visual specialization within or alongside the motor cortex of a mechanism for regulating the action of that cortex itself. Thus arose an organ of attention which co-ordinated with the activities of the whole neopallium so as the more efficiently to regulate the various centres controlling the muscles of the whole body. (1924, p. 32)

Just as the senses are "awakened" by vision, the great prefrontal area is "called into life." Through the "guidance" of vision, the mammalian brain is transformed into an organ of even greater plasticity and power: the mind.

Given such an active role (and vision not only guides but "usurps" and "cultivates" the mind and the body), vision might appear to have a mind of its own. Indeed, expanding the prefrontal area allows for the crossing of the optic tracts and, hence, stereoscopic vision. "Thus the fuller cultivation of the results of the visual powers provides a new stimulus and new means for enhancing vision itself" (1924, p. 146). But the primates also profit from such self-interested deeds, for it is by virtue of stereoscopic vision that the prosimian evolves into a monkey. Nor do the benefits stop there. So as to gain "a more advantageous position by being raised higher from the ground" (1929, p. 28), vision brings about the upright posture which, in turn, brings us apes and the next episode.

BIPEDALISM: IN WHICH
(4) THE HERO PREPARES TO DEPART

Despite the increased power of adaptation,

> The primates at first were a small and humble folk, who led a quiet life, unobtrusive and safe in the branches of trees, taking small part in the competition for size and supremacy that was being waged upon the earth beneath them by their carnivorous, ungulate and other brethren. But all the time they were cultivating the equable development of all their senses and limbs, and the special development of the more intellectually useful faculties of the mind that in the long run were to make them the progenitors of the dominant Mammal – the Mammal destined to obtain supremacy over all others, while still retaining much of the primitive structure of limb that his competitors had sacrificed. (1924, p. 34)

Set above in a literal sense by virtue of their arboreality, the first primates are truly superior, for they have maintained their original mammalian purity of design while developing their special powers. It is by virtue of the primitive primate limb structure that vision is first able to attain its influence. Only in those animals whose limbs have not been subjected to "precocious specialization" can vision cultivate one of its most important powers, muscular skill. Not only does skill enhance the ability to learn by experience, which we have seen to be a basic mammalian property, it also develops the ability to experiment. "Hence it is perhaps no exaggeration to say that high intelligence is largely one of the results of the attainment of muscular skill" (1927a, p. 16). Or, as Elliot Smith announces in a boldface subtitle, **Muscular Skill Begets Intelligence** (p. 16).

Operating on the muscles of the eye itself, vision develops its first skill, stereoscopy. Emphasizing the "vast importance" of this skill (and we saw that it marks the transition from prosimian to simian), Elliot Smith then describes how vision makes an even greater advance when it gains control of the hands. By liberating the hands to perform "skilled movements," vision transforms a monkey into an upright ape. Yet it is unclear just what this ape is doing with its hands, for though Elliot Smith emphasizes manipulative skill, the creature is modeled after the gibbon whose upright body hangs almost entirely by its hands.

Given that the demand for agility and quickness of movement was the original impetus for the growth of vision, one would expect more attention to be paid to the question of locomotion. Considering also Elliot Smith's emphasis on migration (which I will come to), we wonder: how, exactly, did our heroes move around? Yet the whole matter of the erect posture is incidental in Elliot Smith's account; incidental, that is, to other developments.

> The erect attitude, infinitely more ancient than man himself, is not the real cause of Man's emergence from the simian stage; but it is one of the factors made use of by the expanding brain as a prop still further to extend its growing dominion, and by fixing and establishing in a more decided way this erectness it liberated the hand to become the chief instrument of Man's further progress. (1924, p. 41)

So we see in the image of a prop how Elliot Smith places mind over body.

TERRESTRIALITY: IN WHICH
(5) THE HERO IS TESTED,
(6) AIDED BY ITS DONOR, AND
(7) BY THIS MEANS TRANSFORMED

Skilled in the basic arts of life, the ape apprentice is now ready to become a journeyman. With such emphasis on learning by experience, the beginning of human evolution does appear a kind of apprenticeship, and the arboreal environment, nurturing and prolific, resembles a kind of workshop. No wonder that the terrestrial realm appears less productive: a place for testing rather than inventing. Still, it is a creative place for it is "the laboratory in which, for untold ages, Nature was making her great experiments to achieve the transmutation of the base substance of some brutal Ape into the divine form of Man" (1924, p. 51). Mixing metaphors, Elliot Smith tells us it is from "the hard school of experience" (p. 79) that a human being finally graduates.

Thus movement on the ground is a vehicle for the further transformation of the hero. Spreading "far and wide" into Africa, Europe, and Asia, the anthropoids give rise to new kinds of apes:

> In the course of their wanderings the Primates thus encircled the world. Their journeys necessarily occupied a vast span of years because they were obviously not deliberately planned but were such migrations as every kind of living creature was led by force of circumstance to undertake. (1929, p. 55)

Still, it is an internal drive that leads some of them to become human.

> There can be no doubt that this process of differentiation is of the same nature as those which led one branch of the Eocene Tarsioids to become monkeys, while the other remained Prosimae; advanced one group of primitive monkeys to the Catarrhine status, while the rest remained Platyrrhine; converted one division of Old World Apes into Anthropoids, while the others retained their old status. Put into this form as an obvious truism, the conclusion is suggested that the changes which have taken place in the brain to convert an Ape into Man are of the same nature as, and may be looked upon merely as a continuation of, those processes of evolution which we have been examining in the lowlier members of the Primate series. (1924, p. 39)

Just as the tarsier, monkey, and ape are transformed, so the human evolves by virtue of its power of discrimination.

> If one analyses the nature of the changes which the brain has undergone in its passages from the stage represented in the Chimpanzee and Gorilla to the most primitive human condition, the outstanding factor will be found to be primarily a great expansion of the region of the cerebral cortex that is interposed between the areas into which impulses from the visual, auditory, and tactile organs are poured.
> This means presumably that a greatly enhanced power of recording the impressions of these senses and of profiting by experience – in other words, an enormous expansion of the powers of discrimination based upon acquired knowledge – is the fundamental distinction between Primitive Man and the Apes. (P. 63).

Even the development of language follows the path paved by vision.

> While still in the simian stage of development Man's ancestors were already equipped with all the specialized muscles needed for articulate speech and the cerebral apparatus for controlling their movements, and for acquiring the skill to learn new methods of action. All that was needed to put this complicated machinery to the new purpose was Man's enhanced power of discrimination. (P. 64)

Nor is this a selfless act: "Handing on the accumulated products of experience" by means of language, vision extends its dominion beyond the immediately visible.

Despite such apparently radical changes, "Man at first, so far as his general appearance and 'build' are concerned was merely an Ape with an overgrown brain."

> But in virtue of those changes which convert the Ape into Man, his powers of adaptation to changes of country, climate, and food were enormously increased, so that he was able to spread abroad more quickly and roam into climates and into lands which were closed to the tropical forest dwelling Anthropoid Apes. Thus Man was able to make his way into every region of the earth. (P. 63)

And so, by the beginning of the Pliocene, a whole variety of "caricatures of men" roam the Old World. Those "finding themselves amidst surroundings which were thoroughly congenial and called for no effort, lagged behind," while others possessed of a "glorious unrest" continue their wanderings, moving one step further along "the highway towards Man's estate." Still, they follow an ancient route, for

> Man is the ultimate product of that line of ancestry which was never compelled to turn aside and adopt protective specializations, either of structure or mode of life, which would be fatal to its plasticity and power of further development. (1924, p. 34)

So we see in the image of a highway how Elliot Smith paves his genealogy with general principles.

Not that fossils do not appear along the way. Indeed, they illustrate some of Elliot Smith's main themes. For example, the Oligocene primates of the Egyptian Fayum, by their diversity and advanced status, demonstrate the effects of the (supposed) Atlantic crossing of the New World monkeys. The Miocene apes of the Siwalik Hills similarly reflect the "wider triumph" achieved by the primates.

In his admirable review of Dr. Pilgrim's memoir Professor Boule refers to the fact of first importance that is revealed by the new discoveries in India. During Miocene times Asia was inhabited by very numerous Anthropoid Apes exhibiting characters diverging in all kinds of directions, and even, as in *Sivapithecus*, in the direction of Man.

[Quoting Boule:] *"Il y a là un mouvement de vie chez les Primates tout à fait extraordinaire, et l'on a, pour la première fois, la sensation que l'Asie était, à ce moment, le laboratoire où devait s'élaborer la differentiation des ancêtres de Hominiens."* (1924, p. 62)

More recent fossils such as Piltdown, *pithecanthropus*, *palaeoanthropus*, and *Sinanthropus* make the same point. Contemporaneous, according to Elliot Smith's genealogy, they give graphic representation to the spread and diversification of early humans. Interestingly, none of these fossils occupies a directly ancestral spot. Still, they point in the right direction. As Elliot Smith observes, "The outstanding interest of the Piltdown skull is the confirmation it affords of the view that the brain led the way" in human evolution (p. 67).

CIVILIZATION: IN WHICH
(8) THE HERO STRUGGLES, AND
(9) THEREBY ACHIEVES (UNCERTAIN) TRIUMPH

Oddly, the first human appears almost mindless: Possessed of skill, emotions, instincts, and even language, it is strangely less than the sum of its parts. Single-minded, the whole mentality of this early human appears to be predicated on its powers of observation: "In the pursuit of his quarry and in the avoidance of danger the hunter was forced to be an observer of certain things, and was quite oblivious of others which did not affect, or did not seem to affect, his occupation" (1924, p. 119). Using the Punans of Borneo as a model, Elliot Smith describes this primitive man in contrast to the modern European.

Where a European can discover no indication, whatever, primitive natives point out the footsteps of any number of people, enumerating men, women, and children, and even their racial peculiarities and personal idiosyncracies, and will state the day or even the hour at which they passed. To the European who can detect nothing at all, or, at most, faint and confused marks, such powers seem to be almost magical. But it must ever be remembered that the acquisition of these powers of observation and inference occupy the whole time and attention of Primitive Man. As Palgrave says, even of a branch of mankind so far removed from the primitive stage as the Arab: "he judges of things as he sees them present before him, not in their causes or consequences." While the children of civilized Man are engaged in absorbing the fruits of their people's conventions and traditions, those of the untutored savage are acquiring the more vital knowledge of the untamed world of Nature. Each of them, and especially the latter, gives little or no thought to the contemplation of the real significance of natural phenomena. Only a very rare genius amongst either group appreciates the fact that there may be something behind the obvious veil which the majority of his fellows is accustomed to regard as the real world. (Pp. 119-120)

Cast next to civilized man, Elliot Smith's primitive man is cast also in irony. For it is clear that, though oblivious to the "real significance of natural phenomenon," primitive man sees more than the European. Whereas the European "can discover no indication," "can detect nothing," it is the primitive who can see a footstep, who can read it like a hieroglyphic. While the children of the European absorb the "fruits of their people's conventions and traditions, those of the untutored savage are acquiring the more vital knowledge of the untamed world of Nature." Finally, it is not the European but primitive man who "judges of things as he sees them present before him, not in their causes or consequences." Ironically, it is primitive man who looks more like Elliot Smith, the scientist.

But there lurks a third figure in Elliot Smith's passage: the rare genius. Unusually perceptive, he alone sees "behind the obvious veil." Depicted by Elliot Smith as the "visionary," the "man of insight," he is not merely possessed of great power; he is its personification. And so, just as vision aroused the mind, the genius wakes it to the possibilities of civilization. But it is a slow dawn, as Elliot Smith describes in the following passage:

In the early history of the gropings after new knowledge and skill in arts and crafts human nature was probably not very different from what it is to-day. When, after countless thousands of years' experience of the use of stones as implements, some man of clearer insight learned to appreciate the fact that an edge could be given to the stone by deliberately chipping it in a particular way, no doubt he was regarded as a foolish visionary, whose pretensions were resented by his staider and duller companions. Perhaps he was even reproved with the palaeolithic argument that his predecessors found unchipped stones good enough for them, and it was therefore supremely foolish to attempt to supersede methods which experience had shown to be so thoroughly efficient. However, in course of time, the momentous invention was adopted: but although there are scores of ways of chipping a stone implement, the one

> original method was meticulously followed for many centuries to the exclusion of all others. Not only so, but it became stereotyped and adopted far and wide as one people after another learned the technique of this particular method. After this process had been going on for many centuries some new genius arose, and although no Samuel Stiles has put on record the history of the difficulties he had to overcome before he could persuade his generation to adopt a slightly different method of chipping flint, there can be no reasonable doubt that his experience was similar to Galileo's, Watt's and Lister's. He had to fight against the forces of cultivated prejudice and inherent stupidity. In time, however, the new technique became the fashion; and in the course of centuries it slowly percolated to the ends of the earth. (1924, pp. 103-104)

So the process of civilization appears to be a conscious and deliberate pushing. According to this principle of the continuity and diffusion of culture, Elliot Smith traces the origin of civilization to the insight of the first great human.

Rather than mindlessly follow basic urges, these beings of insight begin to examine the conditions of their existence and so become "actuated" by the conscious desire to find the means of transcending them. Conducted as a search for the "elixir of life," this "Life Quest" begins with the worship of symbols of the hunt (the blood and internal organs of animals), and eventually extends to the worship of women, cowrie shells, and gold. Of all these, "the search for gold has been the most potent influence in the development and spread of civilisation" (1923, p. 441), for, as revealed by the discovery of Tutankhamen's tomb, "it was the arbitrary value attached to [gold] for its supposed magical properties that initiated the world-wide search for it which has now lasted for sixty centuries" (p. 441). So the golden mean takes a material turn. Still, it leads in the same direction. For like previous migrations, the search for gold is the means by which genius extends and diversifies its power in the early world of humans.

But it is in the art of extending life beyond death that the life quest reaches its apotheosis.

> The specific activities of the embalmer who preserved the bodies of the dead were in large measure responsible for giving civilisation its distinctive character. The man who dissected the human body for the practical purpose of preventing it from suffering corruption had a much more ambitious aim than the mere preservation of a corpse. Musing deeply on the problems of life and death, he persuaded himself that in making a mummy he was actually prolonging the existence of the body so that it might be reanimated as a living being. (1929, pp. xv-xvi)

Wrapped around the idea of death, Elliot Smith's view of civilization looks rather Freudian. Yet Freud sees human unhappiness to be a direct result of man's raising himself up from the ground, while Elliot Smith sees it to be a later consequence of returning to the soil.

> There are reasons for believing that men were, on the whole, peaceful and happy until the device of agriculture was invented. . . . For the custom of tilling the soil brought many things in its train, good and bad. It created the assurance of a food supply and a really settled mode of life, and the need (and the opportunity for satisfying it) for many arts and crafts – houses to store grain, pots for holding and cooking grain, works of irrigation for cultivating barley, and eventually the emergence of a leader to organize the community's labour and the equable distribution of water for irrigation. Weaving, the use of clothing, amulets, jewelry, the arts of the carpenter, the stonemason, the boat-builder, to mention only a few, created a division of labour, and contributed to the emergence of classes, which still further emphasized the position of the irrigation-engineer, who became the first of a dynasty of hereditary kings, the regulators of irrigation and the astronomers, who controlled their people's destiny. . . . These were the sort of circumstances that put the labour of the community at the service of one man, and conferred supernatural powers on him. Thus were created the social inequalities and the material factors that excited greed, envy and jealousy. Out of such events emerged the social organization that regulated marriage and provoked quarrelling and malicious violence. By putting power into the hands of a ruler this train of events made it possible for him not only to use the labour of the community for his own purposes, but also to exercise the power of life and death over his subjects. (1927b, p. 27)

Invented by man, agriculture becomes man's inventor. By creating the need for architecture, pottery, jewelry, and clothing, agriculture transforms man into the architect, the potter, the jeweler. Similarly by creating property, agriculture invents social classes. But just as it supplants human genius, agriculture is overpowered by one of its offspring, the ruler. For it is the ruler who commands the digging and planting, as well as the embalmer's great invention.

In life and death – as ruler and as mummy – this unnatural (indeed, supernatural) figure lies at the center of civilization. More powerful than the genius, it is the ruler who controls invention. Indeed, this transfer of power from genius to politician can be seen as the next stage in the transformation of the power of vision. For just as vision ruled the brain, the politician harnesses the human mind for its own purposes. But whereas the power of discrimination leads to greater plasticity, the power exerted by the ruler leads to increased specialization. Whereas vision awakens the senses of smell, touch, and movement to strengthen the mind, the ruler weakens it with fear, greed, and envy. Finally, by forcing "a ready-made supply of opinions and ways of thinking," the ruler not only dictates but usurps the power of the mind to discriminate.

Stripped of its natural powers, the hero undergoes its final and perhaps most profound transformation. Indeed, for Elliot Smith, primitive man differs as much from civilized man as from an ape man:

> He has no social organization apart from the family, and no hereditary chiefs. He has no property, and all the food he collects belongs to the family group. He is monogamous. He is a naked, harmless, truthful, overgrown child, kind-hearted, but quick and able to defend himself and to stop quarelling among his fellows. (1927b, p. 30)

With "no houses," "no property," "no social organization" and no chiefs, the primitive appears to be cast in the shadow of civilization. Yet despite such deficiencies, primitive man dwells in a more vital place, a "Golden Age of Peace and Happiness" – a state of mind as well as a state of nature. Compared to this Garden of Eden, the civilized mind appears a truly unnatural growth: overrun by "strife and discontent, dishonesty and greed, envy, malice, and all uncharitableness" and governed by the "tyranny of tradition" (p. 30).

It is not surprising that civilization spreads only very slowly, and that humans should be so resistant to its infection. Indeed, Elliot Smith calls it a tragic "accident" as though, like the plague, it might have been avoided. Yet one might argue that civilization is the inevitable outgrowth of Elliot Smith's logic. With the rise of civilization, the power of the ruler is superseded by the "tyranny of tradition," and mind, now disembodied altogether, triumphs over matter.

Here too, fossils follow lines of thought as Elliot Smith traces genealogical relationships according to cerebral lobes. Nowhere is this clearer than in the fate of Neanderthal: "However large the brain may be in *Homo neanderthalensis*, his small prefrontal region is sufficient evidence for his lowly state of intelligence and reason for his failure in the competition with the rest of mankind" (1924, p. 35). But Neanderthal also sins with his body. Looking at his coarse face, prominent eyebrow ridges, short and thickset build (which Elliot Smith describes as "grotesque," "weird," and "repellent"), it becomes clear "that this peculiar type of mankind had in certain respects become so highly specialized as to make it impossible to regard him as the ancestor of men of our own type" (1928, p. 113). Like his remote mammalian ancestors, Neanderthal succumbs finally to the temptation to specialize.

But nearby stands Cro-Magnon, much as the first primate stood to the mammals: with a "high-domed and well-filled brain" (1926, p. 299) and unspecialized body. Derived from a yet more primitive parent stock which was evolving in either Asia or Africa, "the arrival in Europe of these men of modern type ought surely to be regarded as the greatest event in history" (1916, p. 325), for its signifies "the appearance upon the earth of men capable of formulating plans and of reasoning, men of imagination, and endowed with an artistic sense" (p. 324). With the Cro-Magnon people come the first geniuses. "Thus the new spirit of Man and modern Man himself are revealed in the Upper Palaeolithic Period" (1924, p. 90). But with the invention of agriculture in the following Neolithic period comes the ruler, and, after him, the "tyranny of tradition." And so we might expect to see the demise of civilization.

But in closing we meet another figure, whom we met in our opening passage. For it is the archeologist, in Elliot Smith as in Freud, who holds the keys to the past and thus to the human future. It is the scientist, insightful and skilled, who triumphs over tyranny. Still, looking ahead, we see that the investigator too will be defeated. Despite the struggles carried against the forces of prejudice by people like Galileo, Watt, and Lister, in time their truths become conventions. And so science finally fails to liberate and becomes one more instrument for human enslavement. However, Elliot Smith does not see this paradox or the paradox of his own efforts. Yet it is clear that in constructing his genealogy, he is in the grip of those forces which displease him. Locked between rarely opened covers, he remains in the temple of tradition.

REFERENCES

Freud, S. 1961. *Civilization and its discontents*. New York: Norton.
Landau, M. 1984. Human evolution as narrative. *American Scientist*, 72, 262-268.
Landau, M., D. Pilbeam, and A. Richard. 1982. Human origins a century after Darwin. *BioScience*, 32, 507-512.
Smith, G. E. 1903. On the morphology of the brain in the Mammalia, with special reference to that of the Lemurs, recent and extinct. *Transactions of the Linnaean Society*, 8, 319-432.
Smith, G. E. 1916. Men of the Old Stone Age. *American Museum Journal*, 16, 319-325.

Smith, G. E. 1923. The study of man. *Nature*, 112, 440-444.

Smith, G. E. 1924. *The evolution of man.* London: Oxford University Press.

Smith, G. E. 1926. Casts obtained from the brain cases of fossil men. *Natural History*, 26, 294-299.

Smith, G. E. 1927a. The meaning of the brain. *Scientific American*, 136, 13-16.

Smith, G. E. 1927b. *Human nature.* London: Watts & Co.

Smith, G. E. 1928. Neanderthal man not our ancestor. *Scientific American*, August, 112-115.

Smith, G. E. 1929. *Human history.* New York: Norton.

PART II

Studies of
Narratory Competence

4

Children's
Fiction Making

Brian Sutton-Smith

Although modern children tell each other jokes, rhymes, games, riddles, and tricks as a part of their oral tradition, they do not very often tell each other stories. The words "narrative," "story," and "tale" do not appear in the classic, *The Lore and Language of Children*, by Iona and Peter Opie (1968). On the other hand, when asked to make up stories, modern children can readily do so. The question to be asked here, therefore, is where children's stories come from and how we should proceed to their analysis.

To date there are two emerging perspectives for story analysis. The first is textual or structural and is typified by the work of Jean Mandler in her *Stories, Scripts and Scenes: Aspects of Schema Theory* (1984), within which she contends that the plot structures which children are able to remember (after our story presentations to them) allow us to infer underlying mental structures in the children. In her view there is a parallel between the story "grammars" and the children's mental schema. In my own earlier work, *The Folkstories of Children* (1981), in which the stories that children tell spontaneously were used as a source, there was also a concentration on the structural sequences through which children proceeded with age. It was shown, for example, that between the ages of five and eleven years children proceed from plots without attempted mediation, through plots where mediation is attempted, to plots where a nullification of the threat or deprivation occurs, and plots where there is a complete transformation of the original situation. Judging by the extensive studies of Gardner and associates, which are also largely plot centered (Winner, 1982), it has been easier for psychologists to adopt this more abstract paradigmatic mode of analysis than to analyze stories in terms of their particular occasions and context. Indeed, Mandler protests against the criticism that her structural approaches are too abstract to reveal much about children's stories. She says people always find or impose structures of order on the world which is then constrained by the system that they have invented. See, for example, the alphabet, or, if you will, language itself.

The second perspective, derived ultimately from various hermeneutic traditions (Gadamer, 1982; Habermas, 1983), but found comfortably also in much humanistic scholarship, is the view that if we are to understand the meaning of stories to those who use them, rather than some truth they tell us about the chronology of child plot development or child memory schema, we must study them in their contexts of use. Knowing what these contexts are, however, is not always simple. The accumulating evidence would seem to suggest that in most oral societies, storytelling was an adult not a juvenile tradition, though children might imitate the adult practices in their own peer groups (Erwin-Tripp, S. & Mitchell-Kernan, 1977; McDowell, 1979). Modern children outside the Third World are not, in general, participants or audience in such traditions of storytelling. Instead they participate in an urban tradition within which storytelling has become an educational tool employed by parents, schoolteachers, and librarians for the benefit of children or an amusement vehicle as in television and in films. Hundreds of folktales have been gathered and reworked to accommodate the moralities and sentiments of those who would use them in more modern domestic times. In effect, present-day children's literature, like schools, or toys, or sports for children, is a part of the disjunction of the modern childhood from adult life (Kelly-Byrne, 1983). It serves to socialize and to domesticate the child so that the context of story use is predominantly didactic (Cochran-Smith 1984).

The two kinds of approach, textual and contextual, suggest, despite their diverse epistemological roots, that any adequate analysis of children's fiction should seek to pay attention to both text and context, or as Bruner puts it, to both the paradigmatic and the narrative modes of thought that are illustrated by these alternatives (Bruner, 1984). He suggests that the textual approach (at least in the form of modern structuralism) derives from the history of science as mathematical, logical, concerned with verification, truth, consistency, and noncontradiction. In the present case, it focuses on being able to predict correlations between age and plot structure or age and memory. On the other hand, the contextual approach derives from the history of myth, ideology, literature, the ability to create credible stories, and to achieve meaningful verisimilitude. In this chapter I begin with the contextual approach.

THE STORYTELLING CONTEXT

Children can begin to tell stories themselves in about the third or fourth year of life when this is encouraged by their parents or teacher. Although there is very little published work on this issue, one would suppose this capacity for storying to be a normative outgrowth of the children's own participation in storytelling and story-reading occasions, as well as of their acquisition of symbolic capacities in the second year of life. Unfortunately, the acquisition of symbolic capacities has to this point been described largely in Piagetian-derived terms as a series of stages of implicit mental structures as if the presence of these alone accounts for the ability to symbolize or to narrate. Or, alternatively, it has been suggested that the children's acquisition of the scripts of everyday action is what permits them to symbolize or to narrate (Bretherton, 1984). Both of these approaches make the mistake, in my opinion, of reducing storytelling to either symbolic mental operation or figurative memory when neither of these, while important, is sufficient to account for the complex task of storytelling. At the very least, storying involves the real teller and the real listener in a context in which the teller is using words to refer to fictional actors and counteractors who are not present in that context except as imaginatively entertained by both storyteller and listener. What must be accounted for therefore is the emergence of this theatrical quadralogue (director: audience: actor: counteractor) in the fictional performances of the young child (Sutton-Smith, 1979b). And what is required for this analysis, it seems, is an understanding of the earlier analogous theatrical contexts in which the child participates. It might be expected that participation in such earlier theatrical performances would provide the model that subsequently allows the child to generate narrative on the symbolic level.

The earliest such theater occurs around two to six months when nurturers (parents or peers) and babies play face games together (Stern, 1977). In general, the nurturer provides the proximal developmental zone by imitating the baby and ultimately leading the baby to imitate the adult. At the same time, in order to attract the baby's attention, the nurturer makes highly incongruous faces and performs other actions, following these, by reassuring smiles and laughter. Through incongruity and laughter a situation of increasing emotional intensity and joyfulness is established with the baby. Over time, these mutual face plays extend to action-routine plays in which anticipation is followed by sequences of cumulative intensity leading to emotional climaxes in lap games or hand games. Of these *peekaboo* is best known through the study of Bruner and Sherwood (1976) of a baby developing this game first as audience at eight months and later as director by 15 months. At the later age the child was quite capable of selecting novel situations and novel objects for new performances of the game. From the work of Leila Bretherton (1984) and Judith Van Hoorn (1983) we know that this kind of play is widespread among modern parents in the United States of Anglo as well as Mexican, Chinese, and Philippine origins. It is reasonable to assume, furthermore, that the bulk of play in infancy is this kind of social play with parents or older peers. There is reason to doubt whether much of what an infant does solitarily has the character of play, though it does have the character of exploration or mastery (Sutton-Smith, 1985). With all his observational diligence, Piaget comes up with fewer than ten solitary plays in his study of the first year of life (1951), but he comes up with many times that number for subsequent years. Unfortunately it was his epistemological bias to omit most social play.

The argument being made here is that the parent-child play quadralogue establishes the social scaffolding for later expressive performances. This is the most probable source of both later symbolic play (Sutton-Smith, 1979c) and later storytelling. Here in laughing at incongruities of a facial and motor kind, the baby is learning the sensory-motor rudiments of thesis and antithesis, of frame and reframe which are the necessary precursors for the pretense of both later symbolic play and for fictional narratives. On this account, out of the bathos of laughter and incongruity, play emerges. That there may be other inherent bases for the frame switching character of play as paradox is also possible, but at this point not investigated (Bateson, 1972).

All of this is by way of suggesting that the true source of narrative is play scaffolding, not social picture-book scaffolding alone, as has been more often suggested (De Loache, 1984; Ninio & Bruner, 1976). Indeed in the Ninio and Bruner study those responses of the child which were not pertinent to the mother's picture-book labeling were ruled out as white noise. The predominance of the parents' proximal scaffolding zone, therefore, was in part a function of the newness of the phenomenon to the infant and of the neglect by the investigators of what else the infant might like to do with the book. The baby's interest in using the book for the earlier established exchange routines with the parent, or in using the book for peekaboo would hardly be pertinent to their study. What this implies is that we have again a very one-sided situation with the baby being allowed a very limited role in the interaction, just as the baby plays a very limited role in the first face games at four months. And what that does is make context (the social scaffolding) appear to be the overwhelmingly important part of the variance in this kind of study of picture-book reading. The text is an epiphenomenon of the social context, as it must perhaps always be when we focus on the initiation of a newcomer into a new text (ritual, and so forth) and neglect that newcomer's prior assets.

While there is no available study to resolve the issue of which antecedent – social, play, cognitive operations, figurative memories – plays the greatest role in determining a child's ability to tell a story, there is one study which at least helps to resolve the issue of the relative roles of social context versus the narrated text as determining the kinds of interactions that occur between parent and child. This research, reported more fully elsewhere (Eadie, Sutton-Smith, & Magee, 1983; Magee & Sutton-Smith, 1983; Sutton-Smith, 1984), involved the nine-month study of a two-year-old girl in 28 taped sessions of her parents' storytelling in their own kitchen with no one else present. The sessions averaged 11-1/2 minutes each. The data analysis yielded codings of 21 categories for adult interaction (for example, reading or elaborating text, telling made-up story, play, questions on what the child said), and 29 categories for child interaction (for example, asks questions, makes own interpretations, becomes storyteller, playful transformation of themes). The predominant interaction for the adults was "reading or elaborating a text" (25 percent). The responses of the child were much more heterogeneous. The highest percentage (2.3 percent) was for the category "playful transformation of themes."

Unlike the more didactic situation in the Ninio and Bruner study (1976) this one involved much more playing about, particularly with the father. These categories were then factor-analyzed along with an accounting of whether the occasion involved a storybook, storytelling, a personal narrative (a script), or a picture book. In addition, account was kept of whether the storyteller was mother, father, mother and father, the child, or the visiting teacher. Other variables having to do with the length of the episodes and the child's familiarity with the material were also assessed. All of these variables were then subjected to successive factor and correlational analyses to yield 12 clusters, which we have classified as text clusters, social clusters, and child clusters. The text clusters involved (1) picture books, (2) improvisational storytelling, (3) storybook reading, (4) personal narratives, (5) storytelling, and (6) framing the story. The social clusters were (7) didactic scaffolding and (8) role reversal. The child clusters were (9) child heightened affect, (10) child plot involvement, (11) child pretending with story, and (12) child affirmation. What is important from the present perspective is that the six text clusters commanded the largest part of the variance (approximately 60 percent) and the other two social clusters commanded the rest. This is true even though the adults did most of the speaking (73.5 percent). Despite the apparent importance of scaffolding in this as in other studies, most of the interaction that went on between parent and child was still a function of the kind of narrative (story, picture book, and so on), to which they were attending. In a sense then, in this study text outweighed social context as a cause of behavior. This is a welcome outcome for those who traditionally place the text over its interpretive reading, and for those who consider text as structure more important than text as narrative occasion.

Before speculating too heavily on the implications of this intensive study of only one child, I hasten to add that since Ninio and Bruner's study had a one-year-old as subject and our study a two-year-old, the observed difference might rest solely on age differences. Recent studies of children's intelligence scores, assessed subsequent to parents giving children appropriate toys, show that the parent-toy interaction accounts for most of the variance in the first year, whereas with increasing age the toys themselves begin to account for most of the variance (Brown & Gottfried, 1985). It perhaps makes sense that as children get older, they gain greater freedom from adult social conditioning or scaffolding, and become more intrinsically interested in other media in the world, whether toys or books. In object genesis, transitional objects like toys and books become increasingly commanding of their own patterns of interaction sui generis and decreasingly subordinate to the scaffoldings within which they first appear. It follows that although we have contrasted text and context as two kinds of approaches to the understanding of children's ability to make fiction, what this study also suggests is that at different ages there are different standard patterns of text-context relationships. While there is no work on how these variations change over age, by sex, by ethnic group, and by situation, we have shown elsewhere that such factors as the storytaker's sex, the child's sex, and the child's mental health can make a difference (Sutton-Smith, 1979a). In our research male storytakers evoked more fantasies from both boys and girls. Female storytakers evoked more realism. Both sexes evoked longer stories from the same sex storytellers. Some storytakers, in addition, evoked freer kinds of expression, including obscenities.

THE TEXTS

Although each different context presumably inflects and changes stories to some extent, we were impressed with the great consistency in the stories told by about half the children, regardless of storytaker, or of time, or place of telling. For some storytellers the story overwhelmed the occasion, while for others, their sensitivity to the time and place was of great importance (Sutton-Smith, 1981). In this section, however, I want to discuss some common textual or structural characteristics of children's stories as they emerged in our research on children from ages two to 12 years.[1]

The stories of very young children, for example, were best thought of as a kind of music. They had a "theme and variation" structure as in music and they often had some of the elements of verse. Here are two stories by a boy and girl who were between two and a half and three years of age, which is about as early as stories can be elicited from children. Even then such stories are not given without companionship and friendliness from the storytaker. They are usually given easily to a parent who tells stories or to a familiar preschool teacher.

(1)   The monkeys
        They went up sky
        They fall down
        Choo choo train in the sky
        The train fell down in the sky
        I fell down in the sky in the water
        I got on my boat and my legs hurt
        Daddy fall down in the sky.

(2)   The cat went on the cakies
        The cat went on the car
        The cookie was in my nose
        The cookie went on the fireman's hat
        The fireman's hat went on the bucket
        The cookie went on the carousel
        The cookie went on the puzzle
        The cookie went on the doggie.

In the first story we notice the repeated theme of *falling down*. In the second story we notice the repeated theme of *went on*. Most children of this age level pick such a theme and repeat it (or something of a cognate kind) over many months in most of the stories they tell. It seems that they are preoccupied with a particular, perhaps disquilibrating, vector of human action and that this is what they are trying to deal with in their stories. In story (1), the boy keeps his theme constant but varies his actors. He keeps his location constant (the sky). But what he gives us is a series of small episodes on the same theme. There is no chronicity across the whole story; instead there are four small stories (the first three lines about monkeys; the next two about the train; the two following about the child; and the last line about Daddy).

The girl keeps her theme even more constant. She has three actors (the cat, the cookie, and the fireman), but her predicates are quite variable. Unlike the boy whose style was to center in on his theme and vary only his actors (who came from his home play environment), her style was to attend peripherally to the environment in which she was telling the story and pick up her predicates more or less haphazardly from her surroundings. His is a kind of central strategy of variation, hers is a peripheral strategy of variation.

In short, our way of looking at these stories is to ask (as in music) what is constant and what is variable. It then becomes possible to *score* stories for the number of constant elements (within one story or across a number of stories) and the number of variable elements, and possible also to talk about different kinds of constant and variable ratios and different patterns of variation. These ratios and patterns we can discuss as *styles of storytelling* at this age level.

But there is much more to say. Our discussion so far is about the way children organize their world in terms of themes and variations. We would add that it is our belief that they also organize their verbal world in the same way, their toy world, their graphic world, their song world, and their clay world. In all cases one can see that they tend to organize repeated behavior around one or more central actions (or words), which are then varied endlessly in a patterned fashion. Note that one comes to this conclusion by watching what children do spontaneously and voluntarily. It is a quite different conclusion from the one usually arrived at when one *tests* children within the constraints of some adult experimental or psychometric setting. It is worth noting that in the act of constructing their own worlds in expressive terms children seem to be immensely complex. However, when examined with Piaget or Vygotsky tests, they seem to be relatively primitive and egocentric.

The music in their storytelling cannot be seen on the page of print. But when we listen to these stories what we usually (not always) hear is one or more of the following prosodic characteristics. The children raise the pitch of their voices, they give a slower delivery, there is more word emphasis, there may be exaggerated sounds, there is a regular beat to the telling of the story which tends to come in regular lines as in verse, and they may give a rhythmic delivery and use dramatic crescendoes. In the above examples, both are strongly stressed after the fashion of nursery rhymes (as in "Old King Cole was a Merry Old Soul"). In addition, there are elements of rhyme (repeated sounds), alliteration, consonance, and assonance in both of these stories. So if the stories are taken down on a tape recorder it is possible to go back and score the child for control of the prosodic or expressive features of storytelling. This is something quite apart from the meaning of the story. In some work with older retarded children we find quite superb management of these expressive characteristics, even though the meaning of the story is not always clear to us. This follows the general rule that in human discourse *melody precedes meaning*. Logically minded adults have difficulty in realizing that the infant and toddler live in worlds where the discourse is to them rhythmic and melodious before it is referential and logical. We know that even in the first days of life infants move their bodies in tune with the rhythms of adult speech, that they can also tell their mothers' voices apart from those of others. Furthermore, when adults want to communicate their love or their playfulness to children, they characteristically adopt the expressive mannerisms just mentioned. They "citchy citchy coo" with raised eyebrows, wide open eyes and wide-mouthed smiles, with simple syntax, with raised pitch, nonsense sounds, transformed words ("pwitty wabbit") and the rest as above. This kind of thing goes on endlessly in the world of many little children. Even when adults ask the children to tell a story they often do so by signaling their question, "Can you tell me a *story*?", with raised eyebrows, open eyes, high pitch, and a special inflection of the word story, so it sounds "stor—eee." So the child knows immediately that he or she is to move into the play domain and not surprisingly responds in accord. They then generate the kind of prosodic response described above. Such a response is to adult stories as an eighteen-month-old's pivot or telegraphic speech (Mommy go, Daddy go, Baby go) is to adult language. In each case the child generates a novel form which has never been heard in adult speech, but is representative of the child's own stage of development, and it embodies faithfully the prosodic characteristics of adult play. The prosody appears to be modeled after the parents', but the prose is created out of infant mental cloth. If this is indeed true, we are entitled to argue that the prosody is the carrier for semantics. It is the relatively stable competence which the child uses as a basis for launching out as a storyteller. It is typical in new skill learning (at least in expressive areas) for children to use an earlier developed skill (prosody) to handle a novel emerging one (prose). We call this the *law of genetic recursiveness*. In our studies of preadolescent filmmaking, for example, the story that children compose for their own filmmaking is much simpler than stories they tell just as stories. Because the technical requirements of filmmaking are so difficult, they simplify the narrative task for themselves and that makes the technical work easier to manage. The story carries the film (Eadie, Sutton-Smith, & Griffin, 1983).

As time passes some of these musical aspects of the stories gradually drop out of regularly told stories. The manner of telling may still be dramatic and expressive, but the story itself tends to lose its rhythmic, alliterative, and rhyming qualities. There are other genres in child life where these characteristics persist longer than they do in stories, for example, in riddles, jump rope rhymes, and singing games, though perhaps the most characteristic genre is the parodied television commercial where childlike music continues unabated.

Still we do not want to suggest that the attenuation of these characteristics is too rapid. We know from studies of children's language that children both solitarily and in dyads continue in what you and I might call nonsense play, which has all the above musical characteristics. Some of our children, even after telling quite sober stories, would lapse into sound making, showing again the awareness of prosody and the interest it held in their own worlds. Thus, at the age of four years, after a year of sober storytelling, Cathy came to know her storytaker so well that she reverted to play with story making. Thus,

(3)   Now there was a pa ka
        Boon, goo
        There was a dog doo doo
        And he didn't like dog doo doo
        Then there was a man named Snowball
        And he didn't like snow
        Cha cha
        Doo choo
        Cha cha
        Doo choo
        I named dog doo doo
        Christopher say
        Dog doo doo
        Then there were a boy named Taw taw
        O
        Too too
        There there was a Captain Blooper he had a book and he were
            very bad and it hurt him
        Then there was a blooper pa pa
        Pa pa
        There was Superman coming and he hurt both of him knees
        Then they were flying and they went right in the ocean and he got
            bite from a shark
        And he didn't like when he got bite from a shark
        Then kla kla toe toe
        Tee tah
        Caw caw caw caw caw caw caw caw caw caw caw caw caw caw
            caw caw caw caw caw caw caw caw caw caw
        Now say pah pah kla klee
        Sa see
        Too tee
        Tah tah too tee
        Chee chaw
        Ta klu
        Kli klu
        Kla kla
        Klu fu
        Klee kla
        Koo koo
        Say say

Klee klee
Klip kla
Klee klee
Klip kla
She she
Fik ahh
Tungoo nah
Ka pa
Popeye the sailor man
Bad guy him be very bad to him
And I spit out a words.

Although, in general, after the age of three and one-half years the stories of the children could not well be characterized as verse, the vectorial character of the stories and the regularity of line and other verse effects do not entirely disappear. Our most gifted four-year-old, at the age of 4.1 years, told the following story, which is both a remarkable narrative and a kind of continuing poem on the theme of eating. The sequence follows the chronology of a picnic but almost every normal picnic expectation is defied or reversed. We get an unexpected picnic, unexpected members, unexpected eating habits, and unexpected consequences repeated and repeated. The style is one of variation by reversal of expectation. Nothing goes right, but there is an elegiac quality to the whole piece.

(4)   Once upon a time there was a family of tigers, bears, and lions
        And they went out for a wild animal picnic
        The wild animal picnic was made of baby rabbits
        That's what they ate
        They took the rabbits alive and they killed the rabbits at the picnic
        And when they ate the rabbits the blood washed out all the meat
            where they were chewing so they missed all the parts where
            they were chewing
        When they missed it they only got a tiny bit of their tooth left
        They kept chipping their teeth cause they forgot to take out the
            bones
        They kept chipping their teeth so much they only had one tooth
            on the top and one on the bottom
        Then they swallowed the rabbit
        After they chipped their teeth and had dinner they went home and

had roasted beef rabbit
Then after they swallowed the rabbit and after they had dinner
    they went to sleep and they all dreamt the same thing
And that's all.

Lest there be any doubt of this boy's tendency to conjoin story and verse, as well as to parody both, consider that at 5.1 years he told the following:

(5)   Once upon a time the once upon a time at the once upon a time
            which ate the once upon a time
       And then the once upon a time which ate the once upon a time ate
            the princess once upon a time with the king
       And then the once upon a time died
       Then the end ate the end
       The end
       The end
       Then the end died
       Then the end died
       Then the end died
       Then the end died
       And then the end the end the end died
       The end with a the end
       The end
       The end.

We found that still older children of seven to 11years who did not let their stories be poetic in this way nevertheless often asked us if we could let them introduce interludes of parodied commercials, obscene rhymes, and nonsense rhymes.[2] It is as if the musical or verse-like discourse context, from which the stories first emerged, is ever ready to bubble to the surface in a play setting, now in differentiated and distinct genres.

But the two-year-olds are not only more competent at the prosodic features of storytelling than they are at the logical features, they seem also to be relatively advanced in *staging* their stories in a dramatic way. While this is implied by what we have said of the musical features above (pitch, voice exaggerations, etc.), there are additional features which have to be taken into account. To stage a story there must be a sense of one's self as a storyteller, of the storytaker as an audience, and of the story itself as a stage for the actions of characters. When one realizes that many children have been playing theatrical games with their parents even as infants (peekaboo), it is perhaps not surprising that their management of staging is quite advanced. Clearly they know (a) that there is an appropriate time and place for this activity, (b) that the adult making the request will listen patiently and show responsiveness, (c) that they will be permitted to adopt the center of the stage in the narrative performance, (d) that, as we have seen, a particular style of address will be expected of the teller. In addition to these social presuppositions, the children also understand some cognitive presuppositions, namely, (a) the distinction between narrative fantasy and reality, and (b) that fantasy narratives are distinct from personal narratives (chronicles) and other genres (songs, and so on). Not all of these presuppositions are managed equally well by all children, but in general where storytelling is encouraged most of these are mastered by three- to four-year-olds, even though their stories do not yet meet an adult's criteria of proper narrative sequence.

In our samples, after the first few stories and by the age of about three years, most of our children have stories in which the characters become constant and the actions take place in a roughly chronological sequence. The emergence at this age of initial and/or terminal markers perhaps heralds this sense of a line of chronicity throughout the story, as in the following three-year-old girl's story.

(6)   Batman went away from his mommy
        Mommy said "come back, come back"
        He was lost and his mommy can't find him
        He ran like this to come home (she illustrates with arm
            movements)
        He eat muffins
        And he sat on his mommy's lap
        He fell to sleep
        And then him wake up
        And it was still nighttime
        And his mommy said "go back to bed"
        And he did all night
        And then it morning time
        And his mommy picked him up
        And then him have a rest
        He ran very hard away from his mommy like that
        I finished.

This story now has two vectors running through. One is the theme of going away and coming home, which is a popular one especially with girls in our stories. The other is a going-to-bed-and-getting-up theme. Basically these are both manifestations of the deeper theme of being independent of, or dependent upon, mother. Notice the great extent to which conjunctions as constants (and, then) have taken over the bonding of the lines (rather than just the identical repetition of the action and the location). Pronominal reference (he, his, and him) is also much more extensive and implies an underlying and more continuous deeper structure. But although in the story one thing happens after another without defying our idea of progression in real time (hence, has chronicity), we do not have a clear development. There is an early complication (he was lost), which is apparently resolved without effort, and then at the end we finish on another complication (he ran very hard away). There is no resolution or conclusion. But this is characteristic of stories through about seven years of age: they are stronger on introductions, complications, and endings than they are on development and resolution. Consider the following two stories also told by three-year-olds, boy and girl.

(7)   Batman
       Batman fight
       He crashed in the robber
       He got crashed in the big truck
       Supermarket
       The supermarket flew away
       And batman flew away with his cape
       That's the end.

(8)   She makes pee on the floor
       Then she goes with her mom to the ferris wheel wheel
       Now she went home and saw her dadda
       And now the daddy went away
       Now her grandpa is dead
       Now she crept into her bed
       Now she had a new baby
       The mother said, "no babies allowed"
       Now all the people were stuffy and had medicine
       The end.

In contrasting these kinds of stories with true stories which have a plot, we are highlighting the difference between the kind of chronicity in personal narratives and the kind of chronicity in myths and legends and fairy tales. These younger children's stories seem to borrow their notion of time from personal narratives. The latter come earlier than stories in young children's discourse. Before they can tell stories even two-year-olds can recount what they have just done, or have done yesterday, etc. But the kind of time that is found in myths and legends is something quite different. It is plot time and has to do with cultural beliefs about success. The hero begins by being put to some test, which he must subsequently overcome. In this kind of time there is usually a beginning, a middle, and an ending, or in story terms there is:

Introduction
Elaboration of characters and situation
Complication

Development

Resolution
Complication

As mentioned, from four through ten years of age children go about mastering these kinds of developments, and for a considerable period their stories are an intermingling of *theme and variations* structure with plot structure.

Plot structure requires a conflict, an opposition between characters or between a character and some obstacle, as well as the kind of time arrangement (introduction, middle, ending) just indicated. In story (6) above, we have the beginnings of character opposition (the conflict), but we do not have the temporal structure of plot. And this appears to be the general course of things. Children can state a conflict before they can develop and resolve it. We are able to perceive the child's beginning acquisition of plotting when there is a clear central character who has a clear conflict of some sort. Generally this is not with us until somewhere between five and seven years. Prior to that we will get a central character who will relate in a fairly unsystematic (theme and variational) way to a passing parade of other people and events – as in stories (7) and (8) above.

We have detected four stages in the way children come to deal with their characters and their conflicts: The conflicts are usually over villainy (attack, threat, and so on) or deprivation (loss of love, food, and so on).

Level I: No Response to Conflict

The most common response at this level, typical of five to seven years, is that the subject is threatened or overcome by a monster or there is some lack or loss to which no response is made. In a few cases, we are only told of the presence of the monster with some implied threat, or someone else is hurt, or we are scared, or the monster is described. One thinks of paralysis in the face of fear when seeking the biological counterparts of this response.

(9)   This is a story about a jungle. Once upon a time there was a jungle. There were lots of animals, but they weren't very nice. A little girl came into the store. She was scared. Then a crocodile came in. The end. (Girl, age five)

(10)   The boxing world. In the middle of the morning everybody gets up, puts on boxing gloves and fights. One of the guys gets socked in the face and he starts bleeding. A duck comes along and says, "Give up." (Boy, age five)

Level II: Failure

The predominant responses here are those of escaping or being rescued. The monster may be attacked but the attack is not successful. In this subject group, some children convert the monster into a benevolent creature. One may join with it in attacking others, or simply make it a nondangerous entity. On occasion, the benevolent monster has to persuade the mother (now the negative force) that it may be taken into the home quite safely. Unlike most fairy tales and folktales, there is little reference in this group of stories to the interference of magic or luck, an indication perhaps of the inner- rather than outer-directedness of this particular population. In most cases, those who rescue do not succeed in getting rid of the original threat either, so that these are Level II responses.

(11)   Henry Tick
       Chapter I: A few years ago Henry Tick lived in a hippy's hair but he got a crew cut so Henry had to move. He went to the dog pound but it was closed. He went to the pet shop but it was closed too. Finally he found a nice basset hound. So he moved in. He got a good job at the circus jumping 2 inches in mid-air into a glass of water. One day he jumped but there was no water. He was rushed to the hospital. They put 12 stitches in his leg. Well, he never went there again. The end.
       Chapter II: One day Henry Tick was walking down the street when he was almost stepped on. He was so startled he jumped in the shoe! He was in the shoe for about 15 minutes when the person took off the shoes and put them in the closet. Henry jumped out and ran into the next room which happened to be the bathroom. He jumped into the toilet, by mistake of course. Henry almost went down the drain.
       Chapter III: Henry got out of the toilet. The first thing he did was wash. He found a damp washcloth in the sink. He wiped himself thoroughly and then dried off. He went into the next room and watched the football game. (Girl, age 10)

It should be noted that in the Henry Tick story, Henry escapes his various dangers, but in no way nullifies them. They still exist and may return.

Level III: Nullification

At this level, the story's central character is successful in rendering the threat powerless in some way or in overcoming what is lacking. The enemy may withdraw. The nullification of the threat may be done by the good services of others, as in the following story of a pussy cat, who gets separated from his loved ones but is finally, after many travails, once again absorbed into a loving family.

(12)   A story about a pussy cat
       There was this old cat. It was wandering around the streets and

had nowhere to live. It was pregnant and it has nowhere to stay to have its babies and then it ran into another cat. The other cat said, "There's a burnt-out house where you can go and have your babies." And she said, "Where?" "Down the road and turn left." Two months passed and she had her babies. She died, it was wintertime. All the other babies got took by someone else except one little baby. This baby was frozen. She hardly could move. She got in the warmest spot. Someone dropped something out the window and she took it and it made her warm. She got very sick. Someone took her in and made her better. She was a playful kitten. She knocked over so much stuff and they were too poor and no one to give it to so they let it go in the street. It was springtime. She was able to eat again. And she was wandering around looking for a home to stay in. Once in a while she would see another cat and play with it. And sometimes people would hold the little kitten. The kids would ask their mothers if they could keep it but their mothers would say no – it's too hard to keep a little kitten. One day this little girl came over. She had one older sister and one baby sister. She was 10 years old. She asked her mother if she could keep it. Her mother said no. The girl's name was Lisa. Lisa was gonna be 11 in two days. Her mother did not know what to get her for her birthday. She put it in the box and cleaned it and gave it food, went to the pet store and got a cat box and wrapped it. It was Lisa's birthday. Lisa thought it was an empty cat box and was starting to cry but when she opened it she was glad and the little girl took care of it and fed it milk and food and the little kitten lived with Lisa happily ever after. (Girl, age 9)

Level IV: Transformation

At this level the danger is not only removed, there is a complete transformation, so that there is clearly no possibility of this threat or this lack returning again. In the following example, the ten-year-old writer has a story in three chapters. The first chapter has a Level II ending, the second chapter has a Level III ending, and the final chapter has a Level IV ending.

(3)   Chapter 1: Mr. Hoot and the Married Lady
One night Mr. Hoot was sitting in his house thinking why he
never had any fun. He said to himself, "Maybe I'm too shy." So
he said to himself again that he was going to go out and get into
mischief. He got on his coat and put on his contact lenses and he
was off. There he was strolling from bar to bar. At his fifth bar,
he decided to have a drink. He pounded on the table and said two
martinis on the rocks. While he was waiting for his two drinks,
he took off his shoes and socks and picked his feet. Then he got
his drinks and chug-a-lugged them down the hatch. After his
drinks, he saw a beautiful lady in the corner of the bar. So he
went over to her and said, "Can I buy a drink?" She replied, "No,
thank you. I'm not finished with this one." Then she said,
"Anyway, please sit down and we will talk."
        A big guy walking out the men's room came over to Mr. Hoot
and said, "Are you fooling with my wife? How dare you," and
picked Mr. Hoot up and threw him on the ground. The moral of
the story is – you can't tell a married lady from a single lady.
        Chapter 2: Mr. Hoot and the Stewardess
Once Mr. Hoot was sitting in the bar with his friend Bobby the
Baboon. They were discussing going to Hollywood. Mr. Hoot
said to Bobby, "Let's go next week." So they made all the
arrangements and before they knew it they were on the airplane
going to Hollywood. While they were on the airplane, Mr. Hoot
saw this very attractive stewardess. So Mr. Hoot called her over
and said, "Hi, what's your name?" She said, "Laura Sinch,
what's yours?" "Harold Hoot," he said. Then he said, "How long
have you been working for the airlines?" She replied, "Two years
and seven months." Then they started talking about where they
lived and other things like that. Then a little baboon said, "Hey,
would you stop it with the lady and let her do what she's
supposed to be doing." Then Harold got mad and said, "Shut up,
you little baboon." Then Bobby said, "Hey, are you sounding on
my kind? How dare you." "Oh, Bobby, butt out of this," Harold
replied. Then the little baboon said, "Shut up, you overgrown
owl." Then they really started at it. They were throwing pillows
and suitcases at each other and cursing at each other. Then Harold
gave him a good sock in the face and that was the end of the
adventure.

Chapter 3: Mr. Hoot Gets Married

Once Harold was sitting in a restaurant at a table all by himself. Then he noticed there was a female owl sitting down by herself. Mischievously he walked over and asked her what her name was. She said, "Mary Gline." Then Harold thought for a moment and said, "Are you the girl that broke her wing when you were nine years old?" Then she said, "What's your name and how did you know about my wing?" "Well," said Harold, "I knew about your wing because your name sounded very familiar, so I thought back to my childhood and remembered a girl named Mary broke her wing, and my name is Harold Hoot." Then she said, "You were the kid they called Hoot the Tott." "Oh yeah," Harold replied. "I forgot about that." Then they started to talk about their childhood and ate dinner together.

After that night they went out to dinner, to movies and did lots of other things like that. After about a year, they told their parents they were going to get married. Their parents agreed and they had a wedding. They had the most beautiful wedding you can imagine. For their honeymoon they went to Niagara Falls. Then after that they settled down in a nice house in Poughkeepsie and had boys named Bobby and Peter. Last and not least, they lived happily ever after. (Boy, age 10)

When the stories were classified in these terms there was indeed a significant age trend. Older children in this sample tend to tell the higher level stories. We have now made the same analysis several times and such a chronological age shift is always forthcoming. This time there is no sex difference across the four levels. There is a difference in style of solution but not in level. That is, boys more often reach Level III or IV by having their hero overcome the villain, while the girls more often reach these levels through an alliance.

From the cross-cultural evidence presented by the Marandas (1970), it is also clear that there are many societies where no such belief in one's ability to overcome the fates exists, and in these cultures the stories do not rise above the first or second levels. Again we find that some of our younger children, even five-year-olds, occasionally tell the fourth level stories, and so we wonder whether or not this particular series of steps might not be functionally related to need achievement, or to an inner locus of control.

The changes across these four levels of plotted time is also accompanied by other developments in the stories. In the last story, for example, we saw a series of conflicts take place, although the final resolution of marriage overcame the lack of excitement stated at the outset. There are thus subplots (chapter 2) within the larger story. In general, children learn to handle this kind of embedding of subplots ("meantime, back at the ranch") between nine and eleven years (Botvin & Sutton-Smith, 1977). What one often finds is a persistence of a theme-and-variation kind of wandering story, thinly pulled together by some slight attendance to plot requirements. At the younger ages, three through seven years, the "once upon a time" and "they lived happily ever after" markers are as often as not a substitute for any real plot control.

CONCLUSION

I have presented the thesis that storytelling in this society may have its precursor in the theatrical "playese" of parent and infant. Their melodic interactions, their quadralogic roles, and their management of incongruity and laughter to create the paradoxes of both being and not being themselves may provide the true scaffold for later storytelling. On this playful basis, the parents introduce the relatively more sedentary activity of making fiction from picture books, storybooks, improvised stories, and personal accounts. The evidence appears to be that when this happens the adults dominate the interactions (over 90 percent in the Ninio-Bruner account and 75 percent in our own), with a question and answer scaffolding. Nevertheless, when children tell their own early stories emerging from within this interaction (Magee & Sutton-Smith, 1983), what impresses one is how independent these stories are of the kind of storying that parents have done. As in the case of generative grammars in early language development, the adult storytelling and the child storytelling are simply not the same. And in fact the first child stories are more reminiscent of the first face-to-face plays than of the parents' picture-book storytelling. The child's first stories are melodic as are the first face-to-face plays of infancy. The child's stories are as attentive to the intonative quality of the language as to its semantic content. Furthermore, at the heart of these stories are the dramatic vectors or the crises which they reiterate, just as infant ludic play centers on anticipations and climaxes of faces seen or not seen, or of children tickled or not tickled.

As time goes by these first poetic stories give way to plot stories and with age these approximate to the hero myths of the Western world within which heroes and heroines brought under duress, undertake tasks which resolve their problems. Although thinking within developmental psychology tends to privilege these later plot stories over the earlier poetic ones, because of their greater complexity, the display of stories we have given here shows clearly that the bias on behalf of complexity and abstraction simply does not do justice to the characteristic fictional competences of the young. Nor does that bias recognize the child's highly aesthetic renderings, which still remain sensitive to prosody, when those of their elders do not. The young trained on the bathos and "playese" of their parents or older peers still keep these textural and motivational characteristics salient in their stories, while the older children do not.

NOTES

1. Stories collected by Dan Mahoney and from the Soho Center for Arts and Education, New York, Jeanna Golobin, Director.
2. Collected at P.S. 3, New York, 1974, John Melser, Principal.

REFERENCES

Bateson, G. (1972). *Steps to an ecology of mind.* New York: Ballantine.

Botvin, G. J. and Sutton-Smith, B. (1977). The development of structural complexity in children's fantasy narratives. *Developmental Psychology,* 13, 377-388.

Bretherton, J. (1984). *Symbolic play.* New York: Academic Press.

Brown, C. C. and Gottfried, A. W. (Eds.) (1985). *Play interactions.* Skillman, NJ: Johnson & Johnson.

Bruner, J. S. and Sherwood, V. (1976). Early rule structure: The case of "peekaboo." In R. Harre (Ed.), *Life sentences.* New York: Wiley.

Bruner, J. (1984). Narrative and paradigmatic modes of thought. Invited address. A. P. A. Division I., Toronto.

Cochran-Smith, M. (1984). *The making of a reader.* American Psychological Association, Norwood, NJ: Ablex.

De Loache, J. S. (1984). What's this? Maternal questions in joint picture book reading with toddlers. *The Quarterly Newsletter of the Laboratory of Comparative Human Cognition,* 6, 44, pp. 87-95.

Eadie, F., Sutton-Smith, B., and Griffin, M. (1983). Film-making by "young filmmakers." *Visual Communications,* 9, 4, pp. 65-75.

Eadie, F., Sutton-Smith, B., and Magee, M. A. (1983). The origins of fiction. *Infinity Magazine*. Spring, pp. 64-67. (Also ERIC 249506)

Erwin-Tripp, S. and Mitchell-Kernan, C. (1977). *Child discourse*. New York: Academic Press.

Gadamer, H. G. (1982). *Truth & method*. New York: Crossroad.

Gardner, H. (1984). Is there an artistic intelligence? Annual Meeting of American Psychological Association. Invited address, Toronto.

Habermas, Jurgen. (1983). Hermeneutics and critical theory. Paper presented to the Conference on the Philosophy of the Human Studies, Philadelphia.

Kelly-Byrne, D. (1983). A narrative of play and intimacy. In F. E. Manning (Ed.), *The world of play*. West Point, NY: Leisure Press.

Magee, M. A. and Sutton-Smith, B. (1983). The art of storytelling: How do children learn it? *Young Children*, 38, 4-12.

Mandler, J. M. (1984). *Stories, scripts and scenes: Aspects of schema theory*. Hillsdale, NJ: Lawrence Erlbaum.

Maranda, E. K. and Maranda, P. (1970). *Structural models in folklore and transformational essays*. The Hague: Mouton.

McDowell, J. (1979). *Children's riddling*. Bloomington, IN: University of Indiana Press.

Ninio, A. and Bruner, J. (1976). The achievement and antecedents of labelling. *Journal of Child Language*, 5, 1-15.

Opie, I. and Opie, P. (1960). *Lore and language of children*. Oxford: Clarendon Press.

Piaget, J. (1951). *Play, dreams and imitation in childhood*. New York: Norton.

Stern, D. (1977). *The first relationship*. Cambridge, MA: Harvard University Press.

Sutton-Smith, B. (1979a). The play of girls. In C. B. Kopp & M. Kirkpatrick (Eds.), *Women in context*. New York: Plenum.

Sutton-Smith, B. (1979b). Presentation and representation in children's narratives. *New Directions in Child Development*, 6, 53-65.

Sutton-Smith, B. (Ed.) (1979c). *Play and learning*. New York: Gardner Press.

Sutton-Smith, B. (1981). *The folkstories of children*. Philadelphia, PA: University of Pennsylvania Press.

Sutton-Smith, B. (1985). *Toys as culture*. New York: Gardner Press.

Sutton-Smith, B. (1984). The origins of fiction and the fictions of origin. In E. Bruner (Ed.), *Story, play, text*. Proceedings of the American Ethnological Association.

Van Hoorn, J. (1983). Games of infancy: Their function in cognitive development and enculturation. Paper presented to A.E.R.A. Montreal, April.

Winner, Ellen. (1982). *Invented world: The psychology of the arts*. Cambridge, MA: Harvard University Press.

5

The Acquisition and Use of Narrative Grammar Structure

James C. Mancuso

A radical constructivist (see Gergen, 1985; von Glasersfeld, 1984) accepts the premise that an organized cognitive system occupies a psychological context as definitively as does the energy-emitting event which impinges on that system. Any input, be it a story or a detailed architectural drawing, serves a psychological function only through its cohesion with a person's existing structural representations of events that he or she judges to be similar to the input-related event. In other terms, a stimulus accrues one or another meaning through its assimilation into a person's existing knowledge system. The "sense" of an event derives from the ways in which its input-producing energy patterns are translated into neural impulses at sensory endings and then assimilated to a person's existing cognitive structures.

THE NARRATIVE AS AN ASSIMILATING STRUCTURE

Studies reported over the last decade amply support the belief that the typical adult person assimilates input, particularly textual input, to an acquired, internal representation of narrative grammar structure. Although narrative structure had been analyzed by literary scholars (for example, Propp, 1928/1968), the recent attention given to narrative structure by behavioral scientists has followed upon the promulgation of the major premises of constructivism. Just as the study of general language processes took a radical turn when investigators of syntax development began to take into account personally acquired grammatical structures, so the study of narrative took a new course when constructivist postulates were employed to help understand story grammar. Contemporary investigators (Colby, 1973; Lakoff, 1972) have proceeded from Propp's observations that simple, traditional stories are built around an actor and certain functions. The actors remain constant, but the functional aspects of a story change as the actors complete their enactments. The categories of action have been described (Labov & Waletzky, 1967), for example, as orientation, complication, evaluation, resolution, and coda. Other investigators have analyzed story structure with other formal grammars.

Mandler (1984) states that "stories have an underlying, or base, structure that remains relatively invariant in spite of gross differences in content from story to story. This structure consists of a number of ordered constituents" (p. 22). Using a schematic which parallels that of other researchers (see, for example, Thorndyke, 1977), Mandler proposed that traditional stories begin with a setting, wherein the narrator introduces characters, locale, and time of the events. One or more episodes then follow the setting. All episodes contain a beginning and development. Within development the protagonist reacts to the beginning events, and the reaction takes the form of a cause for continued action. The protagonist sets a goal path to a goal. Each episode includes an outcome of an attempt to reach the goal, and one assumes that a reader would process attempts as causes of outcomes. Thereupon, an episode closes with an ending, which sets the outcome into a broader context. Final ending portions may include a more global ending to coalesce stories that contain multiple episodes.

Investigators working with the concept of narrative structures generally assume that persons acquire, in some way, organized internal representations which reflect the constituents of the proposed grammars. The expression of this schematic knowledge becomes explicit as a person develops expectations about a text which he or she attempts to process. These expectations guide the person in retrieving the information required to make inferences and decisions about the flow of input. Furthermore, the overall cognitive strategies that ensue from use of a coherent narrative schema facilitates long-term memory storage and subsequent retrieval of the text's semantic content.

DEMONSTRATIONS OF USE OF STORY STRUCTURE

As a byproduct of his studies of people's use of causality concepts, Michotte (1963/1946; see Sarbin, this volume) made clear that observers, though not instructed to do so, would impose narrative structure on moving geometric configurations. Participants in Michotte's investigations confidently imposed elaborate cause and effect stories on even the simplest stimulus materials, and they found it worthwhile and enjoyable to do so.

Contemporary investigators conduct direct studies of narrative grammar by first delineating a formal story grammar which should meet two basic requirements. The grammar (1) should specify rules for defining the categories of the text's information units, and (2) should allow definition of the relationships among the story's various isolatable units. After having defined a suitable grammar model, however, the investigator should be able to show that the proposed narrative grammar is employed by the person processing a text.

To complete a direct demonstration of the structure of story grammar, Stein and Policastro (1984) composed a variety of text segments. Some of the segments represented simple collections of words, some represented several, but not all, required grammar categories, some represented "near stories," and some represented a story that contained all the grammar constituents that would appear in a story if it adhered strictly to the formal grammar defined by these investigators. They then asked their participants (1) to indicate yes or no to register judgments about whether or not the text could be classed as a story, and (2) to mark a seven-point scale to indicate the extent of the segments' "storiness."

Stein and Policastro (1984) concluded that "we can say that texts must include at least an animate protagonist and some type of causal sequence in order to be considered a story" (p. 147). Second-grade children did not categorize a text as a story if it did not contain these elements, and teachers generally followed the same practice. Additionally, Stein and Policastro found that the rated quality of a story was consistently related to the number of story grammar constituents contained in the passage. "Those passages with all the parts of an episode were always rated higher than those passages containing permissible deletions of any category information" (p. 150). Finally, "storiness" rankings assigned to the passages by the teachers correlated very highly ·with the "storiness" ratings made by children, despite the teachers' propensity to judge more of the incomplete segments as suitable stories.

By using a multidimensional statistical technique, Pollard-Gott, McClosky, and Todres (1979) extracted a narrative structure which fit very well with the structure that would be imposed a priori on a story. In this study readers sorted the story's sentences into groups which, to them, represented coherent units. The investigators then produced a matrix by entering each sentence as an element which labelled one of the matrix's rows and one of its columns. A number at each intersect of a row and column would provide the index of the similarity, derived from the participants' patterns of groupings, of each sentence/element to every other sentence/element. Using a hierarchical clustering algorithm they then categorized those sentences which participants had judged to be grammatically similar to each other. After such analyses the investigators were able to show, for example, that participants had, indeed, located one group of a story's sentences into a psychological space representing setting and other groups into spaces that could be labelled initiating event, attempt, consequence, and so forth. They concluded that "subjective story structures generated by the hierarchical clustering procedures are consistent with the major features of structure found in the story grammar analyses of Glenn (1978) and Mandler and Johnson (1977)" (p. 270).

DEMONSTRATIONS FROM WHICH THE USE OF STORY STRUCTURE MAY BE INFERRED

Constructivist premises support a principle affirming that the cognitive classification which a person imposes on materials at the time of input will limit the ways in which the material can be used when it is retrieved during memory processes. Furthermore, when persons use *their own input categories* during learning, recall may proceed effortlessly and effectively. Additionally, the ways in which a person organizes input during initial exposure affects the ease with which that information will later become available (Posner, 1973, p. 33).

Numerous illustrative reports (for example, Bower, Clark, Lesgold, & Winzenz, 1969) contain evidence that lists of words are better recalled when the words name objects which a participant can categorize into personally meaningful classes. By accepting a correlative premise, an investigator would expect that a comprehender would show relatively efficient retrieval if he can process a text using his complete, well-ordered, internally represented story structure.

One can now make the incontrovertible claim that participants better retrieve those stories built to include semantic material representing all the properly sequenced story grammar parts of a text (Stein & Glenn, 1979; Thorndyke, 1977). Further, a listener or a reader who encounters a story from which a salient story part has been omitted, on recalling the story, will fill in the missing element with text which preserves the canonical story structure (Mandler & Johnson, 1977; Stein & Glenn, 1979).

To construct another cogent demonstration that persons treat a story in terms of its grammatical structure one can start with the assumption that the organizing process takes time. The reader, using the episode schema, performs particularly important encoding operations at the boundaries of episodes. One can show, then, that "holding other factors constant, the process in load is greater at or around the episode boundaries than at other points in the episodes" (Haberlandt, Berian, & Sandson, 1980, p. 636). Reading speed decelerates at each transition to a new episode as the person's system engages in the macrolevel operations required to shift his or her cognitive guides.

Mandler and Goodman (1982) designed a study of reading times at episode transitions in order to assure that the results would not be attributable to factors other than the load on processing produced by the important encoding operations which occur at the transitions. They used two-episode stories, carefully controlling length of sentences, number of nouns and pronouns in sentences, and so forth. They asked subjects to read the stories, which contained two sentences to represent each grammatical unit. They report the finding, among other results, that comprehenders use more time to process the first sentence than they use to process the second sentence of each story grammar unit. For example, a reader might encounter two sentences of text that serve as the ending unit of an episode, such as: "They made an awful muddy mess in the elephant yard – The zookeeper worked for two days cleaning it up" (Mandler, 1984, p. 39). On average, participants read the second of these ending unit sentences in 105 fewer milliseconds than they had used to read the first.

From their results Mandler and Goodman concluded that readers' knowledge of story structure allows them to recognize a shift in topic as they process the first sentence of new constituents of a narrative. Comprehenders can recognize episode shifts by relying on information such as transitional formalisms and changes in type of information. More importantly, Mandler and Johnson conclude, the reader carries his or her knowledge structure into the cognitive task, and, as a result, a comprehender does not require the presence of such narratory devices to process the content of the tale and to locate the episodic boundaries.

In short, one could set out the postulate that a person's acquired system of narrative grammar directs his or her text processing toward anticipating the flow of the story constituents, just as one's sentence syntax structures leads him or her to expect a predicate to follow the subject of a sentence, and so forth. Stein and Glenn (1979) extended the validity of this postulate by careful study of people's implicit knowledge of relationships within and between narrative grammar categories. They note that state or activity statements occur within setting segments – "Once there was a little golden-haired girl known as Goldbraids." The episode system which follows the setting consists of an entire behavior sequence (including external and internal events that affect one of the story's characters), the character's goal settings and expectation, the overt actions that conform to his or her internal responses, and the consequences of the character's undertaking. Stein and Glenn stress the explicit and implied causal linkages that a comprehender can cognize in an episode. The external or internal initiating events of an episode – "One afternoon Goldbraids saw a bird hopping as if it couldn't fly" – may *cause* an internal response in a protagonist. The *initiate* relation designates a direct causal connection between the initiating event and the response constituent of the story. The protagonist may experience an emotion, or become motivated to draw up a plan, or to set a goal – "Goldbraids felt very sorry for the bird." Setting the goal causes an action, which then becomes the cause of a successful or an unsuccessful outcome – "Goldbraids knew that Daddy could help the bird. She ran to catch it, but it hopped very fast. Then suddenly it jumped up and flew away." Unlike Mandler (1984), Stein and Glenn include a grammar category which is used at the end of a complete episode. A final *reaction* category would describe the affective state which the characters experience as a result of the goal attainment (or nonattainment) described in the story – "Goldbraids was annoyed that the bird had fooled her."

To add further clarification to their propositions Stein and Glenn proceeded from the established conclusion "that story memory was a direct function of the match between text structure of stories (as presented to participants) and an ideal story structure as defined in (their) grammar system" (Stein & Nezworski, 1978, p. 190). They presented four different stories to their participating children. They arranged the stories so that three of the four original story versions contained statements which had been presented in inverted order, relative to their theoretical formal structure. In one story, for example, the initiating event occurred after the character's major goals had been specified, rather than immediately after the major setting statement.

The children first orally retold the stories they had heard. Second, the experimenters asked each child to tell the first, the second, and the third most important parts of the story to be remembered. To collect a third type of data Stein and Glenn asked the children direct "why" questions – "Why did Goldbraids become annoyed?"

Stein and Glenn found that the children recalled the stories in the order dictated by the grammar. Only 7 percent of the recalled statements represented deviations from the ordering of categories as prescribed by the formal theory. Seventy-five percent of the "correcting" reversals which the children had made could be predicted by diagramming the stories into the formal structure. For example, almost all of the category-ordering "errors" occurred when participants "incorrectly" rearranged into "correct" grammatical order the story in which the initiating event occurred after the goal specification. A child might thus "correctly" reposition two sentences which had originally been presented as, "Goldbraids was annoyed. She had wanted to help by taking the bird to her daddy."

By adding new categories, that is, categories which had not been included in the originally presented stories, Stein and Glenn's participants provided additional information about the narrative structure which children bring to a story-processing task. One of the stories presented to children, for example, contained no initiating event at the beginning of the first episode. Thirty-three percent of the first-grade children and 75 percent of the fifth-grade children added information that could be taken as the cause of the actor's plan. In general, children added many statements which would belong to the internal response category. Additionally, 18 percent of the added statements could be classed in the consequence category.

Stein and Glenn's analysis of data from children's judgments of the importance of story parts provided a different kind of index of the ways in which the youngsters had processed the stories. The investigators sorted the statements which the children had judged to be the most important parts of stories to be remembered, and they isolated those recalled statements which accurately reflected story parts which the children had heard. By this method they showed that the children had judged the statements which fit into the direct consequence category to be important. Additionally, the children, particularly the fifth-grade children, had judged as very important the character's internal responses, such as, "Goldbraids felt sorry for the bird."

One must carefully track through the results of Stein and Glenn's efforts to induce the children to report a recognition of the causal relationships between episodes and between categories within an episode. A child's response to a question about the causal links in stories was considered to be an error only if the response clearly contradicted the original story. Children made few errors in recalling the causal linkages presented in the stories. The children clearly reported one or another kind of satisfactory causal link between episodes, whether the episodes were embedded or whether they were sequential. That is, the children tended to report a causal linkage rather than a temporal linkage between episodes in the stories. Yet the children did not report the causal linkages between the constituents of the episodes as they had appeared in the original stories. Instead, they very frequently attributed the cause of internal responses, attempts, and consequences to internal responses. In short, the children appear to infer the actor's internal reaction from hearing the initiating event, and they then attributed the character's other internal responses, attempts, and the consequences of the attempts to those inferred internal responses.

The studies reviewed above exemplify the large and growing literature (see also, Graybeal, 1981; Mandler & DeForest, 1979; Whaley, 1981) which evidences the general proposition that persons fit textual input into a narrative grammar whose basic categories can be explicated. Furthermore, one can readily observe that children as young as age four implicitly use narrative grammar (Brown & Hurtig, 1983).

AN EXPLICATION OF THE DEVELOPMENT OF NARRATIVE GRAMMAR

What explains the acquisition of the narrative grammar which enables an average two-year-old to construct a crude response when asked to tell a story (Ames, 1966)? Fuller, whose method of teaching reading capitalizes on young children's propensity to fit text to story structure (1974, 1979), sets story grammar functioning into a discussion of evolution and the organization of the brain. "If story is the basis of intellectual cohesion, it could be the engram of our species" (Fuller, 1982, p. 134). Mandler (1983) supports the position that one acquires story structure at an early age, and then notes that "From an early age we hear a particular class of stories with highly similar structure and we gradually form an abstract representation of that structure" (p. 6). These responses to the initial question, one can observe, are entangled in basic paradigmatic issues which deserve further exploration.

Mandler (1984) and Fuller (1979) make similar observations as they discuss the criticisms of the concept of story structure. Correctly locating the roots of the criticisms in the long-standing dialectic between the Kantian and Lockean traditions in the behavioral sciences, Fuller writes,

> In spite of the work of [many constructivist scholars] ... IQ tests and education operate as though cognition requires that small segments, "bits" of information, must first be learned before their totality can be understood. Laboriously mastered segments are expected gradually to make a whole, which may be reading a story, or anything else. (P. 223)

Mandler states that "Part of the objection to characterizing story structure by any rule system is that it implies that people have highly *abstract knowledge* about stories. Most of the opponents ... demand more specific *content* to all psychological knowledge" (p. 19). These objections to the use of the narrative grammar concept, I believe, derive from the clash between the basic paradigms which guide the thinking of the commentators. Advocates of the story grammar reason from a contextualist/constructivist (Kantian) paradigm. Critics attempt to reason from a mechanist (Lockean) paradigm.

The exposition rendered below contains an effort to strengthen the narrative grammar concept by presenting a constructivist explanation of the acquisition of story grammar. To proceed, constructivist terms are used to resolve two important issues. First, it is affirmed that narrative grammar develops epigenetically. Second, an intrinsic motivational system directs such epigenetic development.

Epigenesis in the Development of Story Grammar

As stated above, the basic premise of the contextualist/constructivist position is that a stimulus event has no meaning outside of its contact with a person's existing knowledge system. An advocate of the story grammar concept would assume that some form of structure always underlies the continuous evolution of an internally represented abstraction of story structure.

Without doubt, story structure development depends upon the child having acquired a readily recallable set of conceptions about causality. Persons expect and look for causal linkages as they process stories (Mandler, 1984; Michotte, 1963; Stein & Glenn, 1979). In grammatically correct stories the initiating event – "Goldbraids saw a bird hopping" – causes the actor to have an internal reaction – "She felt very sorry," which in turn causes the action "Goldbraids ran after the bird," which in turn causes the outcome – "The bird hopped fast, and then flew away." The centrality of cause and effect are regularly demonstrated by the repeated finding (Haberlandt, Berian, & Sandson, 1980) that the *attempt* and the *outcome* grammar constituent are better recalled by participants in memory-for-story studies.

According to Piaget (1936/1952), nine-month-old infants complete a general psychological development which is critical to a child's understandings of causality. Although, through an earlier development, the infant could "make interesting sights last" by repeating an action which would be regularly followed by one or another kind of sensory input, the nine-month-old infant functions as if he or she can coordinate two internal representations to produce a single pattern of action. "Hence, there exists simultaneously the distinction between the end and the means, and the intentional coordination of the schemata. The intelligent act is thus constituted, which does not limit itself merely to reproducing the interesting results, but to arriving at them due to new combinations" (p. 211).

Aside from forming the base for the growth of the child's concept of causality, the general ability to intercoordinate schemata gives rise to other bases of story understanding. Before the infant achieves the ability to intercoordinate representations he or she cannot successfully treat an object as an entity having a permanent existence. Lacking the cognitive skill to coordinate separate, successive, time-separated sensory contacts with an object, the infant cannot develop a knowledge system to call up and to impose the idea of "same object" in the presence of putatively recurring input from one or another object. How could a person develop a structure that would approach the concept of story without having developed the idea of continuity of events?

Concepts of time, which also form a base for the acquisition of story structure, are interlinked with ability to intercoordinate schemata. Piaget (1927/1969) observes that

When, trying to reach a distant object, [the infant] first gets hold of an appropriate tool (support or stick) it establishes a primitive order of succession between the means and the end. However, this does not mean that time, at the sensory-motor level, is constructed into a homogeneous scheme even on the purely unconscious and practical plane: all the baby does is to correlate the succession or duration of particular actions with spatial displacements. . . . It is only once spatial groups of displacements have been constructed that time itself can become objectivized. . . . (Pp. 280-281).

In sum, a variety of conceptions, particularly those dependent on acquisition of skill to intercoordinate schemata, develop prior to and form the base of the development of story structure. Story structure develops epigenetically out of these basic structures whose early manifestations are observable in the child aged about nine months. One need not be surprised, then, at the observation that two-year-old children can understand the idea of story.

A Motive Principle to Account for the Acquisition of Narrative Grammar

Kintsch (1980) notes that persons enjoy the exchange of stories (see also Sarbin, this volume; Michotte, 1946/1963). He posits that "cognitive interest" (p. 88) motivates story processing; and that a story is interesting if (1) a reader has acquired a general system of cognitions by which to assimilate the particular text input, (2) the input generates uncertainty about how the text is to continue, and (3) the ambiguity which generated the surprise is postdictably resolved. Fuller (1979) frames her motivational proposition in terms of the need concept. "The need to make our life coherent, to make a story out of it, is probably so basic that we are unaware of it's importance" (p. 224).

A person's propensity to avoid ambiguity, or to achieve coherence, stands as the fundamental postulate of a psychology of personal constructs (Kelly, 1955): "A person's processes are psychologically channelized by the ways in which he anticipates events." In their elaboration of this motivational statement, Mancuso and Adams-Webber (1982) have developed the proposition that "one's anticipations are nothing other than the schemata that are assembled to incorporate, integrate, and assimilate the incoming information" (p. 14). They make the case that people, as psychological systems engaging in the continuous process of calling up and assembling schemata to fit over putatively recurring inputs, function to keep high the probability that there will be a match between the patterns developed at the distal sensory systems and those drawn from long-term memory to assimilate the input. When the expected probabilities are not met the system functions to resolve the discrepancy between the recalled schemata and the event-produced input. Though complicated by the distracting body mobilization which takes place to facilitate the discrepancy-resolution process, discrepancy resolution represents the basic motivation of all psychological functioning.

In conditions of moderate discrepancy, that is, in conditions in which slight modifications of a person's knowledge structures must be effected before the input can be assimilated, a person will report that he or she is in a state of interest. When the slight discrepancy has been resolved, the person will report a state of pleasure.

One may easily draw parallels between the position deriving from Kelly's fundamental postulate and the concepts underlying Kintsch's discussion of interest in stories. Kintsch says specifically, "The three factors that determine cognitive interest . . . all point to the importance of the reader's knowledge structure in the comprehension process" (p. 91). And later, in specifying his clearly epigenetic view of learning, relative to text processing, he says,

> We have to start with an initial knowledge structure and then model the comprehension process as a continuous modification of that knowledge structure. 'Comprehension' is thus interpreted as the assimilation of a text into a particular knowledge structure, which through this process itself undergoes change.

Extending these points, one can assert that the epigenetic development of story structure, like all epigenetic development, represents a continuous, intrinsically motivated process.

For purposes of this exposition, the moderate discrepancy hypothesis would stand as a motivational principle which frames the epigenetic development of narrative grammar, just as it supplies a suitable motivational position within which one can construe all learning. As indicated above, children as young as two years appear to retrieve narrative structure in their efforts to comprehend all textual input. One would expect that a discrepancy between the recalled story grammar and input, like any discrepancy, would require resolution. As the toddler's psychological system functions to retrieve the rudimentary bases for its developing narrative grammar he or she will encounter situations which will not be readily assimilated to his or her structures. If, for example, the toddler hears a story in which the protagonist's action is caused by an internal reaction – "Goldbraids felt sorry for the bird. She ran after it" – the child might be unable, at first, to fit that internal reaction into the causality slot; the cause slot in her story structure would remain empty, and there would be an input/system discrepancy. The toddler, thereupon, will be activated and will attend to specific input sources. By such attention those structural schemata which have been called up relative to the input will become linked to those schemata which represent the semantic content of the input-producing event. By scanning the input concerning the protagonist's internal reaction the toddler's story structure system can be elaborated so that she can include internal reaction as the *cause* in a cause and effect sequence.

A young infant, in another example, might successfully intercoordinate direct sensory inputs from two disparate sources, such as the feedback from its leg muscles and the visual input from the shaking of the rattle suspended over its crib. By having acquired the cognitive base of this ability to "make interesting sights last," the infant would have acquired a structure from which cause and effect conceptions would epigenetically develop. At one point, however, the rattle might shake when no muscular feedback has been generated. Or the muscular feedback schemata might be evoked while the visual input of the shaking rattle would be absent. Such discrepancies between input and retrieved schemata would motivate the child and he would scan the situation. New inputs would evoke other schemata that can be intercoordinated with the schemata recalled to process the shaking rattle. By observing that the rattle will shake not only when he kicks his legs, but also when an adult grasps the string by which the rattle hangs and shakes his or her hand, the infant moves toward separating two segments of the situation. The infant's motivation to resolve the discrepancy will prompt him to separate a cause, human movement, from the effect, shaking rattle, and he will move epigenetically toward acquiring the complex narrative grammar knowledge system which will be implicated in his enjoyment of stories.

THE PSYCHOLOGICAL IMPORTANCE OF NARRATIVE STRUCTURE

Current knowledge suggests that people in widely diverse cultures acquire narrative structure (see Mandler, 1984, pp. 50-53). Furthermore, as noted above, most people can use the important rudiments of story structure before finishing the third year. As is the case with the verbal syntax system which develops in parallel with the acquisition of narrative grammar structures, people employ their narrative grammars implicitly and will attend to acquired grammars only under "artificial" conditions. But, in that almost anyone who speaks any language can understand the story grammar of almost every other person, culturally different people will experience little of the motivating discrepancy which is experienced when native speakers of one language attempt to use the syntax of a second language. Such discrepancy would, of course, bring attention to the syntax of languages, and the discrepancies could be resolved by refining personal systems of syntax structures. It is not surprising, then, that formal syntax systems developed in the era around 600 B.C.E., as the philosophizing Greeks established trade routes and colonies among the polyglot cultures surrounding the Mediterranean Sea. One also need not be surprised that the importance of story structures, relative to diverse psychological functions, has only recently become a topic for formal investigation; and that only recently have scholars begun to uncover the psychological implications of narrative structures.

Reading Ability and Narrative Structure

The hypothesis of a totally logical theoretical progression led investigators (Fitzgerald, 1984; Fredericksen, 1979; Fuller, 1979; McClure, Mason, & Williams, 1983) to demonstrate that narrative grammar is implicated in a person's reading skill. Fitzgerald (1984), attacked the perplexing problems of some children's failure to learn to read. She first assessed the extent to which participants supplied continuations or insertions which would represent the same category information that a "good grammarian" would insert into the position of a story text's deleted portion. At each grade level Fitzgerald found a positive relationship between reading achievement test scores and the ability to supply a grammatically correct story continuation or insertion. Furthermore, better readers tended to supply richer, more varied insertions than did the poorer readers, particularly among sixth-grade children. Thus, an acquired narrative grammar of some complexity forms one base for the development of skillful reading.

Self-Concepts and Story Structure

At the same time that investigators have shown that narrative grammar structures are implicated in reading ability other investigators have been exploring the relationships between story structure and self-concept (Gergen & Gergen, 1983; Mancuso & Ceely, 1980; Mancuso & Sarbin, 1983). Mancuso and Sarbin proposed that most people, including William James (1890), have used a metaphoric transformation of a storyteller to conceptualize that aspect of the self which James defined as the *I*.

A number of recently completed studies converge to validate Mancuso and Sarbin's proposition. The first self-descriptive verbalizations, which appear in children aged about 24 months, cast *I* as the cause of an action (Kagan, 1981). One can believe, as Piaget proposed, that children who can conceptualize self as agent promptly set self into the narrative grammar category *actor*, and then proceed to extend self stories by inserting events and objects which fit the grammar category *outcome*. Children in the age range of two years use verbs to describe self as agent before using verbs that describe observed others as agents (Huttenlocher, Smiley, & Charney, 1983). Furthermore, children use verbs that describe overt actions of others before using verbs that describe observed persons altering the status of an object in the environment. This trend continues as children advance through their third to fifth years. Keller, Ford, and Meacham (1978) asked children of this age to say up to ten things about themselves; and after analysis found that over 50 percent of the children's responses could be classed as self action descriptive statements. One statement, recorded by Selman (1980) as he studied developing conceptions of self, neatly summarizes the early childhood view that the self is an action-guiding storyteller. In response to questions devised to probe his conception of his self, one child replied, "I am the boss of myself . . . [because] my mouth told my arm and my arm does what my mouth tells it to do" (p. 95). At about age seven, children begin to act as if they construe self as a storyteller who can compose only a limited range of stories for enactment by self-as-actor (James's *me*). Third-grade children describe their selves in terms of action competencies; and show, at this level in their development, a concern with how their competencies compare to those of other children (Secord & Peevers, 1974).

The typical person's continuing development of the conception of I-as-storyteller is reflected in the average young adolescent's ability to report that he can monitor his storytelling activity, and that he conceptualizes the mind as an active processor of input and as a manipulator of the story that can be retrieved to process self-related input (Selman, 1980). Following Selman's view one could imagine a young adolescent saying, "I (my storyteller self) could fool myself (my actor self) into not wanting a computer. I could say over and over, 'Computers are dumb. Computers are dumb.' That way, I wouldn't care if other kids have computers and I don't."

Finally, in late adolescence people locate an ancillary storyteller self: the unconscious self. When encountering an invalidation created by trying to conceptualize the *I* as a storyteller who follows acceptable narrative grammar rules, the adolescent in our culture adopts the view that the storyteller *I* functions in parallel with an "unconscious" storyteller.

"In adolescence, then, the emphasis on self-understanding shifts away from the constituents of the 'Me' and toward the aspects of the 'I'" (Damon & Hart, 1982, p. 857). The adolescent moves toward establishing a conceptualization of a coherent system for creating one's self stories. By adopting the concept of unconscious functioning the adolescent can believe that contradictions in self story writing can be understood by considering the antics of a secondary author of self stories. By adopting the concept of the unconscious he or she can believe that the authoring of apparently contradictory self stories can be attributed to the functioning of a lawfully ordered, but perhaps "unconscious," aspect of self.

CONCLUSION

The foregoing overview has been presented to validate the proposition that the typical person who has passed through late childhood imposes story structure on all varieties of input. Current thought can be assembled to create a good story about the motivation of the human psychological system as it undergoes the epigenetic acquisition of a complex narrative grammar. Though the "goodness" of the narrative grammar story has been questioned (Black & Wilensky, 1979), other scholars (see van Dijk & Kintsch, 1983) have gone on to refine and to elaborate the descriptions of the processes involved in this complex psychological functioning. Clearly, with the accumulated evidence one would be hard pressed to contradict the proposition that personal narrative grammar structures are involved in the development and use of reading skills. Additionally, the foregoing analysis of the commonly held concept of the self-as-storyteller extends the generality of the psychological functioning which implicates personal narrative grammar structure.

The future of the concept of narrative grammar would be enhanced, I believe, by widespread entertainment of the belief that behavior scientists function as historians when they report studies like those which show that adolescents adopt the view that an ancillary second self, the unconscious, participates in authoring self stories. When reporting the prevalence of this conception of *I*, behavior scientists might better recognize that they have tracked the constructs of incipient adults who live in late twentieth century European-influenced cultures. Like other dwellers in this culture, these adolescents have been influenced by widely propagated tenets that an unconscious mind has been discovered, and that this discovery aids in the explanation of erratic, poorly composed self stories.

The belief in the ancillary mind, I believe, represents a plausible accommodation of the self-as-storyteller concept. When people call up their concept of I-as-storyteller they also retrieve from long-term memory the entire system of narrative grammar which they had developed early in their lives, and they expect *I* to function according to the rules applicable to this grammar system. When self stories appear to deviate from expected grammar structure, the person experiences discrepancy, just as do participants in the formal studies who hear "garbled" stories. In life persons cannot attribute the garbled story to the machinations of a psychologist/experimenter. Aided and abetted by many modern behavioral scientists, however, the participant in late twentieth century European-influenced culture can attribute the garbled story to the unconscious.

Although I believe that behavioral science can offer no conception that effectively supersedes the concept of I-as-storyteller, I hesitate to collude with those who would attribute garbled stories to a secondary mind which functions in parallel with the storytelling mind of which we are aware. Instead, I would attempt to construct a good psychological story to be used by ordinary persons who struggle to understand the ubiquitous effects of the narrative grammar used by their selves-as-storytellers.

REFERENCES

Ames, L. B. (1966). Children's stories. *Genetical Psychological Monograph*, 73, 337-396.

Black, J. B. and Wilensky, R. (1979). An evaluation of story grammars. *Cognitive Science*, 3, 213-230.

Bower, G. H., Clark, M. C., Lesgold, A. M., and Winzenz, D. (1969). Hierarchical retrieval schemes in recall of categorized word lists. *Journal of Verbal Learning and Verbal Behavior*, 8, 323-343.

Brown, C. J. and Hurtig, R. (1983). Children's discourse competence: An evaluation of developmental inference process, *Discourse Processes*, 6, 353-375.

Colby, B. N. (1973). A partial grammar for Eskimo folktales. *American Anthropologist*, 75, 645-662.

Damon, W. and Hart, D. (1982). The development of self-understanding from infancy to adolescence. *Child Development*, 53, 841-864.

Fitzgerald, J. (1984). The relationship between reading ability and expectations for story structures. *Discourse Processes*, 7, 21-41.

Frederiksen, C. H. (1979). Discourse comprehension in early reading. In L. N. Resnick and P. A. Weaver (Eds.), *Theory and practice of early reading* (Vol. 1, pp. 155-186). Hillsdale, NJ: Lawrence Erlbaum.

Fuller, R. (1974). *Ball-Stick-Bird reading system* (vols. 1-5). Stony Brook, NY: Ball-Stick-Bird Publications.

Fuller, R. (1979). Teaching reading with stories vs. cognitive hierarchy. *Journal of Suggestive-Accelerative Learning and Teaching*, 4, 220-226.

Fuller, R. (1982). The story as the engram: Is it fundamental to thinking. *Journal of Mind and Behavior*, 3, 127-142.

Gergen, K. J. (1985). The social constructionist movement in modern psychology. *American Psychologist*, 40, 266-275.

Gergen, K. J. and Gergen, M. M. (1983). Narratives of the self. In T. R. Sarbin and K. E. Scheibe (Eds.), *Studies in social identity* (pp. 254-273). New York: Praeger.

Glenn, C. G. (1977). The role of episodic structure and story length in children's recall of simple stories. *Journal of Verbal Learning and Verbal Behavior*, 17, 229-247.

Graybeal, C. M. (1981). Memory for stories in language-impaired children. *Applied Psycholinguistics*, 2, 269-283.

Haberlandt, K., Berian, C., and Sandson, J. (1980). The episode schema in story processing. *Journal of Verbal Learning and Verbal Behavior*, 19, 635-650.

Huttenlocher, J., Smiley, P., and Charney, R. (1983). Emergence of action categories in the child: Evidence from verb meanings. *Psychological Review*, 90, 72:93.

James, W. (1890). *Psychology*. New York: Henry Holt.

Kagan, J. (1981). *The second year: The emergence of self-awareness.* Cambridge, MA: Harvard University Press.

Keller, A., Ford, L. H., and Meacham, J. A. (1978). Dimensions of self-concept in preschool children. *Developmental Psychology*, 14, 483-489.

Kelly, G. A. (1955). *The psychology of personal constructs*. New York: W. W. Norton.

Kintsch, W. (1980). Learning from text, levels of comprehension, or: Why would anyone read a story anyway. *Poetics*, 9, 87-98.

Labov, W. and Waletzky, J. (1967). Narrative analysis: Oral versions of personal experience. In J. Helan (Ed.), *Essays on the verbal and visual arts* (pp. 12-43). Seattle, WA: University of Washington Press.

Lakoff, G. P. (1972). Structural complexity in fairy tales. *The Study of Man*, 1, 128-190.

Mancuso, J. C. and Adams-Webber, J. R. (1982). Anticipation as a constructive process: The fundamental postulate. In J. C. Mancuso and J. R. Adams-Webber (Eds.), *The construing person*. New York: Praeger.

Mancuso, J. C. and Ceely, S. G. (1980). The self as memory processing. *Cognitive Therapy and Research*, 4, 1-25.

Mancuso, J. C. and Hunter, K. V. (1983). Anticipation, motivation, or emotion: The Fundamental Postulate after twenty-five years. In J. R. Adams-Webber and J. C. Mancuso (Eds.), *Applications of personal construct theory* (pp. 73-92). Toronto: Academic Press.

Mancuso, J. C. and Sarbin, T. R. (1983). The self-narrative in the enactment of roles. In T. R. Sarbin and K. Scheibe (Eds.), *Studies in social identity* (pp. 233-253). New York: Praeger.

Mandler, J. (1983, August). *Stories: The function of structure*. Invited address presented at the meetings of the American Psychological Association, Anaheim, CA.

Mandler, J. M. (1984). *Scripts, stories, and scenes: Aspects of schema theory*. Hillsdale, NJ: Lawrence Erlbaum Associates.

Mandler, J. M. and DeForest, M. (1979). Is there more than one way to recall a story? *Child Development*, 50, 886-889.

Mandler, J. M and Goodman, M. S. (1982). On the psychological validity of story structure. *Journal of Verbal Learning and Verbal Behavior*, 21, 507-523.

Mandler, J. M. and Johnson, N. S. (1977). Remembrance of things passed: Story structure and recall. *Cognitive Psychology*, 9, 111-151.

McClure, E., Mason, J., and Williams, J. (1983). Sociocultural variables in children's sequencing of stories. *Discourse Processes*, 6, 131-143.

Michotte, A. E. (1963). *The perception of causality*. (T. R. Miles and E. Miles, Trans.) New York: Basic Books. (Original work published 1946).

Piaget, J. (1952). The origins of intelligence in children. (M. Cook, Trans.). New York: International Universities Press. (Original work published 1936).

Piaget, J. (1969). *The child's conception of time*. (A. J. Pomerans, Trans.). London: Routledge and Kegan Paul. (Original work published 1927).

Posner, M. I. (1973). *Cognition: An introduction*. Glenview, IL: Scott, Foresman.

Propp, V. (1968). *Morphology of the folktale* (L. Scott, Trans.). Austin: University of Texas Press. (Original work published 1928).

Secord, P. and Peevers, B. (1974). The development and attribution of person concepts. In T. Mischel (Ed.), *Understanding other persons*. Oxford: Blackwell.

Selman, R. L. (1980). *The growth of interpersonal understanding: Developmental and clinical analysis*. New York: Academic Press.

Stein, N. L. and Glenn, C. G. (1979). An analysis of story comprehension in elementary school children. In R. O. Freedle (Ed.), *New directions in discourse processing* (Vol. II, pp. 53-120). Norwood, NJ: Ablex.

Stein, N. L. and Nezworski, T. (1978). The effects of organization and instructional set on story grammar. *Discourse Processing*, 1, 177-193.

Stein, N. L. and Policastro, M. (1984). The concept of story: A comparison between children's and teachers' viewpoints. In H. Mandl, N. L. Stein, and T. Trabasso

(Eds.), *Learning and comprehension of text* (pp. 113-155). Hillsdale, NJ: Lawrence Erlbaum Associates.

Thorndyke, P. W. (1977). Cognitive structures in comprehension and memory of narrative discourse. *Cognitive Psychology*, 9, 77-110.

van Dijk, T. A. and Kintsch, W. (1983). *Strategies of discourse comprehension.* New York: Academic Press.

von Glasersfeld, E. (1984). An introduction to radical constructivism. In P. Watzlawick (Ed.), *The invented reality* (pp. 17-40). New York: W. W. Norton.

Whaley, J. F. (1981). Readers' expectations for story structures. *Reading Research Quarterly*, 17, 90-114.

6

Narrative Thinking as
a Heuristic Process

John A. Robinson and
Linda Hawpe

INTRODUCTION

Our concern in this chapter is with the ways in which stories are used
in thinking. Experience does not automatically assume narrative form.
Rather, it is in reflecting on experience that we construct stories. The
stories we make are accounts, attempts to explain and understand
experience. Narrative thinking is, therefore, a type of causal thinking.
The power and versatility of narrative thinking are rooted in the cognitive
schema which serves as the generative base for any story. The narrative
schema identifies several categories of information (for example,
protagonist, situation, outcome) and relevant types of relationships
among them (for example, temporal, motivational). Narrative thinking
consists of creating a fit between a situation and the story schema.
Establishing a fit, that is, making a story out of experience, is a heuristic
process, one which requires skill, judgment, and experience. When it is
successful, the outcome of story making is a coherent and plausible
account of how and why something happened. Everyday stories are not
fictions, or rather, they are no more fictional than any other product of

thought, such as concepts, since abstraction, schematization, and inference are part of any cognitive act. Stories are a means for interpreting or reinterpreting events by constructing a causal pattern which integrates that which is known about an event as well as that which is conjectural but relevant to an interpretation. In this respect narrative thinking resembles other acts of comprehension and problem solving currently studied by cognitive psychologists.

Specifying the general ingredients of stories has turned out to be more difficult and controversial than was initially supposed. For our purposes, the position argued by Stein and Policastro (1984) is persuasive. They conclude that no single structural definition can account for the wide range of compositions people accept as stories. Stein and Policastro showed that good stories are readily distinguished from poor stories, but compositions that are deficient in many ways may still be accepted as stories. The practical consequence of their demonstration is that there is no rigid recipe of what counts as a story. Stein and Policastro propose that our concept of *story* consists of a prototype and a number of variants which share some features with the prototype. A prototypical story identifies a protagonist, a predicament, attempts to resolve the predicament, the outcomes of such attempts, and the reactions of the protagonists to the situation. Causal relationships among each of the story elements are also explicitly identified in the prototype. The most successful stories include all of the prototypical features. These may be described as structurally complete stories. Other tests of credibility and acceptability must also be met for a story to be accepted as a genuine account or explanation. In our discussion we will assume that most instances of narrative thinking involve efforts to get from an inadequate story to a complete and convincing story. This is not a question of competence in story*telling* or narrative performance. It is a matter of effective causal thinking.

Stories seem to be the natural way to recount experience. We believe that this naturalness is an index of the success of narrative thinking in everyday life. Because we live in groups, we need ways of understanding the actions of others. This requires a cognitive analysis of action in its social context. The categories and relations which comprise narratives are the distillation of such an analysis and represent the properties of social action that are most useful in explaining everyday experience. In effect, narratives are a solution to a fundamental problem in life, viz., creating understandable order in human affairs. This solution has several strengths. Narratives strike the most useful balance between alternatives on several cognitive dimensions.

Economy

With a handful of categories and a larger set of potential relationships among those categories, narrative provides an economical cognitive instrument for understanding everyday life. The story schema can be applied to virtually anything in our social life – to any person or incident in the past, present, or future. This vernacular mode of explaining and recounting human actions makes no distinctions of rank or status. Kings and beggars can both be victims or victors. The domain-specific information bearing on the rights, privileges, and usual behavior of beggars and kings guides the reasoning about cause and consequence in our stories. But that information does not require structurally different stories or different modes of thought.

Selectivity

It is impossible to take in or remember all the information in any episode. Even if it were possible to do so there is little reason to believe that it would all be relevant. On the other hand, omitting or ignoring information can be risky. Important facts or information which could support alternative constructions of the episode could be overlooked. Some criteria are needed to guide the selection of information. The narrative schema identifies categories of information and specifies what relationships between those categories are essential. Thus, it provides a set of criteria of wide applicability.

Familiarity

Storying creates categories out of experience, events that provide a sense of familiarity about one's daily life. In order to perceive order and recognize repetition and similarity we must go beyond the surface features in dealing with the world of concrete objects and human social interactions. A story provides the right balance between uniqueness and universality. Because stories are contextualized accounts they can convey the particularity of any episode. But because they are built upon a generic set of categories and relationships each story resembles other stories to varying degrees. A sense of familiarity is the result of this underlying similarity.

Narrative is the most common form, but not the only one, used to organize and record social and personal experience. Like stories, annals and chronologies construct temporally ordered records of events, but they are deficient as accounts in several ways (compare White, 1980). A temporal record per se does not reveal causal order; indeed it often masks such order by the literal rendering of sequence. Stories, on the other hand, do not replicate or literally recreate experience. As Hill remarks,

> Stories are always inventions or, as Hannah Arendt preferred to say, discoveries. . . . In telling [we would say constructing] a story the minute elements that formed part of the experience or the event have to be sorted out and given an intelligible order. Details have to be sacrificed, information selected, emphasis placed, a sequence created . . . situations viewed from different angles – all in the attempt to discover and reveal what happened in a way that is faithful to reality and at the same time illuminates it. (1979, pp. 297-298)

Narrative thinking also contrasts with scientific thinking (compare Mink, 1978). In both, the goal is the establishment of cause and effect relations among factors. Both are attempts to organize and give meaning to human experience, to explain and guide problem solving. But the products of these two modes of thought, story and principle respectively, are quite distinct. The product of scientific theorizing is a principle, or law. These principles are general, context-free, usually abstract, and testable only by further formal scientific activity. The product of narrative thought, story, is context-bound, concrete, and testable through ordinary interpersonal checking. Theories do not have a generic form. The concepts and relationships which comprise any theory are determined by the domain or phenomenon under study. In scientific reasoning the similarity of one phenomenon to any other is defined by strict criteria. There is no place for the more flexible resemblances which stories can evoke or discover. Unlike the creation and communication of scientific laws, the creation of a story is partially dependent upon who does the storying. Point of view, in other words, is an element of storying with impact upon the product. This fact makes narratives personal, and therefore more useful in everyday life. The story incorporates the feelings, goals, needs, and values of the people who create it. Thus the same episode may be rendered in quite different ways by each participant. The story is flexible where principle is rigid. Unlike a scientific law or principle, a story is open to interpretation. One person can take from it what suits the needs of the moment. Thus the same story can be used as a guide in more than one situation since different elements of it can be applied in different contexts.

Perhaps the most radical difference between scientific and narrative thinking is in cast of mind: the scientist strives to eliminate ambiguity and uncertainty and is uncomfortable when there are two equally credible theoretical accounts of some phenomenon. In contrast, in our everyday reasoning about social reality we live comfortably with apparent contradictions. We want explanations which are convincing enough to be accepted as true, but recognize that there could be alternative accounts which tell a different but equally persuasive story.

PROCESS MODEL OF NARRATIVE THINKING

Narrative thinking involves the projection of story form onto some experience or event. This may occur as the experience is taking place, in reflecting upon the experience, or in recounting the experience at a later time. Our conceptualization of the narrative process has developed out of the work of Rein and Schon (1977) and Bennett (1978). Rein and Schon discuss storying as one of a class of *framing* procedures, that is, strategies for organizing and deriving solutions for problems. Bennett illustrates in detail how judicial trials resemble the construction of persuasive stories.

There are three components to narrative thinking: the story schema, the story maker's knowledge and experience, and a diverse array of cognitive strategies. The narrative schema may be regarded as an implicit procedural plan. By designating certain types of essential information and the need to link them by causal relations, the schema defines the goal of narrative thought. The story maker must then find ways of mapping the situation on to the goal structure specified by the schema. This procedure can be viewed as consisting of a series of questions to be answered, such as, what happened?, to whom?, why?, and so on. Answering each question requires the story maker to examine the information available about the incident in order to identify relevant facts. That information is then entered into the narrative plan. This process of inquiring, identifying, and selecting information is cyclical and provisional, subject to revisions as the narrative act proceeds. Throughout, the story maker must draw upon prior knowledge and experience. As we noted earlier, no story includes or accounts for all of the details. The story maker is guided by experience in judging which details are relevant, which are not. The contributions from prior knowledge are even greater when the available information is incomplete. Then the story maker must fill in the gaps by conjecturing what is plausible under the known circumstances. The kinds of knowledge and experience called upon will vary with the question to be answered. Answers to "why?" involve judgments of motive which may, in turn, derive from knowledge of personality and past behavior. But they may also depend upon experience of the setting. Throughout the construction process, judgments and inferences are required and at two levels: about discrete items of information and about the adequacy of the unfolding story. Selecting, comparing, inferring, arranging, and revising are activities which we regard as cognitive strategies (compare Baron, 1978). These strategies play a pivotal role in narrative thinking as they are the cognitive intermediaries between the goal structure of the inchoate story, the incident which is to be narratized, and the story maker's knowledge and experience.

The outcome of an act of narrative thinking is, of course, a new story. The construction of stories has both cognitive and social ramifications. If the story works, it influences what other people believe and can affect how they may act in the future. The new story will also be incorporated into the cognitive structures which represent the knowledge and experience of the story maker and his audience. Viewed structurally, narrative thinking results in the unitization of experience by establishing temporal boundaries and causal relations between elements within those boundaries. Furthermore, new stories are often linked to prior experiences which may also have been cognitively structured into stories. Thus, narrative thinking can alter the content and the organization of a person's world knowledge and beliefs. And, since prior knowledge and experience is actively used in story construction, each new story enriches the cognitive resources available for future acts of narrative thought.

Narrative thinking is most useful in understanding the actions of others and oneself in relation to others. It is worth noting then that story making is frequently a collaborative activity. Sometimes the collaboration is actively sought, other times it is imposed. We have characterized narrative thinking as an heuristic activity because it is open-ended, constructive, and involves varying kinds of uncertainty. The fact that it is often a collaborative activity reveals a second heuristic dimension to the process. Stories must be tested: the interpretation embodied in a story must be persuasive, for if it is not the story fails and the story maker must either forsake his views or alter them to accommodate the views of others. Robinson (1981) describes several instances of such negotiation and collaboration. The outcome of such transactions is a consensually validated interpretation and account of some event. Thus, narrative transactions are a primary procedure for producing mutual understanding and social cohesion.

CAUSAL MODELS

Suppose that your neighbors dumped their garbage in your yard. You will be angry, of course, but you will also wonder why they did it. What kinds of explanatory procedures are available to you? We propose that there is a continuum of cognitive structures which can be accessed for assistance in explaining events. The continuum is based on degree of generality. We will discuss four points on the continuum: repetitions or precedents, analogues, prototypes, and rules or principles. You might try to explain your neighbors' act by recalling whether they had ever done that before. If they had, you could conclude that their motive then and now is probably the same, and you would review the prior incident to determine whether the circumstances preceding it had recurred. In other words, you would categorize the present incident as a repetition of a prior incident. Suppose, however, that the dumping of garbage is an unprecedented act by your neighbors. Then you would have to apply some other explanatory procedure. It is unlikely that you would have formulated a general rule about such cases. The predicament is sufficiently infrequent and unusual that generalizations would not have developed about it. Instead, you would probably generate some hypotheses derived from your knowledge of human behavior. The process could unfold in several ways. You might label the act an insult and then try to figure out why your neighbors would want to insult you. Or you may think, "this is an act of someone who is angry," and try to infer what could have provoked it. Perhaps, however, your neighbors are alcoholics, or had a heavy party the night before. Maybe, one of them innocently dumped the garbage in your yard while still tipsy as part of cleaning up after the party. Or they may be quite old and nearly senile. Note that an account of the incident will be constructed in different ways depending upon the assumption you select. There are no socially validated rules which could apply unambiguously to such incidents, there are only precedents and hypotheses. Each of them is a contingent prospect. You must decide whether the present case is a repetition of some previous event, and you must select the hypotheses which best fit the particulars of the present case.

This is the kind of cognitive work involved in narrative thinking. The prospective story is about some happening for which an account and explanation is needed. The cognitive strategies of our model are invoked to search for relevant prior experience. If there is none, your knowledge about human behavior is invoked. Hypotheses are then compared with the apparent facts and with your knowledge of your neighbors. Judgments are made about the plausibility of any hypothesis. In reflecting on the incident, trying actively to understand it, you are constructing an account the structure of which is essentially narrative in form. Implicit in this activity is the effort to provide a history, to explain how this event came about, and to forecast the outcome. What you do will depend upon what you conclude about the precipitating circumstances. As in any story then, the ending is foreshadowed in the beginning. Beginnings and endings are choices, however, not incorrigible facts.

We have described two contrasting strategies a person might use in trying to explain an event, namely, a search for precedents and rule generation or hypothesis testing. But there is a middle ground: analogical reasoning. Human beings are curiously ambivalent about generalizations. On the one hand, we try to assimilate the diversity of daily life to a catalogue of maxims and rules of thumb. On the other hand, we emphasize the particularity of each case. We are most comfortable it seems with a point of view based on degrees of resemblance between things or between events. As noted earlier, narrative is a cognitively efficient compromise between uniqueness and universality. Analogical reasoning occupies the same middle ground and for that reason is the strategy most often invoked during narrative thought. The narrative schema identifies the generic features and relationships of events which must be accounted for, and a person's world knowledge provides a storehouse of candidate exemplars of those features and relationships. Analogical procedures can be invoked to probe memory for information that resembles the present case and satisfies tests of plausibility and coherence. Several factors govern the use and effectiveness of analogy:

(1) Human episodic memory exhibits a high degree of contextualization in the representation and organization of events, but also provides a relational structure by segregating experience into domains or rough categories. Thus, the search for analogues to a present predicament will begin with probes of the domain which best fits the present case. In our hypothetical example, a person would be more likely to search for memories of other neighborly interactions than for memories of incidents at work even though the later domain might include analogous experiences (for example, having a wastebasket of trash dumped on one's desk or in a workroom locker).

(2) Analogical thinking, at least initially, operates at the same level of abstraction as the item or incident to be matched (Holyoak, 1984). It is unlikely, for example, that anyone would consider Castro's dumping of refugee criminals on the United States as a suitable analogue of a neighbor's dumping of garbage. The two have comparable features, and metaphors of neighborliness are often used in discussing international relations, but nations are more abstract than individuals and the refugee incident is likely to be encoded at a more abstract level in memory.

(3) When causal relationships are even moderately complex people rely more heavily on specific prior instances which resemble the present case as models for explanation and prediction (Read, 1983). Also, research on concept identification (Brooks, 1978) and acquisition of rule systems (Reber and Allen, 1978) has demonstrated that people can attain proficiency in detecting pattern matches for complex stimuli even though they cannot adequately formulate the structural principles which are the basis of those matches. Thus, the reliance on resemblances between prior experience and present predicament may, in fact, be the most efficient strategy for interpreting the diverse events of everyday life.

(4) Resemblance is not enough: prospective analogues must also pass tests of relevance and plausibility. A prior incident and a present predicament may have several features in common, but the resemblance will be used only if there is a credible causal link between those features in the prior case which matches features of the present problem (Read, 1984).

These four factors summarize when and in what manner analogical thinking typically occurs, but they should not be regarded as prescriptions. Valid and useful analogues may be available in other domains of experience or at higher levels of abstraction, but will probably not be sought or even recognized without assistance. The research of Gick and Holyoak (1980) shows that there is little transfer between problems which are formally identical in structure but drawn from contrasting domains or situations. Rein and Schon (1977) illustrate the value of changing the level of abstraction in their analysis of problem setting and social policy.

Sometimes an event is so salient that it becomes a reference point for entire classes of experience. In these instances the originating incident is schematized and abstracted to form a prototype. Prototypes straddle the upper ranges of the structural continuum: they are more general than analogues, but not so generalizable as to become rules. Kalcik (1975) describes a prototypical story which became a reference point for women participating in a support group which met for regular discussions of their predicaments. The story reported an incident when a female student complained to her teacher of getting too high a grade on an exam. The student's boyfriend had threatened to take back his fraternity pin if she kept getting better grades than he did. The incident epitomized a major theme in the group discussions, namely, male fears of inferiority and the conflicts such fears generated in females. Kalcik reports that other participants began to relate their own experiences to this incident and to use it as a reference point. The predicament – male inferiority – was a common one even though the pretext for it varied from case to case. These prototypical incidents can be exploited for a wide range of uses and situations, rather like the musical structure of theme and variations.

In summary, narrative thinking is driven by the effort to find a useful model of probable cause(s). The model may be drawn from an identical prior incident, a comparable incident, a prototypical incident, or from rules and generalizations about human behavior. The selection of a model of probable cause is an essential part of narrative thought, but it is not the whole story. A proper story must account for how and when as well as why something happened, and detail some resolution of the predicament. The causal model must be integrated with or adapted to the facts of the incident. The choice of causal model is the most important step in narrative thinking. This choice is constrained by credibility tests, but once accepted guides the remaining stages of story construction. In particular, the determination of relevance, and the construction of inferences about missing or ambiguous details will be based on the presumptive explanation embodied in the causal model.

NARRATIVE TASKS

The initial narrative formulation of an incident is not always successful. Stories fail for two reasons: because they are incomplete, that is, they lack some essential information, or because they are unconvincing, that is, the causal model is inappropriate. In such cases the story needs to be repaired. The major test of a story is its acceptance by others. Hence, it is usually true that repairs are prompted by the reactions of others, and in many cases are actually provided by others. Polanyi (1979) describes a story which was rejected because the causal model was clearly inappropriate. The narrator, a woman, recounts an episode of fainting on the New York subway during the rush hour. The subway cars were jammed with people, she was weak from emotional stress and insufficient food, they were all captives. . . . The narrator likens her situation to that of Jews in Nazi prison camps being herded together for execution. The group she relates her experience to rejects the analogy. Not only was her choice of analogue inappropriate, it also was clear that she was implicitly trying to shift responsibility for fainting and its aftermath from herself to the subway environment and other riders. Not surprisingly, her listeners quickly offered other points of view, that is, alternative models of responsibility. The narrator had, in fact, already explicitly identified the probable cause of her faint (lack of food, fatigue). Thus, her account was incoherent as well as inappropriate.

A more extensive repair procedure is illustrated in one of the narrative interactions reported by Gardner (1971) in his casebook on storytelling in psychotherapy. In several examples he shows that in therapy children sometimes tell either metaphoric or actual stories to communicate about their problems. Often, because of anxiety concerning the subject, the child's story lacks the form of a good story. Or perhaps, the goal-oriented actions described by the child are ineffectual for dealing with the problems identified in the story. In response, the therapist retells the same story with modifications that help the child express feelings, and plan action. The case we have chosen for illustration (reported on pages 95 to 99) is that of a nine-year-old boy who is in therapy because of multiple fears, tantrums, and pervasive tension. Gardner asked the boy to tell a story. The boy produced a story about a dachshund taken by mistake to a training class for German shepherds. The dachshund "gets lost" in the class and is nearly trampled by the bigger dogs, but is saved by the man who is conducting the class. The dachshund is removed from the class but then is just left outside. Gardner interpreted the boy's story as an allegory which revealed the probable cause of the boy's emotional problems, namely, feelings of abandonment. Gardner then re-tells the boy's story. He retains the premise, that is, the causal model, but elaborates and clarifies many of the elements of the story, and introduces information and causal links which were missing in the boy's version. In effect, Gardner took an inadequate but convincing story and made it a structurally complete story. The resulting story clarified the feelings of the child, since the child agreed the new version was like his own situation. The goal-oriented actions suggested were ones the child could use to gain the security he sought from persons other than his rather cold parents. The ending, growing up and living happily, offered the child a hopeful vision of his own future. The therapist was able to help the child create a more complete story-reflection of his problem, and to organize action for securing a solution. Haley (1976) describes similar techniques used in adult psychotherapy.

Gardner's technique systematizes an informal but timeless practice used by parents, ministers, and pundits and advisors of various kinds, namely, the construction of narrative analogues to guide a person in resolving some predicament. This strategy works because the story (a) concretizes the problem, makes it explicit and gives it definite structure; (b) provides a natural basis for raising questions about causal relations and for modelling goal-oriented action; and (c) distances the listener (the "target" of the story) emotionally to a sufficient degree to sidestep that person's defensiveness and anxiety. It is one of the virtues of narrative that it can convey information indirectly which would not be understood, or not be accepted if conveyed directly in literal and explicit terms. In effect, the use of analogue stories promotes discussion of a predicament by changing the immediate goal from solving the real-world problem into one of changing a story about a similar problem. Feelings play a prominent role in real predicaments and must also be carefully explored in analogue stories. Feelings provide information about expectations and role relations, and identify the features of a predicament which the person has not been able to comprehend (compare Dyer, 1983). The analogue story strategy will be most effective when it accepts the feelings generated by the real predicament but then explicitly resolves them in a constructive way. For example, if a person expresses shock or surprise about another's behavior, then in the analogue of that situation the protagonist may be portrayed as unwittingly ignorant of facts which would have precluded such a reaction. Basically then, the construction of analogue stories is a form of tutelage in problem solving.

Narrative repair is potentially an unending process. Retrospection, or reminiscing, can be viewed as a process of testing the continued validity of life experience stories. Sometimes new information relevant to an incident is discovered which creates discrepancies in the accepted story, but more often interpretive perspectives change prompting reevaluation of the causal model which organized the original account. These repairs may occur spontaneously during retrospection but may also require guidance and collaboration as, for example, in the life review procedures developed by Lewis and Butler (1974).

Finally, narrative repair may entail overcoming the restrictive tendencies of analogical thinking described earlier, that is, reaching out to other domains or other levels of abstraction for useful causal models.

The two kinds of narrative repair which we have described are probably the most common narrative tasks, but there is another which should be mentioned. The class of stories we will call puzzlements consists of accounts in search of explanations. Experiences that are puzzling or ambiguous may be recounted to a friend with the hope that the friend can explain why the incident occurred or what it means. Such cases require generation rather than replacement of information. In effect, the narrative task has been transferred to someone else.

CONCLUSION

Narrative thinking – storying – is a successful method of organizing perception, thought, memory, and action. It is not the only successful method, but within its natural domain of everyday interpersonal experience it is more effective than any other. Nevertheless, narrative thinking is widely disparaged. The bias against narrative thought has been illustrated in two recent discussions of classroom education. Cazden and Hymes (1978) and Barnes, Britton, and Rosen (1971) both observed that personal anecdotes offered by students during discussion or questioning were rejected by teachers as inappropriate. The schools try to inculcate a style of thinking which emphasizes definition, abstraction, conceptual analysis, and rigorous canons of evidence or proof. There can be no doubt that these procedures are essential for certain kinds of inquiry, but we can certainly challenge the rejection of narrative from the province of rationality.

It is important to distinguish the use of narrative in postdictive explanation from its use in prediction. After the fact, that is, postdictive accounts cannot be expected to satisfy the same criteria which we apply to predictive accounts. The reason is simple enough: stories cannot be tested like hypotheses because authentic events cannot be replicated under controlled conditions. However, mankind has developed both formal and informal methods for testing stories. Consider jurisprudence: Trials try to establish responsibility, settle disputes, and impose some redress. The procedures used in this mode are halfway between those of narrative and those of scientific theorizing. For example, the evidential procedures used in trials resemble both stories and theories. Consistency and credibility are required, but cross-examination and verifiability are also entailed. However, since the events under judicial review cannot be repeated, that is, replicated as required in tests of theories and hypotheses, decisions are frequently based on precedents. That is essentially a process of pattern matching. The judgment of likeness may be more rigorous in trials because several constraints are specified, but it is still the same process used in storying. Equivalent procedures are used informally in checking the stories we encounter in everyday life. Thus, there are accepted ways of evaluating the completeness, coherence, plausibility, and applicability of any story. Given the limitations on absolute proof imposed by the circumstances of everyday life, we believe that postdictive narrative cognition fully qualifies as a rational process.

Two other points may be made about the validity and utility of narrative thinking. First, where practical choice and action are concerned, stories are better guides than rules or maxims. Rules and maxims state significant generalizations about experience but stories illustrate and explain what those summaries mean. The oldest form of moral literature is the parable; the most common form of informal instruction is the anecdote. Both forms enable us to understand generalizations about the social order because they exemplify that order in a contextualized account. Second, stories can also be used as tests of the validity of maxims and rules of thumb. That is, stories can function as arguments. Stories are natural mediators between the particular and the general in human experience. We should strive to improve and refine this mode of thinking, not eschew it.

REFERENCES

Barnes, D., Britton, J., and Rosen, H. (1971). *Language, the learner and the school* (rev. ed.). New York: Penguin.

Baron, J. (1978). Intelligence and general strategies. In G. Underwood (Ed.), *Strategies of information processing*. New York: Academic Press.

Bennett, W. L. (1978). Storytelling in criminal trials: A model of social judgment. *Quarterly Journal of Speech*, 64, 1-22.

Brooks, L. (1978). Nonanalytic concept formation and memory for instances. In E. Rosch and B. B. Lloyd (Eds.), *Cognition and categorization*. Hillsdale, NJ: Lawrence Erlbaum Associates.

Cazden, C. and Hymes, D. (1978). Narrative thinking and storytelling rights: A folklorist's clue to a critique of education. *Keystone Folklore Quarterly*, 22, 21-36.

Dyer, M. G. (1983). The role of affect in narratives. *Cognitive Science*, 7, 211-242.

Gardner, R. A. (1971). *Therapeutic communication with children: The mutual storytelling technique*. New York: Science House.

Gick, M. L. and Holyoak, K. J. (1980). Analogical problem solving. *Cognitive Psychology*, 12, 306-355.

Haley, J. (1973). *Uncommon therapy*. New York: Grune & Stratton.

Hill, M. A. (1979). The fictions of mankind and the stories of men. In M. A. Hill (Ed.), *Hannah Arendt: The recovery of the public world*. New York: St. Martin's Press.

Holyoak, K. J. (1984). Analogical thinking and human intelligence. In R. J. Sternberg (Ed.), *Advances in the psychology of human intelligence* (Vol. 2). Hillsdale, NJ: Lawrence Erlbaum Associates.

Kalcik, S. (1975). ". . . like Ann's gynecologist or the time I was almost raped." In C. R. Farrer (Ed.), *Women and folklore*. Austin, TX: University of Texas Press.

Lewis, M. I. and Butler, R. N. (1974). Life review therapy: Putting memories to work in individual and group psychotherapy. *Geriatrics*, 29, 165-173.

Mink, L. O. (1978). Narrative form as a cognitive instrument. In R. H. Canary and H. Kozicki (Eds.), *The writing of history*. Madison, WI: University of Wisconsin Press.

Polanyi, L. (1979). So what's the point? *Semiotica*, 25, 207-241.

Read, S. J. (1983). Once is enough: Causal reasoning from a single instance. *Journal of Personality and Social Psychology*, 45, 323-334.

Read, S. J. (1984). Analogical reasoning in social judgment: The importance of causal theories. *Journal of Personality and Social Psychology*, 46, 14-25.

Reber, A. S. and Allen, R. (1978). Analogy and abstraction strategies in synthetic grammar learning: A functional interpretation. *Cognition*, 6, 189-221.

Rein, M. and Schon, D. A. (1977). Problem setting in policy research. In C. H. Weiss (Ed.), *Using social research in public policy-making*. Lexington, MA: D. C. Heath.

Robinson, J. A. (1981). Personal narratives reconsidered. *Journal of American Folklore*, 94, 58-85.

Stein, N. L. and Policastro, M. (1984). The concept of a story: A comparison between children's and teachers' viewpoints. In H. Mandl, N. L. Stein, and T. Trabasso (Eds.), *Learning and comprehension of text*. Hillsdale, NJ: Lawrence Erlbaum Associates.

White, H. (1980). The value of narrativity in the representation of reality. *Critical Inquiry*, 7, 5-28.

PART III

The Emplotment of Self-Narratives

7

Self-Narratives and Adventure

Karl E. Scheibe

> Though man lives by habit, what he lives *for* is thrills and excitement. The only relief from Habit's tediousness is periodical excitement.
>
> *William James*

> Those naked little spasms of the self occur at the end of the world, but there at the end is action and character.
>
> *Erving Goffman*

As psychology loses its ahistorical and universalistic pretensions, it becomes not harder but rather easier to recognize the commonness of certain forms. Near the end of his life, William James prepared a series of essays on the paradox of modern wars, where civilized and rational societies are brought to engage in barbaric and primitive acts of destruction. "The Moral Equivalent of War" (1910) is the best known of these essays. In it, he makes a case for the commonness of the impulse to war. He argues also that the war mentality is resistant to reasoned argument: "Showing war's irrationality and horror is of no effect. . . .

The horrors make the fascination. War is the *strong life*; it is life *in extremis*; war-taxes are the only ones men never hesitate to pay, as the budgets of all nations show us" (p. 350).

In presenting an argument against our customary modern wars, James departs from the premise that wars are representative of a much more general class of psychological activity. For this class he suggested no generic name, but its function is the production of thrills and excitement: indeed, he suggests that history and human life itself are interesting because of large and small glories, and that in the past wars have been the chief means for the generation of glory.

Erving Goffman's essay, "Where the action is" (1967) takes up this very same theme, but in an entirely different context. The quotation at the head of this chapter about action and character refers specifically to the conduct of idle youths in amusement park arcades, as they pit their little skills against the determined responses of coin-operated machines. It is a pathetic little adventure to see whether the polished steel ball will strike the light post and thereby register a score. If it seems an absurd stretch to connect the amusement park arcade and the battlefield, a visitor to an arcade will be somewhat reassured by the ubiquity of the battle theme in the names and symbols displayed by the machines.

My claim is akin to that of James and of Goffman – that a very large class of human activity is functionally common, and that the range of this class is suggested by the examples of war and amusement park games. But I wish also to connect this idea with that of "identity as narrative." I suggest that the form of human activity known as adventure has a central role to play in the construction and development of life stories, and that life stories, in turn, are the major supports for human identities.

A claim for the commonness of adventure as a mode for the construction of life narratives should not be misconstrued as a claim for universality. Let it be admitted that in Western culture the idea of adventure – whether it is manifest in sport, in gambling, in the exploration of nature, or in exposing oneself to risk of injury – is strongly associated with the role of male. That this association is largely cultural in origin rather than biological is taken here as an article of faith, but the attendant controversy about origins is in any case not essentially important to the argument to be developed. As a further qualification to the scope of the present treatment, I note that much of the following discussion refers to two stylized forms of modern adventurous activity – sport and gambling. The objective is to establish interpretive commonality within a class of human activities, of which sport and gambling are representative, and for which *adventure* seems the best generic label.

The contextualist view of human conduct is the point of departure for the argument to be developed (see Sarbin, 1977). Human identities are considered to be evolving constructions; they emerge out of continual social interactions in the course of life. Self-narratives are developed stories that must be told in specific historical terms, using a particular language, reference to a particular stock of working historical conventions and a particular pattern of dominant beliefs and values. The most fundamental narrative forms are universal (see Crites, 1971), but the way these forms are styled and filled with content will depend upon particular historical conventions of time and place.

As a justification for devoting special attention to sport and gambling in this treatment of human adventure, I offer the well substantiated observation that such activities are growing all around us – in magnitude, intensity, and variety. Survey data in the United States show that 96 percent of the population is at least minimally involved with sports. About 85 percent of Americans are in some fashion involved with sports *every day*. Finally, sport is no longer a male domain. Women are participating in sports at a rapidly accelerating rate. Barriers to the participation of women in some sports formerly dominated by men are quickly disappearing (Miller Brewing Company, 1982). Similarly, studies have shown beyond all doubt that legal and illegal gambling are becoming ever more popular in the United States, with most states now running legal lotteries. Casinos, horse and dog tracks, jai alai frontons and off-track betting facilities show a steady rise in popularity. Also, there is no sign that illegal gambling activity is in decline.[1]

My fundamental thesis is that people require adventures in order for satisfactory life stories to be constructed and maintained. The variety of adventures has no obvious limit – participation can be direct or vicarious, the venture can carry one no farther than one's garden or to the ends of the earth. Adventures can be conducted in fantasy, as in the case of Walter Mitty, or in hard reality, as in the case of the bullfighter. Such activity can be carried on with a collectivity, as in nature study groups, or individually – the solitary bird-watcher comes to mind. Sport and gambling are singled out here merely as particularly prominent and common examples of the larger class of human activities suggested by the term adventure. The objective is to display the functional significance of adventures in the development, maintenance, and occasional metamorphoses of human identity.

THE ADVENTURE THESIS

In *Meditations on Don Quixote*, Ortega y Gasset credits Cervantes with the invention and development of the figure of the hero in modern fiction. Cervantes, in the boredom of his prison cell, was inspired by reading the legendary tales of Amadis of Gaul, recounting the chivalrous deeds of medieval knights-errant. Don Quixote is now an ineradicable historical reality – fevered brain and all. It is well to remember not only that he once was not, but also that the entire imaginative tradition he represents – the fictional hero – once was not among the presences on life's stage. To be sure, he was preceded by heroes of legend and epic: by Ulysses, by Beowulf, by King Arthur and Sir Lancelot, and many others. But Don Quixote represents a qualitative mutation in the evolution of heroic figures, according to Ortega, and with him the romantic hero is born. Don Quixote is, of course, only a single expression of a more general historical and cultural development; other representations of this same development are the Age of Exploration, the Renaissance, the extension of European imagination and presence over the world. No claim need be made about cause and sequence here – only the observation that in the general round of things, these events occurred in relation to each other. We might say that the sixteenth century ushered in an age of adventure, and that as a sequel, Don Quixote represented the new and pressing role for adventure in the construction of life narratives.

Along with Don Quixote, Cervantes created Sancho Panza: a creature as material, hedonistic, and realistic as his Quixote is ethereal, idealistic, and surreal. In the Western psyche a polarity was established, again in the round of things, without claim that Cervantes is responsible for it. About this polarity, George Orwell observed:

> The two principles, noble folly and base wisdom, exist side by side in nearly every human being. If you look into your own mind, which are you? Don Quixote or Sancho Panza? Almost certainly you are both. There is one part of you that wishes to be a hero or a saint, but another part of you is a little fat man who sees very clearly the advantages of staying alive with a whole skin. (1968, p. 163)

This duality is dynamic. While Sancho is in the ascendant, Quixote recuperates his strength, so as to assume control again when Sancho's vigilance wanes. While the period of oscillation here is not at all precise, the fact of alternations between belly-to-earth realism and starry idealism is easily verifiable in ordinary life. And it is these variations that provide the stuff of life story. In literary terms, Don Quixote without Sancho Panza as counterbalance is not a good story. In terms of psychological biography, a life lived on a single plane is simply insufficient as a story – it doesn't go anywhere, it doesn't move. The socius is constantly testing the individual for the satisfactoriness of the unfolding life narrative, and the particular socius in which we are immersed wants change, wants variation, wants dramatic build and decline.

The sort of self-narrative which this sequence produces is what Gergen and Gergen (1983) call the *romantic saga*, a series of progressive and regressive periods repeating over time. The timing, amplitude, and possible overlay or relation of these cycles with other narrative progressions is not a matter of concern here. Rather, the point to be established is that repose and adventure are inherently unstable states; the sequencing or progression of these states produces the material out of which narrative constructions of the self are developed.

The need for change and novelty or for repose and redundancy must be understood contextually. That is, the extent to which the environment is seen as noisy and too busy will depend not only on the distal environment, but upon the state of the person who is in that environment. Similarly, the felt need for change and novelty is not merely endogenous but depends upon the amount of variation occurring in the stimulus world.

In John Steinbeck's version of the Arthurian legend, the king is puzzled at the unrest of his castled knights, who, "eat well, sleep in comfort, make love when and to whom they wish. They feed appetites only half awakened – and still they are not content. They complain that the times are against them" (1977, p. 249). Here is laid out the fundamental motivational dynamics of one-half of the adventure cycle. The contextualist part of the argument is supported by the observation that not all those in the castled circumstances feel restless – just the knights. The other half of the cycle is also amply illustrated in the Arthurian epic, where Lancelot and his mates leave the docile pleasures of the castle for the unpredictable adventures awaiting in the wild. They continue their quests until their resources for adventure are simply used up, and the wild life becomes intolerable. Although their tolerance levels differ, all knights must return again to haven. We can conclude from the enduring charm of the Arthurian legend in all its many forms that the repetition of this cycle makes a very strong story. So strong is this story, I hold, that our current attempts to construct self-narratives are still pulled and formed by its mythic forces.

The literary theme of adventure and return, as old as Homer and therefore as old as literature itself, has emerged in myriad guises throughout the modern era. Character, as Goffman has it, is built out of repeated exposures to trials, risks, and uncertainties of venturing forth. Withdrawal to domesticity is both a recuperation from the effects of such exposure and a preparation for the next adventure. In specific cultural expression, these venturings range from the "naked little spasms" at the end-of-the-world arcade described by Goffman, to the grandiose venturings forth of Napoleon, seeking to establish his character by the conquest of Europe. We hear two major chords of the human song – risk and accompanying fear, certainty and accompanying security.

Concerning the taking of risks there is, of course, a substantial and informative body of psychological research (see, for example, Kogan & Wallach, 1964). However, the focus here is not on the social determinants or individual correlates of risk-taking behavior, but rather on the contextual significance or participation in risk for the construction of self-narratives. A sense of the psychological consequentiality of risk and uncertainty emerges more clearly from literary sources than it does from the social psychological laboratory.

Thought and attention are wasted in the contemplation of the certain, the fixed, the still. Tours through museums are quickly tiring, and the nostalgic contemplation of the past brings slight satisfaction. If the past can be made to come alive, it is through exploring its interstices of mystery and uncertainty, or by somehow bringing the past to bear upon the mystery and uncertainty of our own lives, as when Herman Melville's *Pierre* examines the evidence of the past to determine whether his lover might also be his half sister. The exploration of this past mystery is but another instance of adventure – in this case a value-freighted exploration of the unknown. Once the mystery reaches resolution, the story is over, and our attention turns elsewhere, seeking always and relentlessly, if in multifarious ways, to reencounter some interesting uncertainty which will repay our watching.

THE SPORTING LIFE AND CONSTRUCTION OF SELVES

Common games of sport and gambling are but stripped down, stylized and abbreviated dramas, inviting the direct or vicarious participation of masses of people seeking for some adventure, no matter how miniscule, to provide story matter for their lives.

The temptation is strong simply to regard sport and gambling as expressive of the ludic impulse – forms of play motivationally sui generis, as Huizinga (1949) would have it. Without denying that sport and gambling are developmentally related to the ludic impulse, continual adult involvement with sport and gambling cannot be accounted for in this reductive fashion. An alternative interpretation is that participation, direct or vicarious, in sport or in gambling provides occasion for what Goffman (1967) refers to as "the generation of character," or for the development of what Mancuso and Sarbin (1983) call self-narratives. Children perhaps begin to play at sports and games of chance for the same motives as kittens playing with a ball of yarn. But transformations can occur from the ludic base. "To display or express character, weak or strong, is to generate character. The self, in brief, can be voluntarily subjected to re-creation" (Goffman, 1967, p. 237). Somewhere in the developmental sequence a transformation occurs, so that activity once pursued out of blind motive is now engaged in with reasoned purpose, however miscalculated that activity might be as strictly hedonic rationalism (compare Allport's 1937 concept of functional autonomy). The guaranteed payoff for sport and gambling activity is that they provide a venue for stylized and reasonably safe adventures, and so provide sequence and story for the lives of the participants.

This argument can be usefully elaborated by considering the self-transforming functions associated with each of the four forms of play identified by Caillois (1961). These are:

Agon. Games or sport played against an opponent involving the possibility of victory or defeat. All professional sports fall into this category, as do such confrontational gambling methods as poker or backgammon.

Alea. Games in which the outcomes are determined entirely by chance – craps, roulette, lottery games, bingo. In sport, chance is not supposed to play much of a role, except in coin flips to determine who gets the ball and other minor intrusions.

Mimicry. In this form of play, the actor imitates another person, role, or object – as when children play cowboys and Indians or pretend to be an animal. Adult theater is mimicry play. Another case of mimicry play is that of the football fan who identifies with the team and symbolizes this identification through use of the pronouns "we" and "our," or perhaps by using team emblems as a part of personal apparel.

Vertigo. Amusement park rides provide a clear example of this form of play. Long-distance running also belongs. Fights and sentimental betting are also classifiable here, for this sort of betting is instrumental in producing a greatly heightened sense of the dramatic impact of the events in question. (See Herman, 1976, for an elaboration of these categories.)

All of the sporting events, gambles, and other forms of play here mentioned have the character of being closed or finished dramatic episodes. These events have a conventional beginning, a middle, and an end. And all are in some way value weighted. The yield is victory or defeat in the agon category. It is monetary wins and losses for chance games. The value weighting for mimicry, I suggest, is one of direct identity enrichment through an amplification of one's repertory for role enactments.

The value of vertigo is revealed through an examination of the nature of the thrill: that which James said we live *for* even as we live *by* habit. Balint (1959) suggests that the thrill involves three essential elements: fear, voluntary entry, and hope for survival.

A Ferris-wheel has just these characteristics, as does a fox hunt, a bobsled run, or sky diving. The value of such action is that the consequences of having enjoyed such thrilling experiences flow beyond the bounds of the occasion. One tells stories about these events, "dines out" on them, elaborates and embroiders on successive retellings. In this fashion, the life story of the participant is enriched.

These elements of the "thrill" are present in the three other forms of play as well. For certainly in agonistic play there is fear, voluntary entry, and hope for survival. Similarly, entry into aleatory games is voluntary, involves fear of loss, and even in the case of Russian roulette one hopes for survival. Mimicry involves the fear of embarrassment, of being caught out, of having one's identity improperly read. Here again one decides to enter the play and one hopes to overcome or master stage fright, or the risk of being exposed.

The thrill is the expected product of adventure. Engagement in the types of thrill-producing play here outlined offers the same kind of potential for self-construction as outlined previously for adventure. Here are confected episodes which are bound to produce swings of value, and thus is time filled and punctuated – existing becomes living. This theoretical view is strongly supported by observation. Guttman (1978) provides a summary of empirical investigations of athletes. The protocols overwhelmingly support the positive self-construction effect of sports participation; "feeling that one exists," "discovering myself," "realizing oneself," "finding an expression of the self," "knowing oneself," "communicating nonlinguistically," "obtaining recognition from others," or "dominating others."

Guttman quotes from Roger Bannister's description of his feelings as he neared completion of the first four-minute mile:

> I had a moment of mixed joy and anguish, when my mind took over. It raced well ahead of my body and drew my body compellingly forward. I felt that the moment of a lifetime had come. There was no pain, only a great unity of movement and aim. The world seemed to stand still, or did not exist. . . . I felt at that moment that it was my chance to do one thing supremely well. I drove on, impelled by a combination of fear and pride. (1976, p. 77)

This is a literary reconstruction of a fleeting moment, but one that succeeds well in showing the dramatic and self-constructive potential of a single agonistic sporting event. The context for this performance was unique and transformed it into the thrill of a lifetime. The accomplishment was ratified by a huge public, waiting anxiously to see who would be the first human being to cause two completely arbitrary metrics, 240 seconds and 1,760 yards, to converge by unaided human pace. Roger Bannister, physician, has a place in the annals of history far more distinguished than that of later and faster runners. As a component of individual biography, surely Bannister's record-breaking run occupies for him a more central place than is commonly the case for middle-aged men who happened to have competed in athletics in their youth.

Direct participation in sports is extremely common among young people. James Michener (1976) makes the point in his compendious survey, *Sports in America*: "Young people need that experience of acceptance. . . . In the United States it is sports that have been elected primarily to fill this need" (p. 19).

Sports in the United States constitutes one of the chief means, if not *the* chief means, by which a young person might construct a life story that is generally considered to be full and complete. As noted previously, sports involvement by means of spectatorship virtually permeates the entire U.S. population – with the vast majority of the population devoting daily attention to occurrences in the world of sport.

Gambling activity in the United States is extremely common, accepted, and shows every indication of a trend toward increasing volume. A recent report states that in 1983 $132 billion was wagered, with about 20 percent of that amount lost to the gambler. In other words, in 1983, something like $26 billion was paid in voluntary taxation and contributions to the owners of legal and illegal gambling enterprises. This figure might be considered to be the price tag attached to the aggregate of aleatory thrills purchased by the U.S. population in the year.

Participation in sporting activity, as player or as spectator, and in gambling activity is pervasive in our world, and at the same time is noneconomic in the narrowly rational sense of that term. Moreover, both of these classes of activity are so heavily stylized and rule bound as to produce events that are esthetically uninteresting and intrinsically boring. Slot machines cycle in about 5 seconds. A hand of 21 is often completed in less than a minute, and almost all casino games complete a cycle in less than five minutes. Baseball, football, and basketball games might be said to command some interest for their pure beauty or intrinsic dramatic quality, but I argue that this appeal is slight and fleeting. Extrinsic context in the form of league or national competitions or comparisons with existing records does contribute to the interest of what is going on, as does a complete knowledge of the intricate possibilities diverging from each moment of play. But the crucial element in a sporting contest is that its outcome is not known ahead of time; and more, that there are those on and off the competing teams who look to the final result with personal interest. An adventure in the small, one might redeem the empty time by investing attention and perhaps money in the unfolding of the minor fates involved. Aleatory gambling events are totally devoid of interest unless one buys part of the action. Then there is thrill to be had, if only the downward thrill of disappointment. Poker is a game of the utmost mechanical simplicity, and is therefore entirely without interest unless enriched by the exchange of tokens of value. When so enriched, poker is one of the few human activities that is commonly sustained over periods as long as 24 hours or more, with few or no interruptions for sleeping, eating, or any purely ludic diversion. These contrived adventures are important. Out of their combination and repetition elements are acquired for the construction and sustenance of suitable self-narratives.

CONSIDERATIONS OF CONTEXT

I have already suggested how the particular web of meaning woven about the four-minute mile barrier imparted a special historical significance to Roger Bannister's accomplishment in 1954. Neither the performance nor even the result of the sporting event determines the power of that event in the construction of self-narratives. Rather, the entire configuration and meaning of a sporting event determines what is to be made of the result. The second Louis-Schmeling heavyweight match, in 1938, was not just a boxing contest, but an event that came to symbolize in complex ways the struggle between U.S. democracy, where a poor black man could become champion, and Nazi Germany, with its arrant claims of racial superiority. This match was cast dramatically as a confrontation of champions, with the victor to carry the day not just for himself but for his entire nation. Never mind that racism was still rampant in the United States, or that Jack Johnson had been heavily abused just 20 years earlier for his effrontery in becoming the first black U.S. heavyweight champion. The Louis-Schmeling bout was witnessed with devout and partisan excitement by the entire Western world. The drama of the 126 seconds it took Louis to knock out his opponent became part of the life story of millions of people. On a similar scale, the finals of a World Cup football (soccer) match draws the attention and anxious interest of everyone in the participating nations. Few could resist the pull of the Italy-Germany final match in 1982, for it seemed within these nations as if something large and fateful were at stake, without anyone being able to specify exactly what it was. Historical and dramatic context often provides sporting events with a rich, if ephemeral, significance. The history of sport is full of thrilling moments, with more to come.

If the significance of sporting events to the individual must be understood in a wide context of meaning, then the very institution of sport and attitudes toward sport must be addressed as a major problem in social history. Indeed, a major new field of history has recently developed and is devoted to the development of just such understandings (see *The Chronicle of Higher Education*, June 8, 1983).

Sport provides adventure, a euphoric release from drudgery, tedium, and the gracelessness of ordinary domestic life. Where routinized and confining dreariness are prevailing conditions of life, interest in sport should be strong when the option is presented. Thus, it is not mere coincidence that the country whose oppressive industrial scene inspired *Das Kapital* should also be the universally acknowledged source of competitive sports the world over (see Weber, 1971; Guttman, 1976). In the context of English life, sport takes its special and very strong meaning:

It may be precisely for their power of contenting some souls that anachronistic English recipes appeared exciting. Action, liberation, adventure and the heroic life were what the colonies seemed to promise. So did sports. Both proposed a way of escape from the drudgery, stultification, and repression of everyday life. Both hold out the opportunity to assert oneself, to expend energies little needed or rewarded in the stagnant situation at home. Both reflected, evident in the little reviews or in the new artistic venture of the *fin de siecle*, against an aging, listless way of life, but largely in terms of a fat boy's revolt rather than a rebellion of the downtrodden. (Weber, 1971, p. 98)

Games do provide an outlet for emotional display in boring or confining worlds, as Elias and Dunning (1970) argue in their essay, "The quest for excitement in unexciting societies." It is not just excitement that is provided by sports, however, but an ongoing series of adventurous episodes, a source of mystery where one's attention and conversation might truly become engaged. The Marxist analysis of competitive sport as escapist, and of professional sport as a capitalistic abomination is limited in that it does not grant legitimacy to the self-narrative producing function of sport. (See Guttman, 1976, for a useful presentation and criticism of the Marxist and neo-Marxist views on sport.)

Competitive sports, it would seem, cannot forever coexist with a system of artificial social elitism. Sooner or later the physical superiority of athletic talent must come to embarrass and cast into ridicule those who would serve as the gatekeepers of traditional privilege. Since raw physical talent is no respecter of arbitrary social classes, sport can indeed serve as a wedge for upward social mobility. One of the great psychological satisfactions of an agonistic sports encounter is the lack of ambiguity in the final result, together with the realization that the final result depends primarily on the quality of play within the frame of the game and not on any inherited privilege. Competitive sports are in this sense democratizing.

Because the results of competitive games bear these features, Hitler's decision to host the 1936 Olympic Games in Berlin is curious and problematic. First, his embracing of competitive sports was conceived as an outrage by the nationalistic Turner movement, for the Olympics were seen as totally alien to the German spirit and to nineteenth-century romantic ideals. Hitler took a calculated risk, for he hoped to show to the world the superiority of the fruits of his system in fair competition, and thereby to reap a huge propaganda advantage. For this he was prepared to sacrifice the noncompetitive character of traditional German sport. But the vertigo element of sport participation did not suddenly disappear with

Hitler's decision. Leni Riefenstahl's brilliant film documenting the 1936 games makes this abundantly clear. Riefenstahl's camera is focused on the beauty of form: runners train on winding forest trails in the crisp mountain air, and their splendidly formed bodies luxuriate in a steamy sauna where limber fronds are applied to naked backs to stimulate circulation. The film shows horses magnificently clearing water hazards in the pentathalon. In another sequence, divers in majestic slow motion seem to defy the law of gravity; in one long montage, many divers are shown in airy freedom, never striking the water. Grace, majesty, harmony, the perfection of the human form – these are the qualities dominating Riefenstahl's film, and only incidentally do we learn of winners and losers. Not once is there mention of the numbers of medals won by the various nations. Even so, it is a work of propaganda for the Third Reich, but more subtle and artful than that which would have been produced by Goering. Of course, for Americans the 1936 Olympic games are remembered for the astonishing four victories of Jesse Owens. Like the Louis conquest of Schmeling to come later, these victories were savored by Americans as a kind of divine signal that in any serious confrontation our system would prevail over theirs. In this as in many other cases, Hitler's strategic decision brought his followers to ultimate defeat. This illustrates a danger of vertiginous play, for from an exalted state of transcendence, one may utterly misjudge one's capacity to prevail in agonistic confrontation.

That the United States has always been in the thrall of the Anglo-competitive mode of play is illustrated by the strategic decisions of another prominent national leader, John F. Kennedy. Garry Wills (1982) has convincingly shown the dominance of raw adventurism in the Kennedy style of government. The New Frontier presented the kind of challenge Americans could understand – missile gaps, space races, the man-on-the-moon program. The Kennedy crowd was young, partied dangerously and often to excess, and played touch football for recreation. Robert Kennedy was a ruthless opponent of the Teamsters Union, Jimmy Hoffa, and many other real and imagined arch-villains. The Cuban missile crisis was broadly played up as a triumph of superior grit, and we came to expect the repeat thrills of "brinksmanship." All of this excitement was created against the background of the Eisenhower decade, which became ever more dull and grey in retrospect as the brilliant sporting and gambling of the Camelot years claimed excited and breathless attention, not only in the United States, but around the world. On the national level, this is an example of a "good opening" period

(Klapp, 1978) emerging from one of ennui. Stories are made of adventures for nations as well as for individuals.

Another instance of the same U.S. thirst for adventure is richly presented in Tom Wolfe's (1979) book, *The Right Stuff*, describing the pioneering space program. The constant tension of this story is sustained by combinations of all four basic forms of play. The astronauts are not interested in being mere passive riders in a traveling can, but want to engage in continual agonistic play, controlling or piloting their craft against the force of natural gravity. The press agentry surrounding the man-in-space program is an instance of mimicry play, for here the astronauts are blown up as superhuman heroes, the elite of the elite, trained to the finest edge of physical and mental perfection, devoid of ordinary and debasing human appetites. The *right stuff* as a concept is bound up with vertigo and transcendence in the escape from earth's bondage. If you have the right stuff you are in harmony with the sublime. And involving as it did a game with ever-fallible machines, large elements of aleatory adventure were involved in the initial space flights, with back-up systems helping to favor the odds of survival while at the same time certifying a real possibility that the gamble could fail calamitously. But with all this complexity, the agonistic element prevailed in the program to conquer space. The United States was first in the imaginary race to the moon, to the incalculable relief and satisfaction of millions of Americans.

No strictly rational argument exists for maintaining a cold war, striving in an arms race, or attaining nuclear superiority. The game is not what it seems. These adventures are required not logically but dramatically – the requirement is that some sort of reasonably coherent and compelling political story line be sustained. The demand for this story line allows talk of "domino theories," "imperialist expansionism," and so on to be taken seriously. The rationale in Orwell's *1984* for the continuing, unstable competition among Oceania, Eastasia, and Eurasia is the same as that being described here. The need for a continued story is paramount, and the government-media combine is insatiable and remorseless. Since story does not emerge from a condition of prosperous security and stability, it is necessary to manufacture insecurity and instability. It is not that the leaders of the world know this in a way that common citizens do not. It is not that world leaders cunningly devise these adventurous shows to keep the masses from falling into an existential abyss. Rather, world leaders are caught up in the texture of the drama in a way that prohibits this cool perspective. Ronald Reagan is so involved in his role as president of the United States, and so aware of the glare of lights on the stage of history, that he has perhaps less capacity than his citizenry for gaining a clear view of the arbitrariness and absurdity of the drama in which he is participating as a chief protagonist. I expect that the hungry media are also largely incapable of gaining a saving perspective on the adventures they so yearn to describe.

World politics is a game, a drama, a series of adventures; it is uncertain, risky, and fraught with weighty consequences. The requirements of adventure for actors on the stage of world affairs is imperative, for it simply will not do to let the narrative collapse. This electronic age could never begin to tolerate a Calvin Coolidge. That this insistence upon action involves certain dangers is quite obvious, but I shall defer further consideration of those dangers until the final section of this chapter, after picking up again in the following section the significance of individual adventures of the sporting and gambling sort in the construction of life stories.

SOME ISSUES AND PROBLEMS IN THE CONSTRUCTION OF SELF-NARRATIVES OUT OF REPEATED ADVENTURES

The biographical aspect of life is not coterminous with the biological. Narrative constructions are the socially derived and expressed product of repeated adventures and are laid over a biological life progression that often extends beyond its storied span. Obviously, this is a social problem of increasing significance in the United States, where a growing proportion of the population enounters retirement while in possession of full physical vigor. Kurt Vonnegut states the problem nicely: "If a person survives an ordinary span of sixty years or more, there is every chance that his or her life as a shapely story has ended and all that remains to be experienced is epilogue. Life is not over, but the story is" (1982, p. 208).

The problem of one's life story being prematurely over is particularly pronounced for the athlete. Two stanzas from Housman's "A Shropshire Lad" will illustrate the phenomenon:

> The time you won your town the race
> We chaired you through the market-place;
> Man and boy stood cheering by,
> And home we brought you shoulder-high.

. . . .

Now you will not swell the rout
Of lads that wore their honors out,
Runners whom renown outran
And the name died before the man.

The problem with athletic fame is that it often sets impossibly high standards for developing the rest of the story of one's life; indeed such a standard can only with great difficulty be sustained through the period of young adulthood. As matters stand, many young lives suffer the brutal, definitive, and unanswerable fate of "not making the cut," of not seeing their names on the list taped to the locker room door and thus being consigned to the sidelines, or worse. Difficult as this can be, things become more difficult still for the athlete who has survived many cuts and has even achieved stardom on the local teams; for the day will inevitably come, and it will not be long delayed, when the local star will find that the competition is too tough and retirement is the only option. Even for the greatest of professional sports stars, age or injury or a combination of both will bring about an end to the active athletic career.

The image of vulnerability is apt, for the athlete retiring after a long and successful career is often ill-prepared to meet the challenges of continuing to structure a life story. After all, an admiring public has largely ceased to be interested in the day-to-day activities of the retired athlete. The wise athlete will be prepared for the transition, with recourse to family and occupational preparation that offers entry into a sustaining and sustainable life story. But because the demands of time and attention are so great for high level athletic performance, it is more commonly than not the case that financial, educational, occupational, and familial preparations for assuming a post-athletic life will have been slighted. The failures in retirement are more common than the successes, particularly in sports such as boxing, where educational background is very commonly minimal. The typical dramatic narrative progression is that of tragedy. (See Michener, 1976, for a number of case histories illustrating this point.)

It is possible to overestimate the traumatic effect of athletic retirement, for with a minimum of prudence, the athlete will be reasonably secure financially; and there are, after all, records. Athletic records comprise a kind of mnemonic for revivifying and improving the past. The notion of "living on one's laurels" is not altogether absurd, for records of past accomplishment can serve as a kind of narrative capital which can be drawn upon again and again. The ex-baseball star who opens a package store or restaurant emblazoned with his name is borrowing on that capital, but it is perhaps a kind of borrowing that need never be repaid.

The cash value of adventures, after all, is only partly enjoyed at the time of their occurring or being suffered, but realizes itself later as the survived adventure becomes the stuff for enriching one's story. Travel to remote and foreign places is partly done for the intrinsic pleasure of beholding the strange and unfamiliar. But without the possibility of redeeming the travel by showing photographs and souvenirs, and telling stories to interested friends of how it was – without these possibilities the traveler is cheated of the major value that can be realized from the trip.

Stories, of course, are often improved in the retelling. Eclea Bosi (1979) remarks on the pleasure with which old people she interviewed regarded their youth. Bosi notes that periods of childhood were often objectively characterized by poverty, deprivation, limitations of freedom, and sickness. And yet the old person often views such a miserable childhood with great pleasure and warm nostalgia. Bosi remarks that the reason for this historical foreshortening has to do with the character of youthful perceptions of the world – perceptions that are fresh and full of adventure. No matter how hard the external conditions, the playful gathering in of fresh perceptions of the world comprise essential features – the fundaments – of the life story as it is to develop. Because the role of early remembered experience is necessarily constructive in this sense – even if the experience itself was negative – it is carried forward into the present as something valuable.

The memory of past adventures is not a faithful transcript of the past, since the memory-record serves a constructive purpose. Even so, the keeping of formal and exact records in modern sports has a very important function, for in this fashion comparative possibilities are afforded which greatly enrich the meaning or significance of present accomplishments. Record and history keeping in sports is a modern phenomenon – basically restricted to the twentieth century (Guttmann, 1978). We cannot compare the performance of today's runners or swimmers with those of ancient times, but we can make direct comparisons that go back 60 years or so. In baseball, the keeping of records reaches manic proportions, and there is an avid interest in the most arcane statistical data; playing with this information becomes itself a sustaining adventure for groups of afficionados (Angell, 1977).

Similarly, horse players are given an overrich supply of information in the standard racing form. For the adept horse player, it is truly fascinating to study the myriad details of past performances of all the horses in a race. The 20 minutes between races seems to the neophyte an eternity, while to the experienced player the whole time is filled with study: hardly enough time to produce a reasoned prognostication and get down a bet. The reconstructions offered by horse players after the race are creative narrative refinements, for the player will typically report having been led away from the correct pick in the last race only at the last minute, having been beguiled by some quirk or whim to follow a loser. Even losers have satisfying stories to tell about their day's adventure. Over the long term, the dedicated horse player develops a scholarly erudition for the chosen subject, and the narratives are densely packed (Herman, 1976).

Narrative enrichment occurs both retrospectively and vicariously. Retrospectively, one revises and selects and orders details in such a way as to create self-narratives that are coherent and satisfying and which will serve as justifications of one's present condition and situation. The autobiographer must describe a story line that somehow or other concludes and coincides just exactly with the known present. Vicarious narrative enrichment is accomplished by the act of identifying with or devoting attention to the myriad adventures occurring or being invented in the world around us. There are sports events, novels, opportunities to gossip with friends, plays and films to attend, and here and there are famous people who sometimes allow themselves to be touched. These are common varieties of vicarious narrative enrichment.

The possibility of retrospective narrative enrichment makes understandable a range of adventurous activities that are otherwise puzzling. Sir Edmund Hillary is said to have responded to a question about why he climbed Mt. Everest with the famous retort, "Because it was there." But he might have replied, somewhat more satisfactorily I think, "Because you are here and are asking the question." Imagine how few mountains would be climbed if the story of climbing the mountain could be told to no one, and if memory could not somehow contrive to select and keep positively valued adventures and to delete or evaluatively transform the unpleasant adventure, for there is a lot of pain and hardship in climbing. An unpleasant episode is suffered, and in time is converted into a diverting tale, as it is selectively revised, burnished, and served up for the dilectation of self and others. Chaucer's *Canterbury Tales* are truly delicious. That their trek could have been thus distilled into pleasure would doubtless have astonished the original pilgrims who were the subjects of the tales.[2]

ADVENTURE AND THE SERIOUS

Leaving the castle to go questing normally involves a cost or a burden to those left behind. Someone must mind the castle while the knights are gone. And here we see an essential element in the feminist protest, for it has traditionally been the role of the male to go aquesting, while the women are left behind to their domesticity. Increasingly today it is the ideal to provide equality of opportunity to the sexes in just this sense – to provide women with the opportunity to leave the castle for the challenge of the wild unknown, and to challenge men to take their fair turn at mopping up the castle. I argue that this can be read as a move to provide equality of seriousness to the possible life stories of women and men.

The athlete who trains for a sport is thereby drawn away from domestic responsibilities and chores. The gambler is likely as not to play with the rent money, with only secondary thought given to who will pay the cost of losses. Those who seek cheap thrills by experimenting with drugs, engaging in profligate sexual adventures, or simply bumming around the land are imposing some increment of cost on the collectivities of which they are a part, with such benefits as accrue from these adventures going only to the adventurer. Touching another facet of seriousness, the scientist, the literary scholar, or the explorer engage in their quests and searches at the expense of the large social collectivity. Here the hope is that benefit will eventually return to the collectivity in the form of advanced knowledge, new discoveries, and fresh insights – or at least in the form of a diverting tale.

Since adventures are in this sense costly, it follows that societies will generally consider it in the collective interest to regulate access to certain forms of adventuring. The ancient Hebrews had no use for pagan sport. Neither did the Puritans. Sport for both societies was considered to be unproductive, costly, and therefore not serious. Recreational drugs are commonly banned, not out of arbitrary meanness, but because of the cost their use incurs to the collectivity. Gambling has a truly ancient history of conflict with the rules of the collectivity, and more often than not is banned. The Crusades of the Middle Ages can be seen as adventurous escapades, the legitimacy of which would have been quite suspect had they not been framed in the context of high religious purpose. Adventures that can bring no rewards to the collectivity are commonly regarded as not serious.[3]

Goffman describes the Calvinistic solution to life's problems as dividing one's activities into those which can have no harmful effect and those which are sure to produce some small gain. On such a plan nothing can go wrong. The problem with this in our current era is purely psychological. We are likely to regard a life lived on Calvinistic principles to be overly serious and very dull.

It is an open question how much the sense of a need for the wild and unpredictable is a matter of individual temperament and how much a matter of the temper of an age. I suspect it is both. The compulsion to avoid complete domestication is neither a cultural nor an individual constant, but something that is itself freely varying and unpredictable. The compulsion to adventure is in a sense a compulsion to play, and is so very often an avoidance of seriousness. The reciprocal compulsion is the compulsion to seriousness. It is possible to have both.

Some forms of staged or play contests pretend to great seriousness – perhaps the bullfight is the most conspicuous example; but grand opera is contrasted with light opera, and serious music from music that is merely entertaining. Goffman (1967) cites Hemingway's description of bullfighting as a kind of ultimate action, complete with the inevitable moment of truth, real swords, real blood, and so forth. But still, I would argue that the whole elaborately staged frivolity is nothing but another example of a domesticated public adding excitement to their lives through vicarious enrichment. I suspect that real struggles to the death normally have a rather different tone, and for the dying person at least, the struggle does not really count as an adventure, for unlike other thrilling experiences, the hope for a return is here quite reduced.

Conrad's description in *Heart of Darkness* expresses the non-sportive character of the struggle:

> I have wrestled with death. It is the most unexciting contest you can imagine. It takes place in an unpalatable grayness, with nothing under foot, nothing around, without the great desire of victory, without the great fear of defeat, in a sickly atmosphere of tepid scepticism, without much belief in your own right, and still less in that of your adversary. If such is the form of ultimate wisdom then life is a greater mystery than some of us think it to be. I was within a hair's breadth of the last opportunity of pronouncement, and I found with humiliation that probably I would have nothing to say. (1981, p. 119)

This is serious. But it is not a permanent or stable seriousness, at least for Conrad or Marlowe, who lived long enough to write about this gray mortal struggle, even finding thought and voice enough to make considerable pronouncements. So it is that just about anything can somehow be assimilated into one's self-narrative, should the adventure be one that is survived.

Adventure is truly described as an escape, as a release from the dead and deadly. It is creative and constructive, even as it is sportive and risky. It is life-creating and enhancing, even as it departs from the hard material seriousness of the rational world. Adventure creates story and contributes to the realization of completed identities. Seriousness is at risk in every venturing forth. But without the venturing forth there is no seriousness. Without the possibility of adventure, domesticity becomes a ludicrous reduction of life, and cannot be serious. Also, seriousness reasserts itself inevitably at the last to characters constructed by even the most frivolous series of naked spasms. Some see this restoration to seriousness as one of the moral advantages of death and war. The search for equivalents continues.

Acknowledgments: I owe a debt of gratitude to Ted Sarbin for reading an initial draft of this manuscript and for making a number of suggestions for change. I also wish to express appreciation to Ken Gergen and John Shotter, who organized a symposium at the "International Conference on Self and Identity" held at Cardiff, Wales, in July 1984. At that conference an initial and abbreviated version of this chapter was presented.

NOTES

1. The source of this and much additional information in this chapter concerning gambling is the report of the U.S. Presidential Commission on the Review of National Policy Toward Gambling, based on survey research conducted in 1974 (Kallick, Suits, Dielman, & Hybels, 1979).

2. The necessity of *relating* the adventure leads to the observation that the photographic industry has probably done more to promote the tourist industry than the tourist industry has done to promote photography, which is the usual way of regarding the matter.

3. It is interesting to note that hunting and fishing, skilled activities which once constituted the most serious of human work, and war, the most serious of human conflicts, have been transformed into sports in the modern era. And activities performed purely for pleasure, such as playing baseball, football, or racing horses, have become serious professional businesses. These are further examples of transformations to and from the ludic.

REFERENCES

Allport, G. (1937). *Personality.* New York: Holt.

Angell, R. (1977). *Five seasons.* New York: Simon and Schuster.

Balint, M. (1959). *Thrills and regressions.* London: The Hogarth Press and the Institute for Psycho-Analysis.

Bosi, E. (1979). *Memoria a sociedade.* São Paulo: T. A. Queiroz.

Caillois, R. (1961). *Man, play, and games.* New York: Free Press.

Conrad, J. (1981). *Heart of darkness.* New York: Bantam.

Crites, S. (1971). The narrative quality of experience. *The Journal of the American Academy of Religion,* 39, 391-411.

Desvuisseaux, P. (1983, June 8). Baseball history. *Chronicle of Higher Education,* 17-19.

Elias, N. and Dunning, E. (1970). The quest for excitement in unexciting societies. In G. Luschen (Ed.), *The cross-cultural analysis of sport and games.* Champaign, IL: Stipes.

Gergen, K. and Gergen, M. (1983). Narratives of the self. In T. R. Sarbin and K. E. Scheibe (Eds.), *Studies in social identity.* New York: Praeger.

Goffman, E. (1967). *Interaction ritual.* New York: Anchor Books.

Guttmann, A. (1978). *From ritual to record.* New York: Columbia University Press.

Herman, R. D. (1976). *Gambling and gamblers.* Toronto: D. C. Heath.

Huizinga, J. (1949). *Homo ludens: A study of the play element in culture.* London: Routledge and Kegan Paul.

James, W. (1911). *Memories and studies.* New York: Longmans.

Kallick, M., Suits, D., Dielman, T., and Hybels, J. (1979). *A survey of American gambling attitudes and behavior.* Ann Arbor, MI: Institute of Survey Research.

Klapp, O. (1978). *Openings and closings.* New York: Cambridge University Press, 1978.

Kogan, N., and Wallach, M. (1964). *Risk taking.* New York: Holt, Rinehart and Winston.

Mancuso, J. C. and Sarbin, T. R. (1983). The self-narrative in the enactment of roles. In T. R. Sarbin and K. E. Scheibe (Eds.), *Studies in social identity.* New York: Praeger.

Michener, J. A. (1976). *Sports in America.* New York: Random House.

Miller Brewing Company. (1983). *Miller Lite. Report on American attitudes towards sports.* Milwaukee, WI: Author.

Orwell, G. (1968). The art of Donald McGill. In S. Orwell and I. Angus (Eds.), *The collected essays, journalism, and letters of George Orwell* (vol. 2), pp. 155-165. New York: Harcourt, Brace and World.

Ortega y Gassett, J. (1961). *Meditations on Don Quixote.* New York: Norton.

Sarbin, T. R. (1977). Contextualism: The worldview for modern psychology. In A. W. Landfield (Ed.), *Nebraska Symposium on Motivation: Personal Constructs.* Lincoln, NE: University of Nebraska Press.

Steinbeck, J. (1977). *The acts of King Arthur and his noble knights, from the Winchester mss. of Thomas Malory and other stories.* New York: Ballantine.

Vonnegut, K. (1982). *Deadeye Dick.* New York: Delacorte.

Weber, E. (1971). Gymnastics and sport in fin de siecle France: Opium of the classes? *American Historical Review*, 76, 70-98.

Wills, G. (1982). *The Kennedy imprisonment: A meditation on power*. Boston: Little & Brown.

Wolfe, T. (1979). *The right stuff*. New York: Farrar, Straus, and Giroux.

8

Storytime: Recollecting the Past and Projecting the Future

Stephen Crites

One of the shorter pieces in the first volume of Søren Kierkegaard's *Either/Or* bears the title, "The Unhappiest." That is the literal rendering of the original Danish title, "Den Ulykkeligste." It stands in the published English translation as "The Unhappiest Man," but no such male preferment in the ranks of the unhappy is implied either in the original title or in the discourse, which celebrates the unhappiness of women and men alike. It is a speech delivered by Kierkegaard's pseudonymous personality, a young man identified simply as A, to the Symparane-kromenoi, a society of the living dead that holds its meetings at ghostly hours of the night. Subtitled "An Enthusiastic Address to the Symparanekromenoi," the speech is received with reciprocal enthusiasm by this company of zombies, who are keen on unhappiness.

The speech has dialectical and perhaps scientific pretentions. "The unhappy person," the speaker explains to his attentive audience, "is one who has his ideal, the content of his life, the fullness of his consciousness, the essence of his being, in one way or another outside himself. He is alway absent, never present to himself" (1959, p. 220).[1] That may do for a general definition, but the speaker immediately goes on

152

to divide the subject: Since "it is evident that one can be absent from himself either in time past or in time future," there must be these two basic types of unhappy people. Neither type of person lives essentially in the present. That is why people of either type are called unhappy. But some are more unhappy than others. If a person who lives only in the past can at least find himself in his memory, recalling a time when he really was somebody, he enjoys at least that much happiness. A woman, for instance, whose life has been blighted forever by her lover's abandonment, may find some satisfaction in remembering the good times before he left. Similarly with the person who lives in the future, if he lives in the lively hope that eventually he will come into his own, either in this world or in the next. He may have no memories he cares to dwell on, and of course the present is a blank, but he is happy in his hope. But if a person who dwells only on the past does so with nothing but bitterness or regret, we have reached a new plateau of unhappiness; similarly with the one preoccupied with the future, but without hope, perhaps with nothing but anxiety.

And so on. Our speaker, who is as systematic as he is enthusiastic, proceeds to sketch a taxonomy of unhappiness along these lines, with numerous literary and historical examples. It is an exciting evening for the Symparanekromenoi, as the brotherhood is presented with ever more exquisite types. At last, in a brilliant stroke, the speaker unveils a dialectical synthesis of both past- and future-oriented unhappiness. Such a prodigy of misery appears

> When it is recollection which prevents him from being present in his hope, and hope which prevents him from being present in recollection. When this happens, it is due, on the one hand, to the fact that he constantly hopes something that should be recollected; his hope is constantly disappointed, but because it is disappointed he discovers that it is not because the goal of his hope is postponed, but because it is already past and gone, has already been experienced or should have been experienced and thus passed over into recollection. On the other hand, he constantly recollects what he ought to hope for; for he has already anticipated the future in thought, in thought he has experienced it, and this experience he now recollects, instead of hoping for it. So what he hopes for lies behind him, what he recollects lies before him. (P. 223)

This baleful combination seems to be awarded the palm as the unhappiest; like all achievements of the highest sort it is perhaps also rare. It would be somewhat more common to find specimens that *either* recollect what they ought to hope for *or* the reverse. Kierkegaard furnishes an example of the former in *Repetition*, another nameless "young man" who has just fallen gloriously in love, but has such an over-active imagination that he already pictures himself as an old man recollecting these glorious days of first love. In fact, from this perspective his entire future life with his sweetheart unfolds before his eyes – as Old Wives say happens at the moment of death. As his confidant, one Constantin Constantius, observes, the young man is essentially finished with the whole affair. A less poetic example might be the veteran member of family, firm, or faculty who dampens every bright new proposal with the inevitable: It's been tried. Such is the recollective overleaping of the future, treating it as a kind of past. The opposite move is to invest one's hope for the future in a condition that can only be past, as in the banal pathos of the middle-aged man or woman trying to become young.

A person who managed to combine both of these moves, with hope and recollection mutually dissolving each other, would indeed be a virtuoso of alienation, well deserving a place in the privileged ranks of the unhappiest. Such a person, says our speaker,

> Cannot become old, because he has never been young; he cannot become young, for he is already old; in one sense he cannot die, for he has not really lived; in another sense he cannot live, because he is already dead; he cannot love, for affection is always present, and he has no contemporaneity, no future, no past, and yet he is a sympathetic nature, and he hates the world only because he loves it; he has no passion, not because he lacks it, but because in the same instant he has the opposite passion, and he has no time for anything, not because his time is taken up with something else, but because he simply has no time at all; he is impotent, not because he has no power, but because his own power makes him impotent. (P. 224)

Although our speaker offers numerous examples of lesser types of unhappiness, it is noteworthy that he mentions no concrete instances that fit this description of the unhappiest. Perhaps none is necessary, since in this suggestive dialectical description the Symparanekromenoi can easily recognize themselves – and their speaker. If the description rings true, furthermore, there can be nothing very concrete about them at all.

Only in the loosest sense can what follows be regarded as an exposition of "The Unhappiest." We will proceed on rather different grounds than those of Kierkegaard's pseudonym, speculating a bit on the story-like way in which we appropriate the past and anticipate the future. That, in fact, will be our primary interest. Yet in an effort to tie some of these speculations together, we will come 'round again to the theme of unhappiness, treating it in a sense that I hope will bear some resemblance to the spiritual pathology diagnosed in "The Unhappiest." By turns so whimsical and so melodramatic in its presentation, Kierkegaard's little piece also offers some suggestive hints about the psychological significance of temporality. Developing these hints in ways that Kierkegaard would not necessarily approve, we will argue that anticipating the future and appropriating the past call for quite different narrative strategies, and that unhappy consequences result from the confusion of these strategies. For differentiation of tense is not merely a convention of language. Language simply registers, in this respect, a peculiarity of the lived time of human beings. Language is tensed because the present in which we exist, individually and collectively, is the point of tension that both joins past and future and also places us in fundamentally different relations to them.

PASTNESS AND IDENTITY

Let us assume, as Kierkegaard would not have, that "selfhood" or "self" is the name for a free-floating life of consciousness, distributed through a network of relationships over time, rather than being the name for a perduring and localized entity more or less coterminous with a single human organism. It is more like the air we breathe, our common *spiritus*, than it is like one of the bodies animated by it, more like the language we share in conversation and continue to share even in our most private moments than like the impervious speaking of a recording device: a difference of which we are immediately aware when we try to phone a friend and are answered by a voice that is his but not he, requesting us to leave our message at the sound of the electronic signal. He is himself only in relation to others. Selfhood is no doubt bodily through and through, but only in the sense that every living body is climatically, chemically joined, through common atmosphere, soil, and nutriment to every other in the biosphere. The self-isolated organism enclosing an atomistic self is an optic illusion, an appearance in a visual field not closely observed.

The more global view of self we are assuming is no doubt debatable, but I do not propose to argue it here. We have other fish to fry. I do concede that it is in some respects counter-intuitive, and that consideration does concern us. For if we take seriously, in the sense we have sketched, the essentially intersubjective nature of psychic life, then the great puzzle is how it happens that I am at least intermittently aware of myself as an individuated identity, as that familiar interior voice that appears to me to be so consistent in its accents, as that center of consciousness that appears so consistent in its point of view, through all the transactions undergone from my childhood to the present. Granted, that is, that "self" is fundamentally a name for a conversation rather than a monologue, how is it that I so unmistakably identify *my* self, this relentlessly persisting "I," this tall, thin pronoun which "I" cannot confuse with any other? How does it happen that out of the great pool of inter-subjective selfhood I can so readily single out that babbling little eddy I call *my* self? No other voice but *mine* babbles with quite that intonation.

Being jostled in a crowded vehicle over bumpy roads for many hours, it is possible to become momentarily uncertain which pair of legs are yours. Putting your hand in your pocket, you may discover that it is someone else's pocket, or even someone else's hand in your pocket. But you cannot, short of amnesia, be in doubt about which is your self. The phenomenon of self-certainty seems intuitively clear, even to those who may find it ideologically embarrassing. But it would be incautious to assume that the phenomenon implies that this individuated self is an unproblematic and self-explanatory entity, much less an irreducible metaphysical substance.

The continuity of memory certainly contributes to this self-certainty. "I" – this self who speaks now – have memories that go back to early childhood, fragmentary and intermittent, but forming enough links with a past to give this present self a sense of having existed over time. The chronicle of memory has many lacunae, yet it gives access to a past that the one who remembers claims as his own, an identity through many metamorphoses. This identity is not simply a matter of the organic continuity of a body through its various stages of maturation. The face I see looking back at me out of a mirror does not remind me much of the one that looked back when I was a child, yet I do not hesitate to claim both faces as my own. Indeed, the presence in my memory of such visual images, not only of that face but of the equally familiar surroundings of my childhood, contributes powerfully to my sense, so obvious that I rarely think of it, that "I" am rooted in a past with which I remain in some sense identical. This sense is reinforced when a lacuna is filled in, for instance when a visual image comes powerfully to mind that had been long forgotten. Recently I visited the house in which I had spent my early childhood, which has long since passed outside the family and has been quite thoroughly refurnished and remodeled. Casting my eye idly over the baseboard in the dining room I was startled to see an oddly shaped crack that I suddenly remembered contemplating as a very small boy playing on the carpet. I had thought it looked like a face of grotesque expression, which fascinated me. I had had no occasion to remember it in the intervening years, but I would have recognized it even if it had turned up in much more unfamiliar surroundings. As it was, it brought back memories of crawling about under the dining room table and of the old carpet on which I had played, in the patterns of which I had traced various ideal topographies, which were incorporated into my games. I recalled childhood friends who had played with me on that carpet as they appeared at that time, in the very clothes they wore then.

But such strong visual images are not the only connecting links between this "I" that writes these words with a past it appropriates as a dimension of temporal depth in its own identity. For me personally, as it happens, the aural dimension, the experience of the ear, is generally more vivid than the visual in my memory. Old jingles and sayings, radio commercials and popular songs of the 1930s, gospel hymns, the precise intonations of voices, the sounds of trains and cars and school bells, will suddenly come back to me, jarred into remembrance by some association.

Not long ago, as I was hiking on Connecticut's Mattabassett Trail with two of my grown daughters, in a mellow family-holiday mood, one of the young women complained about people defacing the rocks and cliffs by writing their names on them in white paint: and out it popped. Without hesitation I said, "Fools' names and fools' faces / always appear in public places." My jingle got the groan and giggle it deserved. But it came instantly and vividly back to me when I had heard it: When I was a small boy, maybe five or six, a rather dour workman was laying sidewalk in front of our house. I asked if I could write my name in the fresh cement. He gave me a severe look and said, "Fools' names and fools' faces / always appear in public places." That was the end of that! Realizing that I'd have to immortalize myself some other way, I withdrew.

The mnemonic power of rhythm and rhyme! So far as I can remember I hadn't thought of that jingle in all the years since, until it came unbidden to my lips that day on the Mattabassett Trail. I assumed it was proverbial, repeated, perhaps, by generations of dour and private people, their revenge on the show-offs and hot-shots of this world. I have since discovered that it still has currency. Anyhow, through all those years I was only its passive carrier. Tucked away somewhere in my brain, it was a small item in the enormous freight of mental baggage all of us carry around unconsciously, most of it never to be called up for use again. This little jingle, for instance, seems to have stuck in my brain by the sheer association of sound, meaning, and situation, joining that corner of my brain with how many generations of dour workmen flinging it at how many exhibitionists. Yet that little shard of sound also linked the little boy eyeing the cement with the middle-aged man hiking on a sunny afternoon in the company of his daughters. It is a minor example of one of the major miracles of language, as a union of sound and sense, that it can forge not only a personal identity over time but also a corporate identity with generations of women and men who share the same linguistic tradition. Both kinds of identity are dimensions of selfhood.

So I cannot conclude from my childhood memories that I was issued this self at birth or in the womb, and that it has simply unfolded like an impervious Leibnizian monad through all its life-transactions from that day to this. It is not as if the child dissuaded from writing his name in the wet cement already contained in germ, like the DNA in his genes, the man hiking with his daughters, the tart saying just awaiting the occasion for its appearance. In the first place, a self-identical self is not the precondition of experience, but its consequence. The sense of self, rooted in a personal past, arises out of manifold interactions with things, some of them, like the crack in the baseboard or the jingle, reiterated over longer or shorter periods of time. In one case, the reiteration of the crack called forth the spontaneous memory of the original situation, in the other case a complex analogy of situation called forth the appropriate jingle. "My" self with its personal past takes form out of just such networks of analogous experience present and remembered. But in the second place, experience is itself mediated by coded sound, image, language, all presupposing a vast social processing of such forms, perhaps long antedating the awakening of the personal self to consciousness.

In the third place, the remembered past is situated in relation to the present in which it is re-collected. The child is not the father of the man. The man, in this respect, is father of the child he once was, who still lives as the remembered eye and ear and voice that is his own, but who must be called up as his own in recollection. This process of re-collecting my own past is conducted by many means, all of them bearing a formal resemblance to the devices by which artists in various media create an aesthetically coherent work. In order for the remembered crack in the baseboard to evoke an otherwise vanished scene with dining table, carpet, and playmates, I had to "recollect" this complex visual image in a manner analogous to the way a painter "collects" the harmonious ensemble of items in a still-life. The recollection of jingle, the voice of the workman, and the temptation to exhibitionism required a similar act of composition, analogous to that of a musical work. By such aesthetic means this "I" that now says "I" actively forges, gathers, re-collects its continuity of experience out of the inchoate intersubjective stream of memory. Narrative, together with other artful devices such as those already mentioned, is one of the primary means by which I construct such a continuous life of experience. The examples already given of visual and aural-linguistic memory are already "narrative" in an extended sense of the term, as it is used, for instance, by art historians of a painting that depicts an episode in history or legend. Crack and jingle each evoked a moment in a definite social situation, with perhaps an implicit story. At any rate, story-like narrative establishes a particularly strong sense of personal continuity, because it can link an indefinite number of remembered episodes from the single point of view of the one who recounts or merely recalls the story. This single point of view is the "I" who now speaks or recalls, and this "I" which situates my story and distinguishes it from others also anchors what I call my self in its identity over time. This story-like remembrance of things past is of at least Proustian length in its full extent, though what I can recollect at a sitting is mercifully some shorter sequence of that whole. The whole story generally remains vague and merely implicit. What I own as my self is always present as the character in the story from whose perspective its episodes are recalled, claimed as its own self by this "I" who recalls. By telling the story from the perspective of this self, as in a first person narrative, usually told in the past tense, I distance this self from the intersubjective matrix of experience in order to claim it as my own, as that personal past with which I claim identity. Still there is always some hiatus between the "I" who recollects and the self who appears as a character in a succession of episodes, a hiatus that I artfully bridge by owning this self, claiming it as my own. Still there remains a point of tension where the hiatus has been bridged, a tension that I express linguistically as a differentiation of tense between past and present.

We become most aware of the break that lies beneath this tension when we are accused of some transgression, or even of some merely embarrassing offense. Can I have done that? – must I own the self that was so brutal? It is entirely possible that the perpetrator of some horrible crime of violence may quite "sincerely" deny having done it, being unable in a cooler hour to avow such a deed as his own or its doer as himself. What have "I" who am now accused to do with *him*? *I* am not violent –

now. The phenomenon of blocking, or the Jekyll and Hyde melodrama, might be described as the involuntary refusal to own the monster as one's own self. Quite apart from perpetrators of violent crime or wartime horror, who does not struggle with the memory of deeds he can scarcely bring himself to acknowledge as his own? Or I acknowledge the deed, that I "did" it (past tense), but I deny the motives imputed to me: I never intended to offend her, I was just joking.

This topic obviously opens up an abyss, into which I have peered elsewhere in a discussion of self deception (Crites, 1979). The reason for glancing into this abyss here is simply because the painful cases of self-avowal bring out most dramatically the aspect of artifice, of storytelling, involved in all identity-formation. The same point could also be made by developing the commonplace observation that autobiographers usually recollect their memories to their own advantage. Their critics claim they lie. The narrative medium of experience is indeed akin to the storyteller's art, not only in its formal properties, but also in that it is a thing made, a modest act of poesis, generally much more rough-hewn and unfinished than a well-told tale, but still a thing that must be formed in the act of recollection. A coherent life of experience is not simply given, or a track laid down in the living. To the extent that a coherent identity is achievable at all, the thing must be made, a story-like production with many pitfalls, and it is constantly being revised, sometimes from beginning to end, from the vantage point of some new situation of the "I" that recollects.

It must be admitted that many things happen to me that I am not able to integrate into my story, and to that extent such things are not experienced, even as at this moment I am not experiencing the functioning of my liver. I experience some of my vital organs only in their malfunction, experience even the beating of my heart only when it is overtaxed by exertion or during very still insomniac nights. Probably most of the physical events in my immediate surroundings suffer similar inattention, even some that are having a profound effect on me, which I will only experience retroactively. Then I "shall have" experienced what I did not in fact experience at the time. In reply to my doctor's interrogation I may say, Yes, now that I think of it, the air was very close and I had a little difficulty getting my breath, but I was too busy at the time to notice. Or: I was working with her all morning under a lot of pressure, and I can recall now that she seemed a little agitated, but I had no idea of her desperation.

Many such things register in my consciousness, are perceived but not experienced, heard but not listened to. Here I must acknowledge a terminological quibble. I think it is useful to reserve the word "experience" for what is incorporated into one's story, and thus owned, owned up to, appropriated. It will follow from this usage that many things are experienced retroactively. The close air, my labored breath, my co-worker's agitation had to be sensed at the time or they could not have dawned on me later, and of course it is common to use the word "experience" for all such sensations. But then we would need another word to signify the conscious appropriation, since the distinction is too crucial to be left muddled. I prefer to say that most of the things that are sensed are never experienced, and that only those that are attended to are experienced, some things only slowly clarifying themselves as I become aware of their significance for my story. From this point of view "experience" is a single, vast story-like construct, containing many subplots, richly illustrated by visual images and accompanied by sounds and rhythms that may already be forming themselves into a kind of music. This narrative construct, furthermore, is constantly changing, shifting its accents; some episodes that had seemed important becoming trivial and others emerging from obscurity into central importance. Again, in speaking of "experience" in this integral sense I realize that in some respects I have ordinary language against me, and that is always troubling. We do commonly speak of "experiences" in the plural, as if the life of experience were an aggregate of modular episodes, a love-affair here, a hamburger there, and an occasional sharp pain at the base of the skull. Yet precisely the lover, or even a professor in a particularly abstracted state of mind, can be unsure whether she has eaten her hamburger or not, and in the throes of either erotic or theoretic ecstasy can absorb many sharp pains without noticing. For her plot-line has quite a different interest, and whether a hamburger eaten but not noticed is actually experienced seems a question of the order of that concerning the sound of a tree falling in the uninhabited forest. Indeed a dieter or a person of vegetarian convictions but wolfish appetite may actively suppress having eaten the hamburger. Whether suppressed or merely overlooked, it can often happen that what has not been experienced can retrospectively take on an importance in the story – What have I done? My God, I am a *lapsed* vegetarian! – and while it is odd to say that the hamburger is only then experienced for the first time, it does seem misleading to say that it was experienced before. Many a murder mystery hangs on just that unnoticed detail that later, of a sudden, comes flashing into awareness and makes a hitherto interestingly muddled plot all too tediously clear. Something similar can happen in re-collecting my experience, sometimes with results that are of the order of a new disclosure of self, and that may not be tedious at all.

So much for the linguistic quibble. The real burden of these remarks is that the self is a kind of aesthetic construct, recollected in and with the life of experience in narrative fashion. There is a provisional dissociation of experience, and therefore of self, from the organic immediacies of life that are always in the present. That is perhaps why people have always been tempted to reify the self as a purely immaterial or soulish thing detached from an equally reified body-thing. It is easy to lapse into that fallacy in ordinary speech even when we know better. The "I" who speaks and recollects is a thoroughly bodily presence, but the self it recollects out of the past, which "I" own as my own, is indeed unphysical, not because it is a soulish substance but because it is a narrative recollection of what no longer physically exists, is no longer present. In the I-me formulation, I is the narrator, me is the narrative figure in the life story. In autobiography, the writer, the I, is the story-teller. The subject of the autobiography is a narrative figure, the me, constructed from recollections.

Yet this recollected self of my personal story has an immense psychic importance. My personal identity, without which I do not know who I am, is at stake in this formative application of narrative art, and the more complete the story the more integrated the self. The poignant search for roots that is such a prominent feature of our rootless age testifies to the acute unease a human being can feel without a coherent story of a personal past. In more stable times, or for people who live out their lives in a clearly defined ethnic community, the sense of self can seem unproblematic, because a person's life story is so powerfully supported by the ethos and mythos of the community. Under such circumstances it is not surprising that people should think of themselves, if they bother to do so at all, as if they were as highly defined and as constant in time as the house they have always lived in. Whether in other respects such a clearly demarcated self-identity is a good thing may be another matter; we will discover that it has its pitfalls. But such a person needs no Socratic guide to hector him about knowing himself, nor does he need a therapist to help him painfully piece together his story at great expense.

Whether the way is rough or smooth in this respect, being a self entails having a story. Self-knowledge, like all other knowledge, is recollection, as ancient wisdom testified. Other things, however, can exist without being known, while it is the uniquely self-reflexive paradox of the self that it comes into existence only to the extent that it can be re-collected out of the past. Nor did the old stories exaggerate the profound unhappiness of not having a soul, not being a self. The self may be an aesthetic construct, but it is psychologically necessary. That person is unhappy, literally a nonentity, who in Kierkegaard's terms cannot re-collect himself out of the past.

FUTURITY AND POSSIBILITY

Our little analysis of pastness is doubtless in many ways incomplete. It may even be wrong. As always in dealing with the past, it is too late to do anything about that! But one unmentioned aspect of pastness is crucially important to our theme, and may serve to introduce the topic of futurity as well.

We have suggested that the present is the pivotal point out of which the "I" who recollects retrieves its own self. But the present is not a static point, or some measurable duration. Presence is always leaning into that vast unknown that we call the future, projecting itself into the future, and that pro-ject in which it is engaged determines the way it is present. I am always active, pursuing some project or other, often a project I would as soon keep hidden from others, and sometimes even from myself. I am active even when I am just sitting there, or sitting there recollecting. We have already emphasized that recollecting is an activity, a kin to the story-teller's art. What we need to add now is that this activity, too, is always interested, part of my project. I recollect the past out of my interest in the future.

It is in general excruciatingly difficult to interest someone in some nugget of knowledge, however golden, if it has nothing to do with the long-term or short-term projects that person may be pursuing. Any teacher can testify to this difficulty. All knowledge is re-collection, but students can be very sullen about recollecting that in which they have no interest. I resist the temptation to draw out the pedagogical implications of this simple insight, though I judge them to be fundamental. Of course it is very difficult to find material relevant to the projects of students whose sphere of interest extends no more than 36 inches from their own navels. But most people have some projects that are more extended than that, and it is gratifying how much they are ready to recollect out of the great reservoir of the collective past.

At any rate, our interest here is in the recollection of self, and this in particular is always interested, directed to the future. We appropriate our personal past, in fact, out of the future. Even an archaeological excavation, aimed at recovering the past, can obviously not be conducted in the past. It is a project in which the archaeologist engages his future, and the deeper into the past he wishes to go, the longer into the future he must dig. So it is with the recollection of the self out of the past. To become a self is to appropriate a past, and that takes digging. Even if I am urgently interested in a new beginning, the evidence of modern psychiatric literature as well as older spiritual writings suggests that I cannot begin afresh by forgetting my past, but by recollecting it. Only a self can amend itself. To amend myself I must repent myself, and only what is avowed, owned, can be repented. But even this archaeological project of recollection and avowal is necessarily directed to the future. The future being unkown, indeed unknowable, the paradoxical result is that self-knowledge, like other knowledge, is mobilized in pursuit of the unknowable.

But that is not to say that we confront the future simply as a blank. We cannot *know* it, because it is not available for recollection. Yet precisely as the lure of all action, including recollection, the horizon of future possibility is patient of imaginative pro-jects, images, lyrical effusions, stories, from the most mundane to the most horrific to the most ideal. Still there is a crucial formal difference between images and stories recollected and those projected. Those recollected are capable of high definition, a large measure of completeness. An image of the future is vague and sketchy, a story incomplete and thin. Sticking to our narrative theme, the story of the past, as what *has been*, is so to speak archaeologically available, while the future, *not yet*, unknown, calls for a different narrative strategy, signified by the difference in tenses when we address it. The effort to narrate the future in the same detail as the past commits the formal error of treating it as if it were past. A story that is projective rather than recollective is properly more like a loose scenario, without a script, on which a group of actors improvises, more like a free, unchoreographed dance than like the New York City Ballet, more like a piece of improvisatory jazz than something *durchkomponiert*. Since it proceeds from the present, it may begin with a certain situation and a few well-defined characters, or a certain harmonic structure and agreement about the key signature, but only as a point of departure, the launching pad for the great leap into the unknown.

But what is this gleam of enthusiasm that glistens in the eyes of the performers? Let us call it hope, though that may be too elevated a term for some of the projects brewing in the fevered brains of our players. Each is scheming and scurrying with all his might, in pursuit of what utopian dreams? what pile of gold for his golden years? what applause from his peers? what dark fantasy? what erotic adventure? what bright wings? Or all of them at once and in no particular order or priority. In hot pursuit of such pro-jects, he colludes or collides with others enflamed with theirs, whom he embraces or adroitly ducks away from, bobbing and weaving, getting deflected, losing interest, coming into fabulous strokes of luck, being thwarted by others, fanning misfortune into calamity, turning into a frog, or a goat, or a member of some learned profession. Keystone cops all the way.

There are several perspectives from which to consider the future, and this is one of them: From the standpoint of an active agent existing in the present but in motion, his momentum even in the present carrying him forward into the unknown. The person who has committed himself, as he must, wittingly or unwittingly, to the improvisatory harlequinade we have described, cannot be certain of the outcome. The artfully shaped Aristotelian plot structure, so serviceable in recollecting a self-identity out of the past, cannot contain this dance into the void. The fully articulated stories are told in the past tense, but Harlequin is subjected to new tension as he ventures on a loose scenario written in the future tense. He cannot count on the perduring of the self-same self he is recollecting out of the past. Future tense is the time of metamorphosis. In precarious possession of that personal past he must appropriate, archaeologically, in just this movement into the future, Harlequin must simultaneously place it in jeopardy, willingly or unwillingly, in that same plunge into the future that has enabled him to recollect it. For from this perspective the future appears to be the universal solvent, in which everything that has been formed in the past dissolves.

We understand backwards, Kierkegaard says, but we live forwards. In negotiating that extraordinary double movement there is both danger and opportunity. It can promise relief for the penitent, release from a self-destructive identity so painfully avowed. But it can also be profoundly threatening to someone who wants to shore up the self he has come to own: who wants his past to be his future. He may lose his self-possession. Perhaps he will die and nourish daisies; he may find it hard to convince himself that this will be a more constructive contribution to the world than he made in life. Perhaps the metamorphosis will be less total. But even if it seems a small change – becoming a year older, grayer, crankier – it will be difficult to sustain the same identity, for even what he re-collects a year hence may from that new perspective be altered from beginning to end. That very prospect, however, implies that Harlequin can hope to be something different than he has yet understood himself to be. With respect to the past the artful act is to reshape what has been. With respect to the future there is the possibility, nourished precisely by possibility, of running toward the open arms of the widest horizon, which dissolves all things and makes all things new, including the self. The present that answers to the indeterminacy of the future is hope. Hope is precisely that openness of the present toward the boundless horizon of possibility.

Wait, someone objects. Futurity is not all that indeterminate. What about five-year plans? What about life insurance, or the accumulation of credits toward the B.A., or getting married and living happily ever after? What about the tickets I've secured for the weekend concert?

May the concert change your life, objector. By all means plan to go. Of course a blizzard may intervene, or an infected toenail. The soprano may catch cold. But I grant you that things do often work out pretty much the way we expected. A five-year plan may be stretching your luck a little, but up to a point the laying of plans and the bending of effort toward their fulfillment are entailed in moving into the future hopefully. Still, a good measure of improvisation is always necessary even to achieve your goals, and the goals are generally amended in the achieving. For a vision of the future functions less as the predictable outcome of all our forward-straining energy than it does as the lure for it. Many a woman lured by love has found herself scraping pots and plotting vengeance. Many a man accumulating worldly goods for a prosperous old age has ended up drooling and babbling in a nursing home. Sometimes, on the other hand, the outcome is fortunate beyond their wildest dreams. Wild dreams are perhaps the best you can do in plotting the future. Plot you must, but be prepared for the plot to thicken.

Before exploring another perspective on the future, let us pause to get our bearings. The perspective on the future that we have been examining is that of the acting agent for whom it is the void into which he plots and projects. From this perspective we have discovered that the future appears as the universal solvent, into which the self-possessed self must quickly or slowly dissolve, and his schemes with him. Kierkegaard's pseudonym in "The Unhappiest" refers to one Anceus, "of whom it is customary to say that nothing is known of him, except that he occasioned the proverb: 'There's many a slip 'twixt the cup and the lip' as if that were not more than enough" (p. 224).[2] But this very indeterminacy of the future, which imperils the passage from cup to lip, also permits hope to spread its wings, with its wild dreams: a hope that only in a proximate sense is directed to some definite goal of a definite self, while ultimately it is directed to the very boundlessness of possibility.

Such a hope comes into view in a more objective way when we consider the future from another perspective, that of the same self whose present is projecting him into the future, but now we are again concerned with this self in his aspect as an experiencing subject. We have seen that this subject secures its experience by digging out, archaeologically, its past in pursuit of its future pro-ject. From the perspective of this experiencing subject the future is the universal fluidity from which everything new is born. The merely possible child, before it is so much as conceived, much less born, subsists in the future of its parents. Of course the child does not actually exist until it becomes present. So all new things come into existence out of the future, become present and pass over into the past where they achieve clear enough definition to be re-collected: understood. That is also true of new possibilities of the existing self. To the extent that they transcend the self-possession of the existing self, they take form out of the future. These children of the future may be born in the present and become past, available for recollection. The future, meanwhile, in its fluid fecundity, never itself becomes past, but remains forever the play of possibility from which all things proceed. It is the land of hope's wild dreams.

If from the first perspective the self that re-collects itself out of the past moves in its present into the future, here the movement appears to have the opposite direction. The two movements are complementary, the dying of what is providing the nutriment for what shall be, but it is difficult to visualize both movements simultaneously.

The concert for which our objector has so prudently secured a ticket may offer him a better example of this double movement, for it can be heard more easily than seen. Listening to the music, the onrush of sound that strikes his ears, out of the future so to speak, becomes incorporated in his hearing into a melodic line, a harmonic progression, a rhythmic pulse, insofar as it passes away into its recollected association with the sounds that have preceded it into oblivion. Meanwhile the musicians, anticipating the sounds at least several bars in advance, are moving forward, keeping time and perhaps improvising as they play, sounding out the future. By the time the sounds have become a piece for the hearer, an aesthetic whole, the musicians are finished with it. While it lasts it is both lured by the future and born out of the future.

Narrative, formally similar to music in this respect, also exists in time. Its temporality is more obvious when the story is told and heard than when it seems to exist on the page; even the text, in fact, exists as a story only when it is being read, word by word, in time. The novels on my shelf are only patterns of printed signs on paper. Suppose, at any rate, that I am going to listen to a story. A similar symbiosis will occur between listener and narrator as that we have noted between hearer and musician, and need not be spelled out again. Let us attend to a different feature of the recital, which also has a musical analogue: While I wait for the narrator to begin, the story exists as sheer future possibility. It will begin out of the future and will continue to proceed out of the future. But the beginning will reach my ears only when the narrator speaks: Once upon a time a king's son. . . . This "once" immediately becomes the beginning in a different sense, the past starting point from which the rest of the story will unfold. The art of the storyteller creates an acoustic illusion, that what has in fact proceeded in his words entirely out of the future seems to begin in a fictive past, which within the specious temporality of the story will function as the beginning of the entire story. The story is coherent to the extent that it formally resembles a recollection from beginning to end. The apparent necessity by which its episodes unfold in this fictive temporality can beguile me into thinking that the later episodes are causally related to the earlier rather than continuing to spin out of pure possibility. The awful slaughter of the Achaians is caused by the wrath of Achilles, in turn caused by a slight to his honor.

This illusion of causality is created by the essential pastness of a well-strung narrative, reinforced by its closure, by the apparent completeness of its action. The specious future of its successive episodes will appear as necessary as the past. This exigency of narrative form may also lead us to think the story of our lives unfolds by a similar necessity, from which there is no prospect of release. The partners in a bad marriage may feel trapped, doomed to invent no more than new variations on a mutually destructive cycle. Hell is the ceaseless reiteration of the past: Abandon all hope ye that enter here. It is easy to forget that a life story has begun in a sheer play of possibility and has taken form at every subsequent instant out of the future.

This acoustic illusion is writ large in the myths of creation that postulate a watery chaos as the primordial past out of which all existing things proceed, often, as in Genesis, by a process of ever sharper articulation and definition. For the mythic imagination is the servant of narrative exigency. The world must begin as a story begins, by the postulation of a fictive past. The story in fact begins as everything begins, out of the unformed future, and this universal fluidity is ironically what is represented *within* the story as its primordial past. Creation is the fictive mirror image of eschatology.

Turning from this dizzying vision of pure possibility, let us call to mind a popular metaphor of a proximate future. A familiar scene in legend and folklore has been the land of enchantment, a dream landscape without causality, touched by magic. Here hero and heroine live for sheer adventure, and for love. Why, my practical friend asked me at the intermission, does Siegfried go looking for adventures? Because he is a hero. What have heroes to do with sensible, goal-directed projects? Hero and heroine alike confront monstrous figures of evil, shining figures of good, grotesques and numenoi, and are rewarded for frightful ordeals by one another's eternal fidelity. And of course they turn into frogs, goats, or members of the learned professions. Nowadays the enchanted landscape is likely to be extraterrestrial. It has always been transmundane. Although it has usually been imagined as having existed in an ideal past, "once upon a time," before the world turned dreary, we suggest that it is always a projection into the future. It is the proximate future, compounded of the boundlessness of unformed possibility and the pro-jected visions and scenarios of human beings. Its specious pastness is due to the reversal we have found to be characteristic of the mythic imagination, owing to the same exigency of narrative form. A story could not be completed without bowing to that exigency. But such a transfigured past, the enchanted landscape where fantastic figures are projected on the great screen of possibility, could never have existed in an actual past, conceived under the law of necessity. It is precisly the future, but a future rendered more finished than the one Harlequin can in fact go careening into.

Once we have adjusted to this topsy-turvy hermeneutic principle, we notice how natural it seems to associate the enchanted landscape with the one we inhabit in dreams. Hearing the fairy tale, we find the topography oddly familiar even if we have never encountered anything like it in our waking life. Here again the causal necessity and, in general, the familiar order of the everyday is suspended. I know I am beginning to fall asleep when that order of connectedness starts to unravel and oddly pixilated sounds and images begin to intrude. Recently, on the edge of sleep, I heard someone say, "Queen Armadillo with chocolate sauce," a remark just silly enough to bring me back so I could remember it. It was answered by a more cynical tone of voice, perhaps the last resistance of everyday orderliness, "But how you gonna find an armadillo queen?" Maybe the time has come, throwing caution to the winds, to revive the age-old theory of dreams as hieroglyphs of futurity: not of the predictable future, which is nothing but an extension of the past, but of the indeterminate futurity of imaginative projection.

Whether or not that suggestion arouses enthusiasm, we do want to insist that dream life and legendary tale offer at least an analogue for the sort of loose-textured, improvisatory scenario which is the lure for action in waking life, if it is to be adjusted to the indeterminacy of the future. We said earlier that for Harlequin, dancing into the void with a scenario largely made up as he goes along, the appropriate posture, adjusted to that indeterminacy, is hope. Considering the future from the opposite direction, the birth of all things out of its play of possibility, we again encounter the passion of hope. For hope is ready to welcome the new-born children of that oceanic mother of us all.

Indeed the inexhaustible mother herself is the ultimate lure of our hopes. As plants, heliotropic, arch their stems toward the sun, so human beings twist from ankle to chin toward the future: not just toward a tomorrow like today and yesterday, but toward the future that never becomes past.

Ordinarily we invest this expectant stretching in more proximate hopes, realistic surrogates of the great hope we can scarcely name. Especially when one is young, the surrogates can suffice very well. What are you waiting for, young woman, that draws that beautiful crease across your brow? Why, for my lover. For my career, for the mark I intend to leave on the world.

But now you are old. Your lover could not sustain the ecstasy of your desire. He has left, he is dead, he is pottering in slippered feet around the house. Your career is past, satisfying at the time and pleasant to recollect. The mark you left on the world is slowly wearing away. Your treasures: "who can tell who shall gather them?"

So why, old woman, do your eyes still have that glitter of enthusiasm, so full of longing? What are you waiting for now? Will you die with that same quizzical squint, those pursed lips?

UNHAPPINESS: A REPRISE

Kierkegaard's pseudonym argues with some elegance that unhappiness is a failure of recollection or of hope or of both together.

The virtuosos of unhappiness, the unhappiest, bring off the feat of hoping what they ought to be recollecting and recollecting what they ought to be hoping. In our terms this fatal confusion might be expressed formally as a confounding of recollective story and projective scenario.

Such a description of unhappiness is apt to seem overly clever. We can think of more vivid discomforts, things like hunger, pain, want, the death of a friend, disappointment in love, the manifold ills to which flesh is heir. Only an insipid sophistry would propose that human beings might be quite cheerful in face of such sufferings. Yet there is a psychic strength the measure of which is precisely its capacity to cope with suffering and adversity. As the foregoing analysis implies, such psychic strength includes both a strong sense of self-identity, rooted in the past, and an equally strong power of self-transcendence, directed toward the future. This strength must be concentrated in the present, which is the point of tension between self-identity and self-transcendence. The extent to which a person is happy may depend as much on this concentration of strength in the present as it does on circumstances. On the other hand there is an unhappiness that can blight even the most fortunate circumstances. This unhappiness, which is the real subject of "The Unhappiest," is despair. Despair is the refusal of either self-identity or self-transcendence, or both. For the despairing person cannot or will not maintain the tension of this double concentration in the present. In this unhappiness, therefore, either self-recollection is absent, or hope is absent, or both are absent. This unhappiness, in other words, is the absence of self from itself in one of these modes.

Self-knowledge, like all knowledge, is recollection. An appropriation of the past that is not re-collective, integrative, self-discovering, is unhappy, self-vitiating, really a form of despair.

All constructive self-activity directed toward the future is hopeful. All projection into the future that is not hopeful, expectant, oriented to a new horizon of possibility, is unhappy, self-confined, again really a form of despair.

The first type of unhappiness consists in the failure to appropriate my personal past by making a connected, coherent story of it. Of course I cannot fail to have a past, but I can let it be forgotten, or I can actively suppress it, or I can be so intent on my future project that I let my roots in the past grow weak. In either case I lose my identity, having no more of a story than the bare chronicle that appears on my curriculum vitae. But identity, recollected out of the past, is the depth dimension of the self, the psychic resonance that gives it character. A self without a story contracts into the thinness of its personal pronoun.

The second type of unhappiness consists in the failure to pro-ject myself hopefully into the future. I cannot, short of death, fail to have a future, but I can ignore or actively resist its claim and live from day to day without any projective scenario, or I can devote all my energy to protecting and reiterating the identity I have recollected out of the past. In either case I live without risk and without hope, doing only what is necessary to subsist more or less in the manner to which I am accustomed. Here the self loses its adaptive nimbleness, and grows too heavy and dense to improvise.

New variations on the same basic types of unhappiness arise when I wittingly or unwittingly confuse the recollective story with the projective scenario. On the one hand, treating my own past as if it were as indeterminate as the future, my story will be so loose and fragmentary that I cannot recollect myself out of it. I make a fairy tale of my past, and become at best an enigma to myself and others, a creature of uncommitted fantasy.

The reverse of this loss of identity is the loss of possibility entailed in the imposition of the tighter-woven recollective story on my future. Attempting to maintain my self unchanged, I impose the "will" of this self on the future. The unhappiness of that is not that I may fail, but that I may actually succeed. For then I will have locked myself into what is after all a construct recollected from the past. The self becomes its own Frankenstein, a monster of its own making, which exercises its control not only over whatever falls within its orbit as it stalks the earth, but also over its very self. I cannot free myself from the self-image I have created, which becomes more confining the more it succeeds in imposing itself.

Once there was a man who looked in the mirror and liked what he saw. Why this fellow is so fine, he said, that he should control everything around him, beginning with his friends and kinfolk, for their own good. The more the man succeeded, the more he turned into the face in the mirror.

Once there was a man who looked in the mirror and did not like what he saw. So he had no friends or kinfolk, but went about in various fantastic disguises. He succeeded so well in losing himself that he no longer even recognized himself when he looked into the mirror.

Once there was a man who looked in the mirror and did not like what he saw. So he decided to impose it on the world anyway, beginning with his friends and kinfolk, out of sheer spite at having been assigned such a face.

NOTES

1. Here and in further quotations I have revised the translation slightly in the interest of a more literal rendering of the original.

2. A learned endnote informs us that "Anceus, King of Samos, just as he was about to drink the new wine, which the oracle had warned him against tasting, was killed by a wild boar." (Kierkegaard, p. 453)

REFERENCES

Crites, S. (1979). The aesthetics of self-deception. *Sounding*, LXII, 107-129.
Kierkegaard, S. (1959). *Either/Or* (Vol. 1) (D. Swenson and L. Swenson, Trans. with revisions and a foreword by H. Johnson). Princeton: Princeton University Press.

9

Paranoia and
Cataclysmic Narratives

Ernest Keen

Steven Marcus (1984b), writing of Freud and his famous case of Dora (1959a), points out that Freud notes the lapses, the amnesias and paramnesias that sever connections and confuse chronologies. These narrative insufficiencies provide Freud with his crucial clue, implying, in Marcus's words, "that a coherent story is in some manner connected with mental health (at the very least, with the absence of hysteria)." Each of us, mentally healthy or not, has a story. My story differs from yours. My story, my past, present, and future, strung out like a plot, is who I am. It is far from incidental. It is central.

Marcus goes on to say that more is at stake than mental health and illness. He attributes to Freud assumptions which here will become propositions "about the nature of coherence and the form and structure of human life" (p. 61). Freud assumed that human life has coherence – and that coherence, the form and structure of human life – is the form and structure of narrative.

Of course, there are many structures and forms to be seen in human life. Like the physical world it follows physical laws; like the biological world, it tends toward adaptation. But unlike either of these, it has yet another form and structure, which can be seen in (and perhaps only in) the structure of human experience. Human experience is languaged, and that language is narratized. Stephen Crites (1975) has put it this way:

> Even if we grant that we may experience something in the utter absence of language, still, if an experienced present is not simply a dissociated "now" but contains at least a vestige of memory and a leaning into anticipation, then an incipient narrative form will be implicit in it, of which narrative language is the irreducible expression. (P. 32)

In 1963, Northrop Frye argued that there are four basic mythic structures that frame human coherence: Romantic (quest, pilgrimage, to the City of God, classless society, etc.), Comic (progress through evolution or revolution), Tragic (decline and fall), and Ironic (recurrence, or casual catastrophe). This list is a remarkable psychological heuristic. One can almost begin classifying one's friends. Such a view is often called "archetypal," echoing Jung's notion that human meaning has a finite number of crucial forms. But such an argument can also be found in Levi-Strauss's (1962) analysis of cultures and even in Kenneth Burke's *Grammar of Motives* (1945). Hayden White (1978), writing on the writing of history, says:

> Not only are the pregeneric plot-structures by which a set of events can be constituted as stories ... limited in number, as Frye and other archetypal critics suggest, but the encodation of events in terms of such plot-structures is one of the ways that a culture has of making sense of both personal and public pasts. .... the effect of such encodation is to familiarize the unfamiliar, and in general this is the way of historiography, whose "data" are always immediately strange. (P. 49)

White says this of historians, who must make sense of their strange data. But I say this of all of us, who also must make sense of data – data which usually do not seem strange because they are already embedded in a narrative. Strange data are exactly those that fail to fit the narrative frame that gives my life sense and coherence. Further, in my making my experience intelligible, I naturally draw on the cultural stock of stories. My personal story is some version of a more general story of how life proceeds in my culture.

PARANOIA

What is *paranoia*? To say it is a disease is to say no more than how our current political system chooses to handle, and to disguise its handling, of social deviance. This point has been persuasively presented by Szasz (1961), Foucault (1965), Leifer (1969), and Sarbin and Mancuso (1980), among others. At the same time, I believe the word paranoia refers to a phenomenon that coheres, points to a pattern that repeats itself, is reliably discriminable and describable. This is surely not true of all diagnostic language, for example, *schizophrenia*. In any case, diagnosis, and the disease metaphor, do not help us to understand paranoia. So while I believe paranoia is a disease in the limited sense of a distortion of human being, our understanding must reach farther than this metaphor.

Let us therefore think about paranoia in terms of how the paranoid person narratizes his life. If we can describe paranoid narratives, and if narrative is as important to psychology as it seems, then we shall have, in our narrative description, described paranoia. Perhaps we shall have understood what is diseased about paranoia as well.

In order to describe paranoid narratives, we shall have to see them as some version of those narratives that occupy the center of your and my personal lives. The structure of those narratives is experiential, that is, stretched out on a time line that carries not only sequence but also motives, reasons, expectations and memories in some complex but orderly relation that makes our experience cohere. That orderly relation, in turn, the structure of experience itself, is exactly narrative. Experience is put together like a story. Experience has a narrative structure as surely as narrative has an experiential structure.

For this analysis, I would like to propose three polarities that constitute some essential part of the structure of experience – and of narrative. Self and other, good and evil, and past and future are each pairs of touchstones around which my experience is organized. In various ways, the parties to each pair must somehow be mediated, be related, positioned, integrated with one other. As we look at these pairs, at what is at stake in their mediation, how they can go wrong, and how they can go right, we appreciate how the stories we hear, tell, and live do the work of this mediation.

Past and Future

Living through a day is a matter of transforming my expectations into memories, the future into the past. The as-yet unlived future is certainly present as I begin my day; I know, roughly, what is going to happen most of the time. Nevertheless, I know that the future has a kind of openness the past does not have, and that once it passes by me, it too, in becoming past, loses this openness and becomes the stodgy fact of the already-happened.

Its passing by me, of course, is often not a matter of indifference to me, as if I were just watching a movie of my life. Instead I know I affect some portion of the day's events; just what gets inscribed as past is at some crucial junctures up to me. My experience of past and future, then, is an experience of movement, part of which is up to me.

I am never exactly in the past or future themselves, but I am constantly on the edge between them, constantly monitoring and affecting (and effecting) the crucial transformation from future to past.

This experience of being on the edge between future and past is also an adjudication between the expectations that I have and the events as they actually unfold. My relegating events, actions, and experiences to the past is a matter of making sense of them, and the sense I make of them is always according to some plot or story. The memories at the end of the day are a compromise, creatively forged out of the disparate quarters of expectation and perception. Inevitably, the day violates my expectations, it specifies what I only vaguely anticipated, and it inserts unforeseen elements. The memory, a mimesis, refers back both to my preconceptions and to how these had to be refigured and re-emplotted in light of "the new," that which in fact never, ever, happened before. The goals I see, the changes I effect, the causality I grasp all have to be gathered and integrated into a narrative; that gathering and integrating makes sense of them.

Turning to paranoid experience, we can say initially that "the new" is not allowed for. The mimesis is dominated by the expectation, the already formulated emplotment which assimilates everything to its preexisting terms. Unlike ordinary experience, new events, that have never happened before, are not plotted in my experience; the possibility of a future in the usual sense does not exist. The whole that is created at the end of the day is not new. Nothing is new; everything confirms the already established plot.

What does this mean for the experience of being on the edge, between future disappearing under me and past accumulating behind me? The edge, where I have discretion, where I can make a difference, loses an entire dimension of its freedom, namely, its ongoing capacity to refigure and re-emplot and thus to take account of the new. I am still far from disinterested; indeed, my participation in the passage of time becomes even more urgent as the number of plots in which I am involved is reduced to fewer and fewer, and eventually to just one. And yet my range of discretion is also reduced as the single plot takes over my experience. What never happened before, the new, disappears as my mimesis becomes more tightly bound to preconceptions.

Furthermore, that plot becomes not only singular, but singularly tragic. The comic, ironic, and romantic (and other) possibilities for interpreting my life and experience disappear. I am condemned to watch a sequence of events whose conclusion, whose tragic finale, I already know and am powerless to change.

A comparison of paranoid experience with depressive experience is instructive at this point. When I am depressed, I hope for, long for, beg my way into a future. The present is unsatisfactory in comparison to a possibility I can still envision. I may be pessimistic about what will actually happen, but I am not fighting against time, resisting the slipping into the future. That slipping, for the paranoid, is a slipping away of life, the inevitable approach of cataclysm.

I have selected the word "cataclysm" (literally, cata = downward + klyzein = to wash; flood, deluge), as opposed to catastrophe, disaster, or calamity, to refer to that eventuality of evil that has no reckoning, no recognition, no future.

Misfortunes are, of course, to be avoided if possible. If they cannot be avoided, they are to be lived through, survived, and recovered from. The post-disaster time is a time of recovery and rebuilding. If the disaster is a moral atrocity, such as a pogrom or massacre, the time after is a time of moral reckoning. Even in natural disasters, a reckoning follows, a time of understanding what happened, of learning to guard against it in the future, as well as a time of mourning those lost and somehow making their loss meaningful. In all these cases, misfortunes and even calamities are understood as happening within a flow of time that will succeed them. My own death is even an example; if it is a tolerable anticipation at all, it is so because of this time after. I will be remembered "as a good and decent man," etc., etc.

A cataclysm, in contrast, has no after. There is no redeeming social value to the story; it will not be remembered; the suffering is for naught; the loss is absolute. There is no mourning, no analyzing, no commemorating; there is no redemption. This possibility does not even occur to most of us, except in our morbid anticipations of nuclear holocaust. For paranoid experience, it is the only future there is. Not only is there no future, then, for the paranoid, but also the present itself is permeated by the tragic sense in a way far beyond the nonparanoid tragic sense of life. Cataclysm is worse than tragedy, and when I am paranoid, I think cataclysm.

It is important to note that there are many empirical exceptions to this characterization of paranoia. Dr. Schreber, for example, whom I'll discuss below, like many paranoids, changed the content of his delusion over time, initially feeling persecuted by his doctor, later by God, and still later honored by God to give birth to a new race of men. This last is hardly a cataclysmic plot, although cataclysm does appear in earlier versions. Even so, cataclysm is not merely content; it is part of the structure of consciousness of paranoia – a particular futureless future whose importance is not the thematic pessimism as much as the way of "timing" which can affirm a future only by over-affirming it, for example, giving birth to a new race of men. I have never known a paranoid who did not have cataclysmic content, but it is the mediation of past and future, the paranoid way of putting together a coherence, part of which is temporal, that interests us.

Good and Evil

A central issue in this aspect of my experience is the locus of good and especially of evil. The paranoid experience places evil out there, in the world, pressing in on my goodness in here – another vivid contrast with depressive experience, which locates evil in myself. (We must of course note the possibility of the combination, not really rare, of a depressive-paranoid delusion that I am the cause of all the evil and suffering in the world.) In paranoid experience I am at war with the world in the spirit of defending good against evil. Self-righteousness, like a tragic sense of life, appears in more experiences than we would care to call paranoid, but again in paranoia its appearance is special.

Good and evil were surely experiences before they were concepts. Pleasure-pain, clean-dirty, strong-weak, warm-cold, safe-unsafe are all names of early childhood experiences that become welded together in the various alloys of adult morality. The *edge* of temporal experience is given another reference point by this polarity and how we mediate the poles. Good becomes that toward which I am supposed to strive and evil that I am to avoid, making my creation of a past not merely an emplotment but a morality play. Inevitably, good and evil also become parts of myself – my impulses, feelings, thoughts, desires, as well as certainly my past, but also my actions, fantasies, plans – in a word, plots.

Ricoeur, in his exploration of philosophical anthropology (1965), and the place in it of our universal experience of good and especially of evil, asks how we mediate between an ideal of goodness, on the one hand, and the inevitable shortfall of human behavior, on the other. Cultures everywhere have myths, concepts, doctrines, and most obviously stories, that make intelligible to human beings the incommensurability between ethical demand and human performance. These mediations (Ricoeur explores them in depth in his *The Symbolism of Evil*, 1967) are also, of course, personal necessities, and we make sense of our own position in the framework of good and evil by adopting some version of a cultural story.

We can say, then, that paranoid stories are usually not cultural, that is, not shared by members of the culture who, like their fellow human beings, must mediate between good and evil in themselves and their world. Paranoid stories emplot a tragic slipping into the cataclysm in which good "in here" is finally wiped out by evil "out there." This plot is hardly a recognizable version of a myth for a culture.

However, the fifteenth century, Foucault (1965) tells us, was the scene of the simultaneous stories of reason and death – the latter being a kind of underground, counter-story that nevertheless was visible in the literature, art, and social institutions of the day. At times it became rampant.

> Up to the second half of the Fifteenth Century, or even a little beyond, the theme of death reigns alone. The end of men, the end of time bears the face of pestilence and war. What overhangs human existence is this conclusion and this order from which nothing escapes. (P. 15)

Foucault's point is that madness comes to substitute for death in this counter-story in the sixteenth century. For our point here, the important thing is that such a "paranoid" story is a counter-story, the dark side of a main stream. Counter-stories, of course, are not necessarily false just because they are "counter." Might contemporary paranoid experiences bear the same relation to mainstream culture? Might our current cataclysmic visions of nuclear holocaust be a cultural version of what appears to us as the private derangement of paranoid cataclysmic narratives?

A final feature of the good-evil polarity is the issue of dissimulation, where evil masquerades as good, thus pushing the nub of the problem from a matter of will ("Can I be good?") to a matter of truth ("What is good, finally?"). Stories solve this problem. In saying this, I mean that everyone has this problem and everyone solves this problem by subscribing to a story. Even in our current period of rationalism, where universal and timeless principles are the touchstones of truth, stories, which are particular (not universal) and temporal (not timeless), are absolutely vital parts of our culture and our lives – particularly our cultural notions of truth and most particularly the truth of good and evil. Even the demythologizing efforts of rationalist scholars participate in a cultural story of mankind's progressive approximation of truth by overcoming superstition, and a personal story of oneself as a hero in that dramatic episode.

Self and Other

We turn now to the celebrated aloneness of the paranoid. We are not, in our everyday lives, lonely in the way paranoid persons are lonely. I am lonely when I miss my beloved, when I'm in a strange city, or when I mourn. I am lonely when everyone else is engaged with someone, and I have no one, or when no one understands or cares about me. But paranoid loneliness is more profound. It does not merely suffer a deprivation; it affirms it, asserts it, even creates it and defends it. Loneliness is not temporary; it is a permanent given. I do not long for contact with others; I want simply to be left alone. This loneliness cuts more deeply into my ordinary sense of life than the word "lonely" usually covers, and it suggests that self-other is also mediated in a particular way in paranoia.

Being alone or not alone is partly a matter of sharing with an other crucial stories about life and truth. Further, the paranoid experience is one that does not share the crucial stories. Years ago, Cameron (1943) described the communicative isolation of the paranoid as central in the development and maintenance of delusions. This view has been supplemented by Lemert (1962), who described the way we exclude those already in communicative isolation, thus making the sharing of stories even more unlikely.

This feature of the paranoid experience has profound implications, for our sharing a story is such a basic element of life that only the most extreme effort of imagination can indicate what it is like not to do so. Even in the bitterest of wars, combatants share the story of the war; they may kill one another, and even hope to kill one another's stories (which is much harder), but even the single theme of your life or mine becomes a shared story which, in weird, apparently irrational ways, surfaces as a note of respect across the battlelines.

Recall that the new, in temporal experience, violates my expectations and forces me continually to refigure the plots I live. Such a refiguring, my constant activity, gives life its growth and movement. Being open to such a task is no more than being a conscious human being, but such an openness is absolutely vital to that consciousness even as consciousness is the necessary conduit of that openness. Without it, my consciousness becomes less adaptive (to say the least) and less human (to say the most). The new, therefore, supplies my life with its fuel for growth, its vital intake of stuff not itself in order to be more than mere repetition. It makes me create as well as merely monitor the stories of life.

Similarly, the other, who is not myself, is a vital source of stuff not myself that makes me grow and keeps me alive. The otherness of the other is crucial, of course; he or she must transcend my self in order to provoke my creativity. But that otherness cannot be absolute. I must have a common ground in order to take the other seriously; I have to share some story or else I would see the other as alien, threatening, fearsome, and dangerous. Paranoid aloneness deprives its carrier of the growth that comes from taking an other seriously. But what is at stake here is not just learning something; what is at stake is letting the other be other, which makes it possible for him or her to be a self, and letting that otherness matter for me, which forces me to create, and continually recreate, myself.

Our accumulating propositions are as follows. First, extreme experiences, like those we call paranoid, differ from our usual lives in ways that throw into relief some of the structure of ordinary, usual life. Second, some of that structure may be stated in terms of polarities I constantly mediate: past-future, good-evil, and self-other. Third, stories mediate, in every case. Fourth, the particular structure of that experience we call paranoia can be described in terms of the particular way paranoid stories mediate the polarities. These are, fifth, that paranoid emplotments position past and future with respect to one another by virtue of a coming cataclysm; sixth, that paranoid emplotments construe good and evil in such a way that the world cannot be trusted; and seventh, that paranoid emplotments cut the paranoid off from that vital completion of self that can come only from the creation and recreation of self forced on us by an other.

We may say, in summary, that it is the story, in each case, that counts. If we are justified at all in calling certain experiences, persons, or lives paranoid, then our justification comes from the kinds of narratives paranoids live, which are discriminably different from what we cheerfully refer to as normal.

COHERENCE

If this is true, then we might turn again to what Steven Marcus referred to as "the nature of coherence and the form and structure of human life" – not, we must modestly note, a small topic . . . but also not, I would argue, one that can be ignored. For it is exactly at this level that I can see the paranoid clearly, and how he differs from myself. The nature of coherence *is* the narrative structure of experience; the form and structure of human life *is* the experiential structure of narrative. Narrative, experience, coherence, structure, form, human life – these are a family of concepts, of phenomena and apparitions of concepts, a family the understanding of any member of which is requisite to understanding any other member or the collection as a whole.

The methodology of these remarks begins with the whole, human experience, and construes these various terms (structure, narrative, etc.) as aspects, aspects that are partial because of the perspective of the various terms, not parts that are separate and fit together. Certainly they are not parts that occur in a causal sequence, which is the most common way to do psychology in this century. This chapter tends to move between parts and wholes differently. The family is wholistic; the polarities described earlier, to which the whole is a response, are not causes. They are analytic units at a more specific level of analysis, but a level that is no closer to clinical data than the whole. Both narrative (the whole) and good-evil (a part) are equally present in the data. Neither is more abstract or inferred.

I would like now to argue for this bundle of claims (about coherence, form, human life, etc.) by turning to the most famous case of paranoia extant, that of Dr. Daniel Paul Schreber, first written by Schreber himself (1903), then analyzed by Freud (1959b), and reanalyzed many times. I will concentrate on Freud's analysis and reinterpretations by Keen (1970) and Schatzman (1973). I will conclude that all these interpretations have merit but that, in every case, the crucial role of narrative is overlooked, and furthermore, when that role is stated it clarifies the particular interpretation.

As sensitive as Freud was to narrative in his concrete approach to patients, his theorizing never focused on narrative and remained instead locked in a pattern of expression borrowed from physics. After reporting Schreber's stories and pointing with fascination to their oddities and their typicality, Freud's interpretation debauches into psychodynamics, which are envisioned as causal antecedents to the narratives espoused and lived by the floridly psychotic Schreber. The defensive distortions of the basic homosexual wish transform "I love him" into "I hate him," "I love her," "She loves her," "He hates me," and so on. Psychodynamics change plots. It is plots that are at stake throughout. It is really plots that Freud understands.

Of Schreber's cataclysmic delusion, Freud (1959b) says: "The end of the world is the projection of this internal catastrophe; for his subjective world has come to an end since he has withdrawn his love from it" (pp. 456-457). Freud is saying here that the internal psychodynamic event came first and the manifest narrative content followed as a projective result. What would be changed in this formulation if we were to say that the breakdown of the narrative (the seeing of cataclysm) caused the psychodynamic catastrophe (loss of love for the world)? Either sequence conceals the best formulation, namely, that the distribution of my love and the narrative of my life are part of one another. We may in fact guess that Freud's devaluing the narrative theoretically, even though he took it quite seriously practically, expresses the rhetorical style of the times more than it expressed Freud's insight.

One more example: "The delusion-formation, which we take to be a pathological product, is in reality an attempt at recovery, a process of reconstruction" (p. 457). Freud here glimpses the narratizing of the human mind as healing, although the process can, and for Schreber, did go awry. But the narrative aspects of this attempt at recovery, and of what went awry, is overlooked. A cataclysmic narrative is the result of narratizing *nothingness*, emplotting in the absence of the future, in the absence of that part of human experience that leads narrative on, gives it direction and force, that part of human experience and of narrative necessary for a human life to have meaning. The cataclysmic outcome appears pathological, to be sure, but the failure of self-healing lies in the absence of a future, which in terms of human meaning (that is, in terms of narrative) can only be a cataclysm.

In 1970, I reinterpreted Schreber's life in terms of possibilities and necessities (Keen, 1970). Eschewing the physicalistic theorizing of Freud's psychodynamic theory, I interpreted Schreber's delusion that he had been selected by God to satisfy God's voluptuous sensations. I saw the delusion as a desperate attempt to reconstruct an "existential platform," a place of standing, some assumptions about life and truth and self upon which one can stand.

In the absence of an existential platform, one has only experiential chaos and panic (as in an acute psychotic crisis). All existential platforms construe some things as under my control and in the realm of the possible, and other things as given to me from without and in the realm of the necessary. We usually envision a range of possibilities within a framework of necessities; I can be a vegetarian or beef eater, but I cannot live unless I eat; I can become wise or foolish, but I cannot avoid becoming older.

Schreber's delusion, from this perspective, is an attempt to avoid the panic of an acute psychotic crisis, engendered by the breakdown of his existential platform, and by the construction of another one. It is pathological because it places the greatest power (he was God's lover, not a neighbor's lover) with the greatest powerlessness (he was selected; he had no choice) side by side, not really integrated but rather jammed together in a fashion different from, and alien to, the usual understanding of possibility and necessity in polite society.

As in the case of Freud's analysis, this interpretation is less wrong than it is incomplete. What is missing is the narrative aspects of the delusion, which expresses the temporality (past-future), the morality (good-evil), and the sociality (self-other) of human experience. Existential platform is a nice concept in contrast to the free-fall of nothingness and panic, but it completely misses the temporal, moral, and social aspects of experience – aspects which are at once fundamental to human experience and invariably expressed in terms of narrative. Having been chosen by God to fulfill His voluptuous sensations, the outcome of which is to bear a new race of men – this is a past and a future, a self and an other, a good and an evil, in a word, it is a plot, a narrative. This is not to deny that it is also an existential platform but it is to say what more it is and what it is more specifically.

Finally, Schatzman's (1973) reinterpretation of Schreber was written in light of a careful study of Schreber's father's theories of childrearing – theories that were well known in bourgeois Germany, for they were widely read and followed. Their author was widely respected. The fact that his older son committed suicide and the younger son became the most famous psychiatric case of several decades did not diminish the high esteem in which German parents held the senior Dr. Schreber's doctrines.

Their flavor is one of a military campaign against "rotten spots" in the soul of the child, which, if left unattended, will "eat away, and the roots get so strong" that the "deeply dormant weeds of the soul will in earlier or later life easily become dangerous" (quoted in Schatzman, p. 143). This strident program for childrearing included various braces, straps, and other paraphernalia for assuring good posture and persevering discipline. Exercises and routines all supported the central tenet of absolute obedience to the parent, which Schreber simply believed was necessary protection against vague and ubiquitous evil that besets those not rigorously trained.

Being a child under this regimen is for most of us barely imaginable. Schatzman sees the program, and its author, as paranoidogenic, and he argues his case carefully and persuasively. Again eschewing the physicalistic language of Freud, and here preferring the language of interpersonal communication, Schatzman reconstructs the processes and understandings between father and son as ones in which (1) the parent persecutes the son (in zealous opposition to evil), but (2) insists that the son experience this persecution as love, which (3) forces the child to misinterpret his own experience and (4) to conceal from himself that he is doing so.

Such persecution goes on, we can surely say from the older Schreber's published program and its popularity. Some children suffered it and were, or are, doubly victimized into misinterpreting their own experience. They are, then, persecuted but do not know it. What appears later as a delusion may be the person's attempt to deal with what he knows (that he was persecuted) but also has been prevented from knowing. And he may then perpetrate on his progeny the same strident campaign against unseen evils deep in the human soul – evils which, if not rigidly constrained, threaten to destroy the fabric of the world built on their containment.

Schatzman's very suggestive thought here becomes much more vivid when the narrative properties of the communication are made explicit. The childrearing practices communicate a world design, and a set of possibilities, a definition of good and evil, and a model of human relationships, not to mention multiple images and slogans, all of which are not listed as much as they are enacted. And they are organized in both their presentation and recollection in terms of narratives. I do not mean only fairy stories and morality tales; I mean also the daily object lessons, disciplines and punishments, whose meaning is related to one's action and oneself in the fashion of a *denouement*.

Schatzman concludes that paranoia is "hereditary" not via genes but "by each generation teaching the next one to fear certain possibilities of the mind." When such fears are taught, they are taught through cultural narratives, narratives of which we eventually assume ourselves to be a part, and narratives some specific version of which we aspire to enact.

These considerations do not argue for a single best interpretation of Schreber or even of the life of paranoia. Rather they suggest that the narrative is the mode of articulation that best captures in each case the interpretation offered. If narrative has this facility, then what was understood by Freud, by Keen, and by Schatzman was really the narrative properties of the person of Schreber, even though the various theoretical languages used failed to make this clear. It is really plots that Freud understood because understanding stories is how human beings understand one another. It is really narratives that protect us from the panic of nothingness, for they formulate a future without which human experience would have no hope. It is really narratives that are taught as I pass my culture on to my children – even as I pass my psychopathology on to them.

This line of thought then bears on the nature of coherence and the form and structure of human life. Narrative surfaces here as an inescapable "form" of the "coherence" or the "structure" of human life. When we understand someone, we understand his or her stories; when one's stories are obscure, the person is misunderstood or incomprehensible. Psychologists have always relied on stories. Through them alone does the human bespeak herself or himself.

THE COHERENCE OF CATACLYSMIC NARRATIVES

Narratives enliven our lives; their projection into a future, which is shared by others and sees the possibility of good surviving evil, is exactly the projective thrust built into human experience. These elements (among others) produce coherence. The experience of being human is a coherent experience and an experience of coherence.

Being on the edge between the arriving future and the disappearing past not only makes life tolerable but itself is tolerable because, and only because, there is a future. That future makes even my death tolerable. People will remember me. Their memory, anticipated by me now, extends my life beyond the point of my death, and softens the uncompromising inevitability of death.

In cataclysm, I lose the future, and the edge I am on is the gaping emptiness of nothingness, an experience more devastating than my personal death, for the softening, made possible by the future, has been washed away by cataclysm.

This future is not only a theme – the future time of the lives of those around me, who will remember me. This future is also part of the structure of my experience, its narrative structure, which builds a future into the present no matter how close I am to death. And it does this exactly because my life's narrative is also intertwined with the narratives of those around me, and with the more or less public narrative we share. The other's consciousness of me and the future's redeeming of the present are part of each other. They are built fundamentally into my experience – and they are lost in cataclysm.

The narrative of cataclysm therefore articulates thematically the futurelessness and the loneliness of paranoia. This narratizing effort attempts to mediate past and future, good and evil, self and other, and it fails on all three counts. The future cannot redeem us, good will not survive evil, and my loneliness will not be healed. The loss of time passing will not be compensated, the possibility of good coming through evil times is closed, and the fulfilling, yea even saving contact with others will not materialize. Cataclysm thematizes nothingness and, as a narrative, embodies it structurally as well. The present is not going anywhere, good has no chance of survival, and the contact with others that makes life liveable is simply absent.

What kind of coherence, then, is this experience we call paranoia? It fails to mediate past-future, good-evil, and self-other, and thus it fails, we may say, to be coherent. Indeed, those failures do justify our seeking to change, to heal, and to prevent paranoia. And yet we see in paranoid narratives, perhaps in the failures as efforts toward coherence, something crucial about nonparanoid experience, that is, its coherence and how it is created by mediating the polarities. And we see the effort, the struggle toward coherence. Schreber's most floridly insane moments were still attempts to create coherence.

Why do they fail? Is there some change in the structure of experience such that the futureless narrative can only come out cataclysmically? Exactly what change makes cataclysm the narrative result? Nothingness seems to loom up and finally to permeate experience. But what is nothingness? Indeed, naming it is merely negative, and other articulations of it seem best to resort to narratives of cataclysm. To say that something called "nothingness" lies behind cataclysm falsifies both. Cataclysm articulates nothingness, and there is no better definition or articulation than cataclysmic narrative.

There is, then, a certain coherence even to this articulation. The paranoid does not merely surrender to chaos and panic. He or she struggles to build a narrative that will articulate his or her experience sufficiently that it can be experienced, that it will register, fit in, make sense, and even ground a life. But the coherence of the cataclysmic narrative is a building without a foundation. There is no future, no other, no good upon which to build, and so life hovers, threatening to rush toward an absolute and irredeemable end.

Our best grasp of the paranoid experience comes to us, I think, in our own contemplations of nuclear holocaust. This capability, perhaps available to us now for the first time in several centuries, is not pathological in a clinical sense. The event is an actual possibility and our anticipation of it a cultural possibility. As such, it loses some of its "pathology" in being shared. But not all. The loss of hope, of future, and the living of cataclysm can be a cultural pathology. What happens to a culture whose technical capability to end life forever generates such a cataclysmic narrative? We ought to worry about widespread hopelessness and the human propensity for self-fulfilling prophesy. What therapy is available to an entire civilization?

Superficial affirmations of optimism do not help, for the counter-narrative, as in the fifteenth century counter-narrative of death, thrives amidst such noise and eventually embodies itself in human action. I do not have an answer. But I do believe that the paranoid, in his glimpse of, then his surrender to, nothingness, and yet his struggle to sustain a narrative, nonetheless, embodies something of all our lives in this violent and possibly cataclysmic century.

REFERENCES

Burke, K. (1945). *A grammar of motives.* Englewood Cliffs, NJ: Prentice-Hall.
Cameron, N. (1943). The paranoid pseudocommunity. *American Journal of Sociology,* 49, 32-38.
Crites, S. (1975). Angels we have heard. In J. B. Wiggens (Ed.). *Religion as story* (pp. 29-50). New York: Harper.
Foucault, M. (1965). *Madness and civilization.* New York: Random House.
Freud, S. (1959a). Fragment of an analysis of a case of hysteria. In A. and J. Strachey (Trans.). *Sigmund Freud: Collected papers* (pp. 13-146). New York: Basic Books.
Freud, S. (1959b). Psycho-analytic notes upon an autobiographical case of paranoia. In A. and J. Strachey (Trans.). *Sigmund Freud: Collected papers* (pp. 387-470). New York: Basic Books.
Frye, N. (1963). New directions from old. In N. Frye, *Fables of identity.* New York: Harcourt, Brace, and World.
Keen, E. (1970). *Three faces of being: Toward an existential clinical psychology.* New York: Appleton-Century-Crofts.
Leifer, R. (1969). *In the name of mental health.* New York: Science House.
Lemert, E. M. (1962). Paranoia and the dynamics of exclusion. *Sociometry,* 25, 2-20.
Levi-Strauss, C. (1962). *The savage mind.* London: Wiedenfeld and Nicolson.
Marcus, S. (1984a). Freud and the rat man. In S. March, *Freud and the culture of psychoanalysis* (pp. 87-164). Winchester, MA: George Allen and Unwin.
Marcus, S. (1984b). Freud and Dora: Story, history, case history. In S. Marcus, *Freud and the culture of psychoanalysis* (pp. 42-86). Winchester, MA: George Allen and Unwin.
Ricoeur, P. (1965). *Fallible man: Philosophy of the will* (C. Kelbley, Trans.). Chicago: Henry Regenery.
Ricoeur, P. (1967). *The symbolism of evil* (E. Buchanan, Trans.). New York: Harper and Row.
Sarbin, T. R. and Mancuso, J. C. (1980). *Schizophrenia: Medical diagnosis or moral verdict.* New York: Pergamon.
Schatzman, M. (1973). *Soul murder: Persecution in the family.* New York: Random House.
Schreber, D. P. (1903). *Denkwurdigkeiten eines nervenkranken.* Leipzig: Schloss.
Szasz, T. S. (1961). *The myth of mental illness.* New York: Hoeber Harper.
White, H. (1978). The historical text and literary artifact. In R. H. Canary and H. Kozicki (Eds.), *The writing of history* (pp. 41-62). Madison, WI: University of Wisconsin Press.

PART IV

Constructing and Deconstructing Self-Narratives

10

The Narrative in Psychoanalysis: Psychoanalytic Notes on Storytelling, Listening, and Interpreting

Frederick Wyatt

In taking up the adoption of a fashionable term in psychoanalysis, narrative, one has reason to ask: what is so new about it? What will help us to conceptualize our subject more parsimoniously, to understand it more profoundly, and to connect it in all its variations before we extoll it as a promising new acquisition? The fact is that psychoanalysts have known all along that we are dealing in stories and with stories all the time; that we offer ourselves to listen to stories and thereby call them forth; and that through a method contrived for this purpose we can carry listening to a point where it transforms storytelling into the life history of a person. The unreflected life may not necessarily be an unlived life; but it surely will be an inarticulate and very vulnerable life, especially when powerful traditions no longer have the power to bind it and hold it together. The psychoanalytic method, interpretation, thus may do more than assist needy storytellers in learning to come to themselves. Interpretation establishes a viable context between a person's past experiences and his engagements in the here-and-now. Even more astounding, interpretation establishes a context between the psychic origins and development of the individual and his present personality organization. We may therefore claim that people, once they perceive our readiness to listen, seek us out because of an inner unrest: they know they carry stories with them, inside as it were, stories that prompt them to become storytellers, to narrate stories that want to be told as in that magnificent paradigm of the analytic process, Pirandello's *Six Characters in Search of an Author.*

In spite of our established role as hermeneutic listeners to people wanting to tell it all – *hermeneutic* because we promise to help them bear these stories in two distinct senses of the word – we may have something to gain by recognizing the role of the narrative in psychoanalysis. A renowned psychologist, E. G. Boring, in an address two generations ago scored psychoanalysis and related endeavors in psychology as "the more conversational brands of psychology."[1] Having been a needy storyteller of inarticulate psychosomatic stories himself (Boring and Sachs, 1940) he still could not acquiesce to the personal context psychoanalysis proffered, holding implacably for the promised land of science to be attained in the psychological laboratory. In spite of this rebuff he inadvertently paid psychoanalysis the compliment of establishing the relationship of the narrative to psychology.

The issue of the concept "narrative" will in any case remind psychoanalysts of the close kinship of the concept to other subjects such as literature and history, a kinship the more physiological or the more sociological psychoanalysts seem to spurn or to overlook. This neglect is quite strange for the kinship between psychoanalysis and literature is so obvious that Freud and the early generations of his students accepted it like a gift, an endless treasure-trove of stimulation and confirmation. Similarly with history, though it took a little longer for the systematic application of psychoanalysis to historiography (Wyatt, 1959; 1963; 1969). Yet it is clear, that even the traditional history "from above" is an enormous collection of life stories with all the problems inherent in such narratives (Stone, 1979), but also with a literally unending procession of destinies and their twists and turns, that is, with a profusion of real life.

Let us accept then the narrative as a psychoanalytic *familiar.* The double meaning of familiar is, tongue-in-cheek, intended; because as will soon become clear, it also holds potential dangers for the psychoanalyst and even more for the act of collaboration in psychoanalysis, involving as it does, not only the fancies of one, but the productive, if risky cooperation of two people over a long time. It *is* a potential danger to become spellbound by the idea that the narrative is the essence of psychoanalysis and that, as psychoanalysts, we listen to stories without end and meet their fancies with our own. Listening to stories is not enough, however. Listening to what stories and for what purpose? And to what end? Are all stories equal, or is narrative a particularly elementary form of organization, not more and not less, a term which at this point leaves much to be defined? Nor is it clear from the outset, *what* the psychoanalyst should or can do with the stories of his patients. What in psychoanalysis has special bearing on listening to stories, on drawing them out and finally on interpreting them? What is interpretation and what is it good for? Some of these questions I should like to examine in the following remarks, especially those aspects of psychoanalysis which matter in the transformation of stories in the psychoanalytic process. What is the fundamental orientation, or attitude of the psychoanalyst when he listens to stories? What of the interlocking system, of the rather arcane-sounding theorems in psychoanalysis which are activated or realized in dialogue with an analysand, that is to say, in the realization of his stories? For it is clear at the outset that stories or narrative are somehow jointly produced, and not by the patient alone, as it might appear on first glance; but *between* patient and therapist through a subtle and elusive interaction of the two.

The idea that psychoanalysis draws from the narrative, as I said before, was not voiced in the earlier writings on psychoanalysis. Instead, it is conventional for psychoanalysts to speak of the "materials" of psychoanalysis – a fatal term when one acknowledges its lifeless and impersonal sound. Materials are produced or mined, then they are worked upon, and product is made of them. With such a conception there is little room for interaction. The analyst as *homo faber* determines the analytic process and gives the product its final shape. This formula may be suitable for plastics, but not for the rehabilitation or reeducation of persons, and especially not for the restoration of their autonomy from self-estrangement.

Recently there has been a movement to stress the narrative in psychoanalysis, a movement given form mostly by the writings of Donald Spence (1982) and Roy Schafer (1983). Their emphasis is on the distinction between historical truth and narrative truth, or *validity* of the life-data recovered, on which any claim to the reconstruction of these histories must necessarily stand. The original attitude, as we know, was that of a somewhat naive faith that the analysand is holding the truth locked in himself. If properly assisted in its unlocking he will be able to recover that truth in the end. Only late in his creative career did Freud cast doubt on the recoverability of the repressed; he even went so far as to suggest that the individual past, instead of being recovered, might have to be *reconstructed* (Freud, 1959). He observed that the events of childhood as reconstructed in analysis effectively take the place of the remembered events. He touched thereby not merely on one but on several fundamental problems of psychoanalytic epistemology.

(1) The belief in the preservation of the repressed and the forgotten, which, like the treasure in the fairy tale, is only waiting to appear again and be recovered is suspect. But *if* it cannot be recovered, and *if*, instead, it can with some effort be replaced by a conclusion just as contemporaneous as the analytic process itself, this assumption must surely be modified. For then the past can no longer be thought of as preserved, locked away like the treasures and tell-tales in a pharaoh's tomb, or, like the Dead Sea Scrolls, waiting in their caves to be recovered and read. We are compelled to conceive of the past as not literally preserved. The past cannot be said to *be*. Instead, we should say rather the past is *made* whenever it is reconstructed. The epistemological change of perspective from a past waiting to be discovered, to a past reconstructed right now in the light of present consciousness (Wyatt, 1963), obviously signifies a fundamental reorientation.

(2) If the independence of analytic *material* can be efficiently replaced by a suggestion of the analyst, which, in turn, is based on the preceding interchange between analysand and analyst, then the whole idea of patient's material is specious. Then there is no such thing as material, unless the term be used to cover everything the analyst can observe of the regularities and repetitions in the analysands and their interaction over many hours.

(3) With the premise that reconstruction replaces recovery, the entire theory of psychoanalytic treatment must be re-thought. We cannot easily speak of the healing effect of the recovery of the repressed, when what seems to matter more is meaningful coherence.

(4) If the past cannot always be retrieved, and if the retrieval of the past is more frequently achieved with the help of reconstruction, then, as acknowledged before, we are up against the question: what would the retrievable past be like? Is there such a thing? The German historian Ranke once wrote that it is the task of history to establish "wie es denn eigentlich gewesen," how it really, authentically, veritably, was when it happened. Since then it has turned out that we can, at best, hope to put into the coherence of a meaningful narrative what documentary evidence we have of that past: testimony of eyewitnesses; artifacts; institutional

changes; and, last but not least, those consequences which we need to explain to ourselves as having followed from preceding events.

Concerning the testimony of eyewitnesses, we surely must assume that it is as biased and limited by the geographical and social locus of the eyewitnesses as we know ourselves to be; biased, last but not least, by their particular persuasion, their orientation in the world, and their ideology mostly without even being aware of their bias. Mark Twain, that keen observer of human foibles and pious fraud, reminds us that the very ink with which historians write "is merely fluid prejudice." The report of eyewitnesses and contemporaries, in other words, is a narrative and not the historical truth, a concept which quickly shows itself to be a many-splendored thing, but extremely vague and uncertain in what it really is supposed to mean. Historical truth can only be an approximation, not to a real object, the past (which nobody can reproduce so that we might judge which of our conclusions are veridical and which are not) but to a plausible conjunction of all available data about the event to be studied. In that instance data are to be understood not as particularly hard and fast, but as reports and things pertaining in some way to the object of study. The conjunction itself will obviously depend on viewpoints and categories held *in the present moment,* not in the past, and will therefore have to be modified whenever newer viewpoints arise. For example, whatever the people in the thirteenth and the fourteenth centuries made of the epidemics they called "the plague," they did not and could not think of the slow migration of rodents from east to west, rodents which happened to be suitable hosts to a certain type of flea which, in turn, was a suitable host to the plague bacillus. Conceivably, we may yet be up to discovering changes in immunity and resistance to infection dependent on ecological factors or, conversely, on changes in the virulence of microorganisms not recognized before. When changes are systematically elaborated, they may unexpectedly throw new light on the events and traumata of that period, and thus compel modification of the historical narrative.

Artifacts would make good data if we but knew what their particular meaning was for their contemporaries and users. When we put them in context, we again have to fill an empty historical space with conjecture, and link what we have to what we presume to know about the period in question. In other words, we have to put the putative significance of artifacts into a *narrative context* – coins, statues, warrior's gear. Consider the various meanings of the relatively profuse sampling of neolithic figurines, of which one of the earlier ones is known as *Venus of*

Willendorf. Were they fertility symbols in a ritualistic context, or something in the nature of worry beads, or a viable form of domestic pornography?

The same questions apply to institutional events. Was the expulsion of the Jews from Spain after the *reconquista* a consequence of the Jingoism inescapable when war efforts are mounted over many centuries until their successful conclusion? Successful, that is, at least in terms of the ideology of the conquerors. Or was it a useful move in strengthening the authority of the crown against feudal barons and jealous allies; or was it a burst of irrationalism caused, among other things, by social and economic changes and brought on by imperceptible tensions in the psychological balance of a society? The consequent exclusion and suppression of a segment of the population must have amounted to a severe social disruption. It does not seem that anybody living at that time and in that place was aware of the sociological and institutional issues. They could be introduced only by historians quite a few centuries after the fact (Wyatt, 1963).

The conclusion is inescapable that the past is retrieved only in bits and pieces, the weight and validity of which diminishes, the further back the past has slid. There is no "eigentlich Gewesenes," no "how, exactly, it was" in Ranke's sense. Epistemologically speaking, the past is a *borderline concept.* There must be a "has been," but only as a necessary assumption, an extension of reasoning about the present, forcefully supported, of course, by the intense and enduring universal experience of "I am continuous," and "I have a past like every other person," yet a specific and singular one that only I can remember. How reliably I can remember is a very different and challenging question.

How reliably I really *can* remember depends, according to what has just been said, on my inter- and intra-personal variability in remembering. The validity of my rememberings again rests on a number of basic propositions. For instance, how much can the sense of continuity be trusted? It persists rather obviously as a belief in having been continuous as a matter of course, rather than on the actual continuity of memories. All my memories unmistakably are *my* memories. The feeling "that was I" is simply a central and inalienable part of them. That is where continuity resides. On further reflection, however, that past "I" sometimes seems to belong to a rather strange fellow. From the vantage point of the present it is by no means easy always to identify with him. He may not even bear much immediate relationship to the next consecutive memory in time, although that, too, has the byline "that was

I." Continuity thus is as much as *reparative reconstruction* as it is an elementary condition of remembering. It may also be motivated by the wish to be continuous, as one would conclude from the intense anxiety when that continuity is thwarted or when, suddenly, the past appears to be fragmented and the will which, until now, succeeded in pulling it all together, is in jeopardy. The reluctance of psychoanalysts to face such conundrums shows up in the credulity of many psychoanalytic narratives and in the rather extensive confusion about the logical (or veridical) status of the life history and its meaning (Schafer, 1983; Spence, 1982).

Historians and psychoanalysts have in common the creation of unified narratives. Historians write collective, or political, or social histories; psychoanalysts, personal histories. Both kinds of narratives come into being in the process of putting together more elementary bits and pieces, the historical elements of research, of which we spoke before, and the individual fragments our patients present to us. As they deal with events and states of mind and moods, we may reasonably liken them to tales. These tales may not be shaped in the same way as tales that are created for the purposes of entertainment, especially when analysis has progressed and when transference has become a joint concern; but they are still sufficiently similar so that one can say that in one important respect at least, their aims are consistent.

That the storyteller of psychoanalysis may not be aware of the true complexity of his aims makes no difference. In fact, the reporters and tale-bearers of historiography do not seem to be more aware of their subjective aims and attitudes; neither are the novelists and dramatists – the writers of fictional stories – as we can see when we scrutinize their texts with appropriate care.

Psychoanalytic experience, including the skillful use of empathy, is inevitably acquired in conjunction with, and under the guidance of, psychoanalytic theory. It is born of the expectation that psychoanalytic theory will manifest itself in the tales of the analysand and prove itself in the connections established between the recurrent themes of these tales. Inevitable, too, this situation leads to a critical ambiguity in the analyst, a kind of unintended duplicity. The listening analyst should be unprejudiced to the point of self-denial – for it is surely the indispensable condition of analytic empathy that it be as uncommitted and undirected as possible. On the other hand, the analyst is supposed to be vigilant as to hints and recurrences to similarities and correspondences, ready to relate them to the established fundus of psychoanalytic observation and theory. At the same time he should not be drawn unawares into settling on preconceived notions. Psychoanalytic writing is full of the shards of mass-produced idols of the day – theoretical presumptions, as it were, enforced out of hand, and out of mindless predilection. The clanking, mechanical quality of ever so many interpretations in psychoanalysis is due to this liability – but how to avoid it?

Listening in psychoanalysis is supposed to be of a special kind, "with the third ear," as Reik suggested. It does appear sometimes that one listens, or is being listened to, more searchingly than anywhere in life, which may indeed be the existential distinction of psychoanalysis in a time of hypertrophied and therefore debased communication. The silence of the analyst, at any rate, has provided one of the stock occasions for jokes, gags, and humorous anecdotes about psychoanalysis.

In spite of all the patient waiting and listening of the analyst there is something in his attitude which goes beyond mere listening and passive availability. The listening analyst silently conveys a demand and transmits the message: "I'm here to activate stories and induce their telling!" He broadcasts on an inaudible frequency: "More! Go on! There is much more to tell about all this!" The attentive listening of the analyst, one could say, draws the stories out of their hide-away, from the recesses of the client's past, draws them toward himself and into articulation. To put it differently, expectant listening seems to be an indigenous part of all stories or narratives. In the analytic process, at any rate, the stories would not progress beyond the inchoate and fragmentary stage, would never grow into an increasingly authentic presentation of self, without the prompting of the analyst. *Active listening*, as described, leads to, but should nevertheless be distinguished from, *active intervention*. The latter is generated by active listening. Interventions in their continuity will connect listening, the stories told (narrative) and interpretation. If all goes well, they will make an approximately authentic *personal history* out of groping and defensive story elements.

Psychoanalytic theory presents itself as a uniquely complex system of "Instincts and their Vicissitudes" as Freud (1925) called it in an important essay. It treats of the development of consciousness of self, its structure and its confines. The variety of contemporary schools in psychoanalysis may easily confuse, to say nothing of the changes in the development of the corpus of psychoanalytic theory where new observations and conceptualizations gingerly and retroactively revise old principles. When these new conceptualizations are applied or even appealed to in a contemporary context, their meanings are different from their original meanings. This process goes unnoticed most of the time even though it is countermanded by frequent reference to Freud's own writings – as if the analyst pleading his point wanted to assert that Freud could have meant this or that only in the sense the contemporary psychoanalyst wants to understand it.

THE PSYCHOANALYST'S SET TO LISTEN

Fortunately, something lies *before* and *above* psychoanalytic theory proper, Freudian and contemporary: the basic orientation, a way of listening and organizing. I should like to call it the *psychoanalyst's set*. There is nothing new to it. Any psychoanalytic clinician will subscribe to it as a matter of course and without being especially aware of it. This may be the reason why so little has been written about the essentials of clinical psychoanalytic procedure as distinguished from theory and system. I believe, this set-to-listen-and-organize describes the orientation and basic attitude of the psychoanalyst more accurately than elaborate theory. I note six features.

(1) Consider the distinction of latent and manifest significance which coincides with the hypothesis of unconscious motives. In the context of the narrative this means that we shall not ever take stories *as* they are being told. For each story points beyond itself to something the storyteller did not intend to say. Its additional or central significance may actually not be accessible to him. As analysts, we are on the look-out for the unconscious intent, for the subtext, of the story. To tease it out of the manifest story, to smelt it out of crude ore, is the purpose of interpretation.

(2) All stories, then, tell not only of what goes on here and now, or what is being remembered here and now. Stories do not speak of an isolated event in the past, like a nugget or a relic of ancient time, even though we are often given to understand that such isolated events make up a case. The tales of psychoanalysis always report a psychological process or development, its many faces and stations, and its manifold changes. In other words, the stories do not speak of something that happened once or that has just happened recently, but, in point of fact, testify to a *continuous transformation*. They speak of something that *is*, and *has been becoming*, not of a fixed event, but of the unending process of coping and experiencing.

Closely connected with what I described before is the psychoanalytic principle that the early shaping of our experiences is bound to affect all later ones. If conflict had an overly strong bearing on them, similar kinds of conflict will tend again and again to impose themselves on new conditions, thereby reactivating and repeating the old problem. Also closely connected is the principle of context in the flux of ideas and flow of images (representations). One should speak here of the *primacy of context* in psychoanalysis. No single event or so-called fact can have as much significance as the origins from which it sprang and the new experiences and images and behaviors to which it will lead – whence it came and whither it will go. The design of the event, the context between past and present will have more significance than the event as such. A stricture is implied here on a belief all too frequently voiced – that of the fatal trauma of childhood which, when discovered and retrieved from the maw of unconsciousness, will change the entire mental state of the afflicted. If nothing else, the dramatic air of this hypothesis should give us pause. For nature, if it has to be addressed in the vocabulary of literature, proves not to be dramatic; it is, if anything, rather epic: it proceeds slowly and in the impalpable transformation toward new modes and forms tends to repeat the old ones. The reason why it can be at all meaningful to speak of the narrative in psychoanalysis seems to me to lie in the primacy of context. Without context, or before it has been established, that which is being told, tale or report or dream, will only convey a fragment, a *narrative inchoate*, but not yet a narrative.

(3) Whatever we have experienced, we are bound to elaborate, or *process* subsequently in unending sequences of images and acts of cognitive organization, commonly referred to as *thinking*. Analytically, we usually say: It will be elaborated in fantasy. The "it" is correct, at least in the sense that *it* happens to us without special resolve or inclination. We often use fantasy to imagine once more what gave us pleasure before, expecting, of course, that it will give us pleasure again. But fantasy does not concern itself only with the pleasurable; the unpleasant, hurtful, humiliating, frightening also comes back to mind. All input needs to be processed. That means it has to be completed, which means it has to be elaborated in thought and adapted to previous experience – adapted, that is to say, to the image a person holds of himself and to his expectations as to how things will work for or against him. Assuming there are not major obstacles, restrictions, or deflections interfering with this ongoing process we can say that new experience has

been *ordered and integrated*, eventually to become part of the self. The ordering and integrating of experience is thus as important as the pleasure it sometimes yields. *Coping with experience*, so that it can become part of the self, without straining and disquieting it, seems to be everybody's continuous occupation. As a result, we see the tendency to be repetitive, to do the same thing over and over again, even if it is some original stimulus no longer perceptibly there – as with Lady Macbeth's spot. The less successful the coping, the stronger and the more insidious the urge to repeat.

(4) The human being wants to know who he or she[2] is. He wants just as much to know what he should be like. As he strains for order, continuity and coherence of what he has experienced, so will he strive for coherence in his own self, between his subjective past, his present and a possible and desirable future, one that he/she may sensibly strive for. This means that he will have to deal in thought as well as in conduct with the qualities that make him appear to himself as good or bad, as lovable or miserable; deal equally with how and what he would like to be and how he imagines relationships with other people, and what he anticipates their actions toward him. Thus the person's stories testify to the state of his identity and its wants, frailties and foibles, mostly without consciously intending to do so. But he may wish to tell his story just because he hopes to assert his identity in the process, to defend it or at least to clarify what it could and should be like.

(5) Individuals strive for *unity and consistency* of the experiences that make up their selves. The incompatibility of divergent motives and tendencies encroaches upon the self, causing stress and discomfort. To be at one with oneself, therefore, is the elementary goal of the continuous stream of mentation, the aim of its persistent *effort at coping*. Fantasy and reflection strive to process what has been experienced and suffered, so that the self will not be troubled too much by contrary and conflicting impulses. Affected not only by what is happening right now, but also by what is long by-gone, the experiencing self will have reason again and again to apply itself to all that is divided, contradictory, split within oneself, in order to cope and adapt. This posture of the experiencing (and narrating) self makes clear the central position of conflict in the individual's experience, and, similarly, of anxiety and of guilt.

(6) About a person's plural aims and goals one can at least state that they all signify a basic tendency of human conduct: always to be striving for something. The person is *appetitive*, in a state of dynamic unrest, desires something that lies, contrary to popular understanding, rather

between pleasure and displeasure, and not just on the tropic of lust. What we crave usually is multifaceted: instinctual needs and satisfactions of self-love; discharge of tension, but also its maintenance and coddling; self-challenge and the gratification implied in functioning effectively, that is *with mastery* (White, 1963). Striving for gratification surely belongs to man's instinctual life, the discovery of which helped from the beginnings of psychoanalysis. Especially in Europe, in Germany and France, there is now a trend, commonly represented by non-clinicians either romantic or ideologized, purporting to recognize in the theory of drives the true and authentic essence of psychoanalysis – the more conceived in terms of a cauldron of untrammeled instincts, the more persuasive (Lohmann, 1985). This emphasis[3] is contrary to the fact that for the last 50 years, and as initiated by Freud himself, psychoanalysis has turned its attention equally to the precarious balance of self-regard, to destructive rage, to atonement for real or imaginal transgressions, and especially to the conditions under which the fragile and overtaxed ego may or may not succeed in integrating experience into a viable coherence. This does not alter the dynamic quality of human conduct, of striving for goals and objects and multiple gratifications. It only puts striving into a larger context.

Psychoanalytic listening thus means listening with this set in mind. The listener's concern is to get to the point when the tales in psycho-analysis – no, the elements of an unfolding tale – may emerge and become articulate, with as little constraint and hindrance as is possible. This is the function of the psychoanalytic setting, to provide the basis and ambience for the kind of listening that will facilitate the telling of stories, as well as invite and evoke them in preparation for the ensuing psycho-analytic conversation. The psychoanalytic orientation described before functions to provide a preliminary order, a grid. The activating impulse which issues from appropriately listening functions to prompt the telling, to make the tale move on. This is the task especially of the early, intro-ductory phase of psychoanalytic treatment. Through his interventions the analyst makes the tale gain momentum and depth; that is, he helps expand it toward plural contexts with which it proves to be connected. His comments serve to point out to the story teller, increasingly caught up in the job of getting the story out against many obstacles, where the story strains to go, often indicating its true direction by the most paradoxical signs. To put it differently, the emerging story, while being told, begins to recognize itself. The paradigm of knowing through telling reaches far beyond psychoanalysis into ancient and modern philosophy, as well as into magical and mystical practices. It is universal and axiomatic. The modest and whimsical "How should I know what I think before I hear myself say it?" is still a very apt paradigm. The purpose of a therapist's interpretative intervention is *to create sense*, that is, to establish a meaningful context and thereby comprehensive, personal meaning.

CREATING THE PERSONAL STORY

Developing in this manner the personal narratives are products of all the needs and strivings described before, when we referred to the analyst's set or orientation. The narrative of psychoanalysis thus results from the efforts at adapting to, or avoiding and of turning away from inner promptings and external demands, a perpetual condition for scuttling between subjective and external pressures or restrictions which biological and social necessities impose on the individual. Personal tales, therefore, are first of all fashioned according to one's self-image, how one would like to appear before others – in this case before the analytic listener. How the person best copes with this desire before self and analyst as audience will primarily shape and qualify his tales. The analytic listener needs to help him to discover behind the coping and make-do version of his tale an increasingly authentic one. The latent subtext will emerge once one has begun to tell one's stories – first *stories*, later *the* more or less coherent *story* urging to be told – especially under the conditions of the impartial analytic setting. Under the inner pressure of being able to tell one's tale in order to know it at long last, to which is added the pressure of the discomfort that induced the analysand at the outset to call on the analyst, the latent context will inevitably manifest itself, even against repression and reversal which the trials of development may have imposed. The unfolding story will intimate something of its real intent. When it becomes clear, however, that topics long repressed and deeply suppressed will now be touched upon, resistance against continuing with the story will intensify. It is as if an oarsman suddenly noticed that the current is becoming stronger and his boat is driven faster and faster: he will grab his oars and push against the current as forcefully as he can, to escape and to return to moving on calmly and safely as before.

Resistance is a normal and necessary event in the dialectic progress of psychoanalysis and will accompany it from the beginning to the end. To call it by name, to point it out again and again and define its hidden links and aims – in other words, to bring it back into the analytic setting demands more time, effort and skill than the *passé retrouvé*, the rediscovery of the forsaken past and reconstruction of that vanished intensity of childhood (Schachtel, 1959) which colored and helped shape so much of subsequent experience. Yet the analysis of that resistance procures an understanding of structure and development of personality we would not be able to reach without the expedients of that often maligned force. Its introduction into the scope of psychoanalysis forebodes the classical swing from a classical theory of instinctual drives with attention focused primarily on the Unconscious, to a *theory of experiencing* in a psychoanalytic Ego Psychology, centering upon the experiencing self. There is no reason here to enter into the details of the clinical approach to resistance. But it should be stressed anew that the authentic, idiosyncratic story of the individual will only take shape when its various, seemingly far-fetched, ends and means are properly understood. Only then will the sense of stories in analysis disclose itself and, in the end, perhaps lead to the authentic story of the self, including its urges and anxieties, with all its disguises and transformations, thereby disclosing an identity which under the pressure of conflicts and self-imposed restrictions could not be fully realized before.

It belongs to the tasks of analytic listening to insist on the authentic story – shall we say, on the best approximation thereof – and not to run aground on the rocks of resistance or on the shoals of a muddled conception of the analyst's part in the enterprise. For on top of the authentic story waiting to be divulged there are usually several other stories waiting, for which Ernst Kris (1975) aptly coined the term "personal myth." Independently, Max Frisch wrote in 1960: "Every man invents a story for himself which he then often and with great cost to himself, takes to be his life; or he invents a whole series of stories verified by names of places and dates, so that their reality will simply defy doubt."[4] The stories of psychoanalysis, therefore, remain fragments of a great, though for the longest time preliminary, confession – until through the analysis and interpretation of resistance (and, of course, through the medium of transference) meaning and secret intent of the personal myth can be grasped. It would be correct to say that seizing the authentic psychoanalytic story is the goal we can and should aim for; but we should also understand why it cannot be fully realized. The stories of Pirandello's six characters could not be adequately realized – on the surface – for dramaturgic reasons, but in the end for a more basic reason:

the complexity of the world of inner experience with its many contradictory impulses and its divergent identifications which barely ever fuse well enough as to make up one coherent and continuous self, and the ever-elusive and evanescent quality of experience which by its continuous changing and passing cannot be securely grasped, apprehended, defined and formulated.

Between the analysand and analyst there is also too much liability for masking, pretending, and denying so that the self-estrangement in the end cannot be fully overcome. The conditions of coping and adaptation initially leading to it are too deeply ingrained to allow for much modification later on. That is why Freud spoke in that late, somber and magnificent summary of his work of "Analysis, Terminable and Interminable" (1937). We may conclude that stories in psychoanalysis are on the way to becoming authentic, as long as they continue to transcend themselves and recast themselves in the light of every new step of self-discovery.

In this sense only does the concept of the narrative in psychoanalysis seem fruitful to me. It was seized upon when reflective minds at large grew impatient with the scorn of laboratory psychology and the pretensions of science in general, when they tried to clarify the human spectacle without recourse to measurement and rigid systematization. Those familiar with laboratory psychology also were disappointed by how little psychological science had to say about human experience as it is really experienced, prior to its being flattened out in the laboratory: hence the inclination "to return to the origins," to what seemed elementary and thus of enduring validity. "Alles Vollendete fällt heim zum/Uralten." "All that is completed bends back upon the pristine," says Rilke in the *Sonnet to Orpheus*. Added to this was a more general dissatisfaction which, without reference to psychology, also showed up independently as a newly conceived interest in the narrative in history (Stone, 1981), in literary criticism, and even in theology (Kepnes, 1982). In psychoanalysis the introduction of the concept "narrative" had a somewhat different rationale. As remarked earlier, it helped to define the nature of communication in psychoanalysis and thereby focus on its validity and on the limitations of the latter – especially for the conclusions habitually and all too faithfully based upon them when psychoanalysts report their clinical experiences and the theoretical conjectures drawn from them.

We should, however, not fall prey to the belief that anything narrative must needs be relevant, just because so much abstraction is not. We tell tales all day long and we are being told stories until our ears ring. We are accustomed to say scathingly: "What kind of a story is this?" Evidence, it seems, that narrative does not hold a lien on ancient truth and wisdom. In fact, it is my aim to show that this is not so, and why it cannot be so. Thus we cannot leave our story as an uncritical espousal of a rather vague concept. We must not resign ourselves to distinguish among different types of narratives, most of all, to identify that measure of deception and evasion to be found in almost all stories, mixed in with what seems to be the stuff of authenticity. In its own precincts, psychoanalysis is quite often capable of recognizing and undoing the disguises in which most stories will present themselves at first, but if the trumpery is not checked, it will persist. It remains to be seen to what extent the skills of psychoanalysis can be transferred to other domains. As it appears, we do have a basic parable to offer, namely, that all storytelling tries to deny and be silent about just as much as it strains to convey. When we think about narrative, we need to acknowledge at once the inherent resistance, and maintain that a worthwhile story should proceed from uncertain beginnings to approximate the "true" or "indigenous" story which for the longest time has been muffled and cloaked. Speaking for psychoanalysis we would be well advised to adhere to the concept of the narrative. We need to be watchful, though, that we listen to people through their stories in order to understand them, and that we accept these stories appropriately but not become pawn to them. If we failed to listen critically, we would collude with the false story clouding the potentially true story. We would fail, like Pirandello's Director of Theater who condemned his characters to futility because he wanted to oblige them while at the same time trying to wring a successful play from them.

NOTES

1. If memory serves, Boring presented this address during the annual convention of the Eastern Psychological Association in Providence, RI, in 1941.
2. [*He*, which linguistically speaking also signifies the *universal* pronoun, will stand in this paragraph as well as in (6) for *he* as well as *she*, for *his* as well as *hers*, for *him* as well as *her*, equivalent to the impersonal pronoun – *man* in German, *on* in French – so awkward in English.]
3. The criteria for this position are nothing short of baffling. They consist of a mysterious disdain for adjustment, finding frequent expression in cavil with Hartmann's germinal essay "On Adaptation" (1958). The argument seems to confuse *adaptation* with *adjustment*, (either word can be translated into German as Anpassung,

which may explain some of the confusion) and adjustment with uncritical submission to the dominion of power holders. Such a view of psychoanalysis would, of course, facilitate and promote its ideological coupling with the several versions of Marxism and the Frankfurt school of *Ideologiekritik* now in vogue. The advocates of "return to the Id" register at the same time their opposition to any kind of *Herrschaft* (dominion), to the "administered life," and their pleading *for* the self in danger of expropriation. At the same time they tend toward collectivist and anti-elitist sentiments, which does not go well with the preservation of a nonadministered self. Psychoanalysis in this argument is treated like a doctrine of salvation in danger of being adulterated through shifty and impious additions. There is no hint anywhere that the usefulness of psychoanalytic propositions first and last must rest on its clinical practice. It has to be tested empirically, or it would quickly decline into philosophical speculation with mystical overtones, similar to the speculative philosophies of nature of the nineteenth century from Schelling to Schopenhauer. There is not a hint in the espousal of a psychoanalysis of the Id that Freud had already transcended the "seething cauldron" view in good time, proceeding to the propositions of ego psychology when they seemed to accommodate clinical experience better than the earlier, drive-oriented or "topical" concepts. For a characteristic sample of discontent, see, among others, Lohmann, *Das Unbehagen in der Psychoanalyse* (1985).

4.   English translation by F. W. (Frisch, 1972).

REFERENCES

Boring, E. G. and Sachs, H. (1940). Was this analysis a success? *Journal of Abnormal & Social Psychology*, 35, 1-16.

Freud, S. (1925). Instincts and their vicissitudes. *Collected papers* Vol. 4, pp. 212-227 (J. Riviere, Trans.). London: Hogarth. (Original work published 1915).

Freud, S. (1937). Analysis terminable and interminable. *International Journal of Psychoanalysis*, 18, 373-405.

Freud, S. (1959). Constructions in analysis. In J. Strachey (Ed.), *The standard edition of the complete psychological works of Sigmund Freud* Vol. 5, pp. 358-371. London: Hogarth. (Original work published 1938).

Frisch, M. (1972). *Tagebuch*. Frankfurt: Suhrkamp.

Hartmann, H. (1958). *Ego psychology and the problem of adaptation* (D. Rapaport, Trans.). New York: International Universities Press. (Original work published 1939).

Kepnes, S. (1982). Erzahlen und Wiedererzahlen: die Narrativitat in der Psychoanalyse. *Concilium, Internationale Zeitschrift für Theologie*, H. 6/7, 390-396.

Kris, E. (1975). *Selected papers*. New Haven, CT: Yale University Press.

Lohmann, H-M. (1985). *Das Unbehagen in der Psychoanalyse*. Frankfurt: Fischer (TB 6782).

Schachtel, E. G. (1959). *Metamorphosis*. New York: Basic Books.

Schafer, R. (1983). *The analytic attitude*. New York: Basic Books.

Spence, D. P. (1982). *Narrative truth and historical truth: Meaning and interpretation in psychoanalysis*. New York: W. W. Norton.

Stone, L. (1981). The revival of narrative: reflections on a new old history. *The Past and the Present*. Boston: Routledge & Kegan Paul.

White, R. W. (1963). Ego and reality in psychoanalytic theory: A proposal for independent ego energies. *Psychological Issues*, 3 (monograph no. 11), p. 210.

Wyatt, F. (1961). A psychologist looks at history. *Social Issues*, 17, 65-77.

Wyatt, F. (1963). The reconstruction of the individual and of the collective past. In R. H. White (Ed.), *The study of lives*. New York: Atherton Press, pp. 304-320.

Wyatt, F. (1964). In quest of change: Comments on Robert Lifton's "Individual patterns in historical change." *Comparative Studies in Society and History*, 6, 384-392.

Wyatt, F. (1969). Notes on the scope of the psychohistorical approach. *Int. J. Psychiatry*, 7, 488-492.

Wyatt, F. (with William Willcox). (1959). A psychological exploration in history. *William and Mary Quarterly*, 16, 3-26.

11

Narrative Smoothing
and Clinical Wisdom

Donald P. Spence

In an imaginative analysis of Freud and Henry James, Hertz compares their treatment of two noteworthy women: Dora and Maisie.

> James and Freud alike anticipate being reproached for both the nature of the stories they have to tell and for the manner of the telling. And both meet these imagined reproaches in ways that suggest that the two faults might be one, that they run the risk of being accused of a perverse and distasteful confusion, of not striking the right balance between the child's world and the adult's. (1983, p. 65)

But there are more interesting comparisons to come. We take it for granted that because Maisie is a character created by James (in *What Maisie Knew*) she is necessarily a part of the author. We are somewhat startled, however, to hear the same argument applied to Freud with reference to Dora.

> Suppose what went wrong between Freud and Dora was not just a matter of unrecognized transferences (and countertransferences) but also of an unrecognized – or refused – identification? Suppose what Freud missed, or did

not wish to see, was not that he was drawn to (or repelled by) Dora, but that he 'was' Dora, or rather that the question of who was who was more radically confusing than even nuanced accounts of unacknowledged transferences and countertransferences suggest? Is it possible that one of the sources of energy and distortion in the 'Fragment of an Analysis . . .' is to be located here, in the confusion of tongues between an author and his young surrogate, and that we can find in Freud's text some of the extravagant tones as well as some of the gestures of sacrifice and self-location that inform James' writing about Maisie? (1983, p. 67)

Hertz goes on to make a further comparison between Freud and Dora. They were both reticent and neither told the whole story. There is, furthermore, a certain vagueness about the source of both Freud's and Dora's knowledge; in the case of the latter, it is often untraceable, whereas Freud often chooses not to reveal because it "would have led to nothing but hopeless confusion" (see Freud, 1905/1953, p. 27). And even granted that Freud's aim is to fill in the gaps in her account and provide us with a story which is "intelligible, consistent, and unbroken" (p. 18), we are still left with a number of rather arbitrary interpretations and puzzling conclusions that do not seem supported by the evidence. In another place (Spence, in press), I have discussed some of these lapses in more detail; here I only want to emphasize the rather arbitrary nature of Freud's account and how often he argues for an interpretation rather than allow the facts to speak for themselves.

To put it bluntly, how much of the Dora case can we believe? The parallel with Henry James makes us uncomfortably aware that both accounts are stories of a certain kind, and if narrative appeal explains why we are persuaded by Dora, does it also imply that we are presented with a good story more than a faithful account? If it is true, as Hertz argues, that Dora is at times part Freud, to what extent does Freud project his own problems and issues onto his patient? Where does Dora leave off and Freud begin?

We are confronted with a problem of narrative smoothing and it is useful to distinguish between two types. On the one hand – we will call this Level II – there is an attempt to bring the clinical account into conformity with some kind of public standard or stereotype. Since Freud, that standard has been represented by such specimens as the Dora, the Wolf Man, and the Rat Man cases, and each of these, in turn, is largely a narrative account which attempts to tell a coherent story by selecting certain facts (and ignoring others), which allows interpretation to masquerade as explanation, and which effectively prevents the reader from making contact with the complete account and thereby prevents the reader (if he so chooses) from coming up with an alternative explanation. Level II smoothing would seem to consist of two kinds of omissions. On the one hand, there is a kind of selective reporting which uses the clinical material to exemplify a particular principle or axiom; anecdote is chosen for its illustrative power and for its ability to further the argument. Quite a different kind of narrative smoothing results from the assumption that what is clear to the treating analyst is clear to the reader – in other words, that privileged competence is equivalent to normative competence (see Spence, 1982). By failing to provide the background information and context surrounding a particular clinical event, by failing to "unpack" the event in such a way that all its implications become transparent, the author runs the risk of telling a story that is quite different from the original experience. This kind of narrative smoothing comes about because we fail to realize that the facts are not fixed, that the referents are never unambiguous, and that each reading will depend on the preconceptions and prejudices of the reader. This kind of narrative smoothing results from a failure to take into account the hermeneutic properties of the clinical account, and we will discuss this problem in more detail in another part of this chapter.

Since Freud's time, Level II smoothing has significantly increased. The narrative structure of the average clinical case in a current journal is buttressed by only a handful of anecdotes (in contrast to the very detailed accounts of, for example, Dora's two dreams and their analysis). In the face of such smoothing, we are presented with clinical impressions that must be accepted almost entirely on faith; by conclusions that are discovered by undescribed technical procedures; and by observations so heavily mixed with theory that it is almost impossible to form a second opinion. Clinical specimens are notably lacking.

The second kind of narrative smoothing – Level I – takes place in the consulting room, long before the case is ever published or considered for publication. This kind of smoothing begins with leading suggestions ("Could you have been jealous of your brother when he came home as an infant from the hospital?") and continues, in more subtle form, in a variety of guises – pressing certain interpretations more than others, supporting the patient in certain kinds of explanations, or "hearing" one meaning in a tone of voice or a dream as opposed to others, to name only a few. Grünbaum suggests that "a 'confirming' early memory may be compliantly produced by the patient on the heels of giving docile assent to an interpretation" and that, in general, "each of the seemingly independent

214 I NARRATIVE PSYCHOLOGY

clinical data may well be more or less alike confounded by the analyst's suggestion so as to conform to his construction, at the cost of their epistemic reliability or probative value" (Grünbaum, 1984, p. 277). But despite his concern for such influence and the obvious impact it would have on our view of the theory, Grünbaum can cite only one specific example (pp. 212-214), which greatly weakens his case. To give him credit, however, the lack of evidence either for or against Level I smoothing is a direct consequence of Level II smoothing – as we will see shortly.

Even if we assume for the moment that both kinds of narrative smoothing take place, it seems clear that the second level is much more insidious than the first. Evidence of suggestion within the hour can frequently be detected by inspection of the transcript (some examples are provided by Gill & Hoffman, 1982; Spence, 1982, p. 194). Pieces of the transcript which are subject to such influence can then be systematically discounted in a further analysis. Merely to claim that such influence *is possible* need not prevent us from taking precautions which guard against that influence; thus Grünbaum's charges must be held in abeyance until more data are in. Second, it would seem as if the psychoanalytic method, with its emphasis on silence, neutrality, and minimal comment, would tend to guard against overt suggestion. Third, what looks like suggestion may sometimes be something quite different. Some of the more refined techniques that have been developed for analyzing the transference (see Gill & Hoffman, 1982) can also be used to uncover the grounds for apparent compliance, and it often occurs that what is superficially seen as agreement with the analyst may contain different motives or assumptions. If the analysts are alert to these differences, they are often in a position to clarify the interaction and translate apparent compliance into something more combative – and more complex.

Whether or not they always behave above suspicion, it seems fair to say that analysts as a group are increasingly alert to the dangers of undue influence and the way in which the analyst's thoughts and feelings come to influence the patient. By contrast, we are relatively naive with respect to the dangers of selective reporting, unobtrusive narrative revision, argument by authority, or the use of interpretation for explanation. Because of the esteemed position of Freud's five cases ("the five pillars on which psychoanalysis now rests," to quote Eissler, 1963, p. 678), they still serve as our specimens of clinical reporting. As a result, we tend to underestimate their faults and minimize their capacity for mischief. And because of our respect for confidentiality and for the wisdom of the analyst, we have no way of challenging the clinical report. Where the traces of suggestion or leading the patient or other kinds of Level I narrative smoothing can often (if not always) be found in the transcript, the traces of alteration in the published report are almost always invisible. Once the record has been changed and the case report is published, it is almost impossible to reconstruct what really happened and to isolate actual cause and effect from what might be called narrative sequence. Where conventional history has the benefit of different historians trying to analyze the same set of events, psychoanalysis has the rule of one analyst : one case; we never have the benefit of second opinions or alternative explanations.

In both kinds of narrative smoothing, accepted concepts are treated as axioms, stereotype is given precedence over more sophisticated observation, and evidence that does not fit the received wisdom is usually not reported. The findings under these circumstances have nothing new to tell us because they are influenced by an outdated framework which is projected onto the clinical material. Because the raw material of the clinical happening is never exposed to public scrutiny, there is no way for theory to change because disconfirmations are never made visible. As a result of the two levels of narrative smoothing, it would appear as if the reported data are fully in agreement with the received theory. Because of this agreement, there is no reason why theory need ever change, and it may be for this reason that references to Freud tend to dominate the literature despite the fact that he is no longer active in the field. (As of late 1984, plans are being set in motion for a new standard translation of Freud's collected works.)

CONSEQUENCES OF NARRATIVE SMOOTHING

The two levels just described have important implications for the future of both psychoanalytic theory and clinical practice. They can also significantly influence one another. So long as Level II smoothing is in effect, for example, we will *never* be aware of how much damage is produced by Level I. Ignorance of its true nature may lead to unwarranted pessimism about the possibility of ever testing clinical propositions within the clinical session. Grünbaum has taken the position that psychoanalytic truths can only be tested *outside* the clinical setting ("it would seem that the validation of Freud's cardinal hypotheses has to come, if at all, mainly from well-designed *extra*clinical studies, either epidemiologic or even experimental" Grünbaum, 1984, p. 278). This conclusion might follow from the finding that the clinical data are flawed by an "irremediable epistemic contamination" (Grünbaum, 1984, p. 127) – in other words, that Level I smoothing is irreversible in its effects. But just because we are not always aware of the original texture of the clinical dialogue and just because it is perfectly possible for Level I smoothing to take place does not mean that it presents us with an impossible methodological obstacle or that its effects cannot be isolated, when and where they occur, and kept separate from the other clinical data.

Turning to Level II smoothing, what are its consequences? Quite early in the Dora case, Freud addresses himself to the issue of technique and how it should be reported.

> There is another kind of incompleteness which I myself have intentionally introduced. I have as a rule not reproduced the process of interpretation to which the patient's associations and communications had to be subjected, but only the results of that process. Apart from the dreams, therefore, the technique of the analytic work has been revealed in only a very few places. My object in this case history was to demonstrate the intimate structure of a neurotic disorder and the determination of its symptoms; and it would have led to nothing but hopeless confusion if I had tried to complete the other task at the same time. (Freud, 1905/1953, p. 27)

We read these lines today with a certain amount of tolerant skepticism. To reveal technical procedures might have, in fact, clarified some of the more obscure passages in the case and given us ways of understanding how Freud arrived at certain conclusions. We might also suspect that full disclosure might have revealed interpretations that did not produce insight; clarifications that were rejected by the patient; and other examples that would tend to disrupt the flow of the narrative and interfere with the kind of story Freud was trying to tell. Whatever the reasons, failure to report specific technical procedures has plagued the psychoanalytic literature up to the present time, and the tendency to report clinical insights without paying attention to precisely how they were arrived at is one of the more grievous examples of Level II smoothing. Where Sterba has referred to this omission with the forgiving label of "scientific tact" (see Gray, 1982, p. 622), we have come to see, with the recent disclosures by Gill and Hoffman (1982) and Dahl, Teller, Moss, and Trujillo (1978), that much more than tact is involved.

Level II smoothing has produced what Gray calls a "developmental lag" in technique (see Gray, 1982, pp. 621-655).

It has for some time been my conclusion, rightly or wrongly, that the way a considerable proportion of analysts listen to and perceive their data has, in certain significant respects, *not* evolved as I believe it would have if historically important concepts concerned with the defensive functions of the ego had been wholeheartedly allowed their place in the actual application of psychoanalytic technique. (1982, p. 622)

Although he attributes this lag largely to a failure to bring the insights of ego psychology to bear on problems of technique, it can also be argued that the lag would never have developed if technical moves were made public as soon as they happened and were given as prominent a place in the literature as other kinds of clinical material.

The reporting of technical considerations tends to take two forms. On the one hand, there was (and is) heavy reliance on Freud's early papers on technique, and this reliance on tradition has directly influenced the lag in technique, as Gray makes clear. A second factor has to do with level of language. When technical changes were reported, as with Anna Freud's monograph on defense (Freud, A., 1937), or in later papers by Sterba (1953) and Hartmann (1951/1964), they tended to be couched in such abstract (metapsychological) language that it was hard to decide exactly what was being described. Consider Sterba commenting on the need for more attention to defensive processes:

We are still very much impressed, even fascinated, by the id contents which psychoanalysis enables us to discover. The working of the ego is so inconspicuous and silent that we are hardly aware of it. . . . It has been my observation that it is a most difficult task to teach students to pay attention to these mute and subterranean workings of the ego. (Sterba, 1953, pp. 17-18; quoted in Gray, 1982, pp. 633-634)

How are these id contents discovered – and are they "discovered" correctly? How would they appear in the clinical material? What are the "subterranean workings of the ego," and how are they detected? How does one discriminate, in the clinical material, between id and ego? Almost no paper on technique or changes in technique concerned itself with the specifics of where attention should be focused, which part of the patient's associations should be addressed, how the meaning of these associations varies with the context of the session, how defense can be recognized, and a host of other technical details. Even Gray's paper, admirable in calling attention to the lag, does not offer any verbatim examples of patient-therapist interchange, examples which proved so edifying in his earlier paper on ways of viewing intrapsychic activity (see Gray, 1973).

We are faced with something more than scientific tact. This kind of Level II smoothing might more fairly be called a conspiracy of silence which perpetuates several unwarranted assumptions. First, it seems as if technique is so well understood and sufficiently refined that no discussion is in order. Second, it seems as if all trained analysts are largely in agreement on how to listen and how to interpret. When examples come to light that call this refinement and agreement into question, a common reaction is that these must be bad examples, the exceptions that "prove" the rules (see Malcolm, 1984, and her review of Gill & Hoffman; she considers the possibility that the bad examples are "merely exceptionally inept" but concludes that there is no way of deciding for sure, given the state of the literature). In other words, the possibility of Level II smoothing raises the question but leaves the answer in doubt.

But the converse should also be noted. Creative, insightful clinical work is also buried behind abstraction and other kinds of Level II smoothing, and as a result, little of the clinical wisdom generated by experienced analysts in the course of their careers will ever be documented or passed on to younger colleagues. Clear exceptions to Freud's technical procedures most likely occur at a much higher frequency than is assumed in the popular press, but these exceptions, or disconfirmations, are never reported and thus disappear as soon as they happen. We are faced by the final irony that the most detailed accounts of patient-doctor interaction appear, not in the psychoanalytic literature, but in popular fiction such as the novel *August*. These accounts naturally mesh perfectly with the prevailing stereotype.

A further consequence of narrative smoothing concerns the hermeneutic nature of the clinical enterprise. Despite the determined efforts of Grünbaum to "expose the exegetical myth" of hermeneutics (Grünbaum, 1984, pp. 1-9), there is every reason to believe that hermeneutic principles are used every day in the process of clinical discovery. The precise nature of this process and the particular way in which the analyst listens, conceptualizes, and interprets have remained unexplored, largely because of Level II smoothing. But even though the data are in short supply, it seems clear that the analyst does not function in a hypothetical-deductive fashion to arrive at a specific interpretation. Despite the tendency to present a case history as if it were some kind of detective story, the actual manner of listening – of choosing what to listen for, of deciding how large or how small to make the units, and which kinds of pattern matches carry weight and which do not – is much more hermeneutic than deductive.

Hermeneutic in what sense? The task of the analyst, first and foremost, is to understand rather than explain, and to understand meaning above all. But meaning is not necessarily "out there" in any clear and defined sense, and even when the referents are clear, their meaning is quite different whether viewed by analyst or by patient. We have technical procedures (of a kind) which tell us that we should interpret resistance before content or defense before wish, but these states or concepts do not come with labels attached; they must be discovered in the clinical material and the process of discovery is largely a hermeneutic endeavor. But the details of this discovery are hidden by narrative smoothing.

Narrative smoothing, finally, tends to turn hypothesis into axiom. In one of his early papers, Freud tells us that the early ideas of his science, like any science, are entirely provisional and can be replaced at any time without damaging the rest of the structure. He speaks of "nebulously elusive, barely imaginable basic conceptions" which are conceived as a temporary framework that is not part of the final structure and which can be later discarded if the need arises (Freud, 1914, p. 77; translation provided by Weber, 1982, p. 21). The history of psychoanalysis paints a quite different story. Provisional ideas and explanations have been reified and accepted as fact because the disconfirming evidence does not exist – not because there is none, but because narrative smoothing prevents it from appearing. We have seen that both types of smoothing tend to perpetuate the prevailing stereotype and uphold the status quo; thus they tend to minimize embarrassments to the theory and support partial confirmations of the central hypotheses. Given the lack of countervailing evidence, it is only natural that central postulates gain strength and support and thus gradually evolve from provisional scaffolding to basic concept.

NARRATIVE AND PARADIGMATIC MODES

Freud's cases can be read in two quite different ways – as transparent accounts of a particular patient with particular symptoms which are treated by a certain technique, or as an evocative recapture of mood and atmosphere, often vague as to specifics. The first reading corresponds to

Bruner's paradigmatic mode of thought (see Bruner, 1984) which is concerned with general causes, general categories, and general principles, and which attempts to reduce the specific symptom or complaint to a broader rule and fit the individual details into a larger pattern. A case account of this kind attempts to minimize ambiguity and emphasize "reference at the expense of sense. It aspires to the astringent goal of singular definite referring expressions with severe restrictions on alternative senses" (Bruner, 1984, p. 14). What happened and how it took place is given first priority; the writing attempts to be as transparent as possible so that we, the readers, are given a ring-side seat in the consulting, examining, or operating room. Language must be denotative rather than connotative, and precision of reference and simplicity of style is the sought-after goal. Cases of this kind are often written in a standard format (see, for example, the Clinical Pathological Conference [CPC] regularly reported in the *New England Journal of Medicine*), and as a result, similarities and differences between cases can be identified and interpreted.

The second reading corresponds to Bruner's narrative mode of thought. It

> Maximizes sense at the expense of definite reference . . . sacrifices denotation to connotation. It is for this reason that the metaphoric richness of a story or a line of poetry is as important as the events to which it refers and why . . . a story cannot be reduced to a set of atomic propositions derived from its particular set of statements. (Bruner, 1984, p. 14)

The narrative account of a case, if done successfully, will give us a feel of what it was like to be Dora and have her dreams interpreted by Freud; it will give us a sense of how he approaches her presenting problem (but not necessarily provide us with the precise manner of treatment); and it will often evoke different reactions in different readers because it tries to evoke a mood or a feeling rather than provide the reader with a flowchart or blueprint of the ongoing treatment. Such accounts depend heavily on a highly developed style, using a figurative and metaphoric language which goes far beyond the facts. Each report bears the stamp of the author and our view of the case is necessarily colored by the particular theoretical and rhetorical stance. As a result, it is almost impossible to consider similarities and differences between cases of the same type, or to build up a coherent set of specimen reports; each narrative impression is more or less unique.

Each mode of reporting brings about its own kind of narrative smoothing. If the focus is on reference at the expense of sense, the facts in the case will be organized with an eye to logical consistency and coherence and the prejudices of the author/observer will be minimized. Transparent language will be used where possible and the report written *as if* the conclusions reached were the *only* possible conclusions to be gathered. But, of course, this objective stance carries with it its own kind of smoothing. It tends to leave out of account the ways in which the facts are not completely clear and to minimize the contribution of prejudice, bias, or preconception to understanding. By treating the case as a closed set of facts to be reported, the author is committed to an impossible position which assumes that all meanings are "out there," ready to be described and put into words, and that all observers would take the same view of the proceedings. A smoothing which maximizes facts over feelings may, ironically, end up by doing an injustice to the facts because they frequently do not speak for themselves, and no amount of transparent, referential description can bring them alive. The paradigmatic account may earn high marks for objectivity but low marks for rhetoric, and the final impression may be much less than the author had hoped, simply because it lacks narrative appeal.

If the focus is on sense at the expense of reference, we come away inspired and even enthralled – but not necessarily informed. Crucial facts may be misrepresented and consensus slighted in favor of rhetoric, but we are wiser in significant ways. We may not be able to identify the source of this wisdom or test its truth value, but our horizons have been extended – often irreversibly. After reading the Dora case, for example, it is never possible to go back to hearing the reports of a crazy patient as so much nonsense and take up once again the modal stance of the alienist in the middle of the nineteenth century. The revelation of the Dora case lies in a significant shift in mode of listening which Freud illustrates over and over again, showing us how it is possible to "read between the lines" and listen to several contexts at the same time. The truth value of his discoveries matters much less than his demonstration that symptoms can be treated as words, that repetition can be treated as remembering, and that Dora's comments to Freud can also be treated as comments intended for her father or Herr K. Only a narrative account could bring these impressions to life and allow us to enter into the interaction in a way that reveals the possibilities of this new way of listening.

It can be seen that many or all of the heard "voices" in the Freudian conversation can be easily lost if we try to pin them down too soon. When Dora speaks with the voice of her governess or addresses Freud as her father, the sense evoked by her words is probably more important than the words themselves; thus any attempt to get the record straight could easily end up by losing the most important discovery of all – that Dora is speaking in many tongues. Rorty tells us that "we have not *got* a language which will serve as a permanent neutral matrix for formulating all good explanatory hypotheses, and we have not the foggiest notion of how to get one" (1979, p. 348). If all accounts are more or less misleading, then it would seem better to smooth the narrative in favor of what makes it distinctive rather than in favor of what makes it trivial.

Accounts in the narrative mode work best by illustrating rather than by specifying, and we turn to such accounts to find new ways of understanding or accounting for what we already know. The Dora case continues to be read as literature because it allows us to participate in Freud's discovery that patients talk in many tongues and gives the reader a chance to share his surprise at Dora's response – particularly his surprise at her decision to abruptly terminate the treatment. But giving the rhetorical account high marks for evoking this kind of surprise does not mean that we must go on being slaves to metaphor and figurative language, just as we would not take seriously an attempt to rewrite *Great Expectations* in a more modern context. Part of the charm of a favorite narrative lies in the sense it conveys of surprise and wonder. But we can be surprised only so often.

We have noted that the narrative mode conveys a highly personal statement about a specific experience, and it is not designed to categorize this experience or account for it in more general terms. How can its wisdom be extracted and put to more general use? It would seem as though the narrative cannot be generalized into a set of findings because the two modes of thought are not interchangeable (see Bruner, 1984); a generalized statement of narrative findings would be, after all, a contradiction in terms. We have also seen that Freud's various moves in the Dora case should be read more as illustrations of his new way of listening than as specific examples of correct interpretations; thus the truth value of his reading of Dora's two dreams is less important than the fact that he can manage that kind of reading in the first place. Again the parallel with literature is instructive. We go back to Tolstoy to recover the confusion of battle, but not to learn where specific regiments were deployed or exactly why one side lost and the other side won.

But to read Freud as literature raises a groundswell of concern in many circles because it implies that we value his narrative appeal more than his respect for the facts. This conclusion seems justified, for reasons we have given, but it does *not* imply that there are no facts to be discovered or that there are no better ways of uncovering or presenting them. And just because Freud discovered a significant new method of listening does not imply that each of his examples should be cherished forever; many of his interpretations are simply wrong and leave important readings out of account. The history of Freud (particularly in the United States) shows us, time and again, an inability to separate the two modes of discourse. We still tend to confuse narrative and paradigmatic modes of presentation and conclude that because an account is enthralling and mindstretching we must assume that it is right in all particulars. The opposite would seem to be closer to the truth: where an account produces a significant dramatic effect on the reader, it should be viewed with even greater skepticism because its narrative appeal probably is achieved by a certain kind of narrative smoothing.

How then do we extract its general wisdom? Certainly not by telling more stories, no matter how fond we are of this mode of discourse and no matter how much we envy Freud's narrative gift. A change in our mode of reporting brings us back to the question of narrative smoothing because the two are closely connected. I would argue that although smoothing comes first in time, its particular nature is determined by the kind of story we want to tell and how we want to tell it. Looking ahead to reports in the narrative mode, we choose to listen in anecdotal fashion with an ear to revealing incident and the kind of detail that would give a story point, color, and suspense. We listen not for chapter and verse but for revealing example, choosing the incident that will clarify our point even when it is not exactly typical. We are describing what might be called a narrative mode of listening, and this kind of stance is always asking itself, what is going on here that has the greatest appeal for my audience?

The paradigmatic mode of listening is something quite different. To say that it is more faithful to the facts is to prejudge the issue unnecessarily, but this approach certainly aims at more evenly balanced coverage. Freud was probably searching for such a mode in his early papers on technique, but his advice to listen with "free floating attention" flounders on the fact that we always listen with a certain amount of pre-understanding (or prejudice in the nonpejorative sense; see Gadamer, 1984). Gadamer makes clear that meanings are always being constructed from impressions and are always influenced by context; thus we must be aware of these contexts and how they contribute to our constructions if we are to come closer to an evenly balanced account. But despite the problems with Freud's conception, the goal is still the same – to listen in a way that allows for surprise, puzzlement, and contradiction, and to reproduce what is happening in a way that gives the most room to the observable referents. Or to put the matter in the form of a question, "How can a text be protected from misunderstanding from the start?" (Gadamer, 1984, p. 238).

Treating the clinical encounter as a text and placing the problem in the context of Gadamer's discussion of the problems of understanding makes us realize that we must come back to the problem of meaning in deciding how to listen. Does the meaning reside in the sharable anecdote? If so, we listen in the narrative mode. We organize the material around these anecdotal highlights because we assume that they best capture the texture we most want to convey. Does the meaning reside in the specific response to the specific interpretation? If so, we report the exchange exactly as it occurred, even at the risk of telling a tale with no point and no surprise. It may leave the audience bored or unimpressed, but such is the risk of paradigmatic reporting. (It is worth noting that the dull nature of archives in general derives in large part from the fact that nothing is left out, an indication that the need to collect information did not give way to the need to amuse or entertain.)

THE HERMENEUTIC TURN

Closer inspection makes it appear that neither the paradigmatic nor the narrative mode completely account for the process of clinical listening; they exhaust some of its intricacies but leave a residue unexplained. The remainder is best captured by Gadamer in his description of how to read an unfamiliar text:

> A person trying to understand a text is prepared for it to tell him something. That is why a hermeneutically trained mind must be, from the start, sensitive to the text's quality of newness. But this kind of sensitivity involves neither "neutrality" in the matter of the object nor the extinction of one's self, but the conscious assimilation of one's own fore-meanings and prejudices. The important thing is to be aware of one's own bias, so that the text may present itself in all its newness and thus be able to assert its own truth against one's own fore-meanings. (Gadamer, 1984, p. 238)

Gadamer goes on to explain that prejudice does not necessarily mean "unfounded judgment" but can be understood more broadly to refer to the set of assumptions, witting and unwitting, which we bring to any new experience. Both Gadamer and Heidegger before him have argued that these assumptions will inevitably color our understanding of a new text; that it is simply impossible to listen with "evenly hovering attention"; and that we must constantly be on the alert for the effect of prejudice and the way it closes our eyes to the full meaning of the text. One test of this openness is measured by our sensitivity to the newness of the text; awareness of what makes it different and distinctive can only operate when we are not searching for standard meanings or validating favorite hypotheses.

When analysts listen to the text of the 50-minute hour, they try to listen for newness in a variety of ways. First, they may notice the difference between their reading of an episode and the way it is reported by the patient; disparities of this kind often serve to initiate an interpretation. Second, they may be struck by the way the patient's response to them (as analysts) does not match their sense of what the patient intended to say or do; the newness of this response can be used to gauge the amount of distortion and may lead to a transference interpretation. Finally, they may be struck by disparities between the patient's history and the standard psychoanalytic account, and if this newness strikes them with enough force, it may be worthwhile to publish the discrepancies and what they imply.

In each of these instances, the appreciation of newness must come after an understanding of meaning, but the meaning is rarely on the surface. Thus it must follow that to listen clinically is to listen hermeneutically and we need to identify two senses of the word.

> According to one pole, hermeneutics is understood as the manifestation and restoration of a meaning addressed to me in the manner of a message, a proclamation, or as is sometimes said, a kerygma; according to the other pole, it is understood as a demystification, as a reduction of illusion. (Ricoeur, 1970, p. 27)

He goes on to argue that psychoanalysis concerns itself with the second, but further reflection will indicate that it is also interested in the first. Dream interpretation can be seen as the restoration of a hidden message, whereas a transference interpretation may have the goal of reducing illusion.

The two senses of hermeneutics differ with respect to what is uncovered. According to the first pole, hermeneutics is the process of uncovering one or more hidden messages and can be compared (in one of

Freud's favorite metaphors) to the work of the archeologist in recovering the past. This reading would suggest that truth values can be attached to each of the discoveries because either they existed once or they did not. According to the second pole, hermeneutics is the process of reducing illusion, and since there are an almost infinite number of ways of going about this task, the truth value of each attempt is much less certain and the creativity of the analyst much more an important variable. According to the first pole, we listen to the patient in the spirit of asking, Why is he saying this to me at this time and in whose voice is he speaking? According to the second pole, we listen to the patient in the spirit of saying, Less is more, and asking, Where is the simple core of this complexity? To reduce a complicated life to a theme and variations is one way of reducing illusion. But notice that now the search has shifted from newness to repetition or, rather, the newness sensed by the careful listener is reduced to a pattern of variations. It would seem that the ability to sense variation and repetition when the patterns are somewhat ambiguous and imperfectly displayed is a highly creative act and one that differs significantly from making and breaking codes or detecting hidden meanings.

If we listen in both hermeneutical senses, we are always doing two things at once. The target utterance may contain a hidden message which might be revealed through association or gesture or slip of the tongue, and in that case, we look beneath surface appearance and listen with the "third ear." Listening in this mode captures the popular image of the psychoanalyst, but it is only half the story. The target utterance may also be less than it seems, not more; it may simply be a variation on an old theme, the nth repetition of a familiar complaint or ambition. Listening in this vein demands less suspicion and more déjà vu, an ear for overtones and an eye for pattern matches, an ability to detect similarity in differences and a sensitivity to transformations and permutations. Listening in the first vein, we listen vertically because the target utterance is assumed to take the place of something else; to listen in the second vein, we listen horizontally because the target utterance belongs to a family of utterances which have appeared at some earlier time, and we must keep the old images intact in order to spot a new member. To listen in the first vein is to listen to the harmony of the hour; to listen in the second vein is to listen to its melody.

These are some of the lessons of the Dora case which were elaborated and clarified in Freud's later clinical papers and amended (slightly) by his followers. But we have seen how Level II smoothing tends to give us the findings from a session and little of the procedures which produced the findings; as a result, we are still largely in the dark as to how an analyst listens most of the time. Conspicuously lacking is an insider's account which describes the analyst listening to the hour, now vertically and now horizontally; an account which would tell us how one goes about choosing how to listen and what to say, and how one amends one's response in the face of new clinical material.

The failure to report details of the listening process is perhaps the most serious consequence of narrative smoothing (Level II) and reflects a grievous misreading of Freud's central contribution. As we noted in an earlier section, his revolutionary discovery was less content and more process; as a result, his specific interpretations in the clinical papers should be read more as illustrations of how to proceed than as truthful interpretations which made a significant difference to the patient and which should be slavishly copied. Narrative smoothing reduces the process to a handful of trivial conclusions and leaves out of the record the clinical wisdom of the treating analyst who is always finding new ways of combining horizontal and vertical approaches. Edelson (1983) correctly reminds us that "a psychoanalysis without surprises cannot properly be termed a psychoanalysis at all" (p. 93), but the number of surprises in the average case report tends to approach the vanishing point.

The distinction between horizontal and vertical listening makes it clear that free-floating attention is only one part of the analytic stance. Decoding manifest into latent content – the popular image of the "mind-reading" psychoanalyst – may take place from time to time, but to focus on the vertical approach to the exclusion of everything else tends to give a mystical flavor to the proceedings which they do not deserve. It also underestimates the sheer lawfulness of the interpretive process, just as the failure to report the complete context of discovery leaves the impression that good psychoanalytic work is essentially ineffable and beyond description, the godchild of genius which cannot be taught.

A full report of the context of discovery would also make us aware of the creative component in good interpretations and the variety of choices which are available at any given time. The standard case report makes it seem as if the interpretations cited are necessarily the right answers; alternative explanations or "readings" of the material are almost never provided. But if we are listening for theme and variations, the number of repetitions we hear will depend on our tolerance for transformation and our choice of unit, and these are clearly individual choices which are rule-governed in a general way but which also contain many degrees of freedom. We have described how Hertz found a way to map the Dora case into *What Maisie Knew* and how this comparison raises a new series of questions about the relation between author and central "character." In a somewhat different reading, Peter Brooks has compared Freud with Sherlock Holmes (see Brooks, 1984) and enables us to look on the case report as a kind of detective story which begins with mystery and incoherence and ends with many questions answered and a sense of final understanding. Each of these comparisons managed to find points of correspondence between apparently dissimilar texts; each comparison provides a new reading of Freud and helps to enlarge our understanding of his approach.

What is the truth value of these readings? In his critique of the hermeneutic approach, Barratt calls Ricoeur to task for not specifying

> Criteria by which rival interpretations with psychoanalysis might be adjudicated. . . . Implicitly and subtly, Ricoeur seems to identify truth and the movement of psychoanalytic interpretation . . . [and] circumvents the question raised by interpretations which are efficacious yet wrong. . . . (1977, p. 462)

Barratt goes on to argue that

> It is wholly unsatisfactory to assume, as Ricoeur seems to do, that truth somehow emerges by necessity within the psychoanalytic situation. It would be equally unsatisfactory to suggest that truth is to be discerned solely on the basis of personal resonance, or to argue that idiographic interpretations are to be validated by reference to certain fixed universal types, which are actually not the concern of the psychoanalytic endeavor. Freud's psychology as a hermeneutic system does imply a set of criteria for the arbitration of conflicting interpretations. (Pp. 462-463)

Does it follow that Freud's system implies a set of criteria? It may be closer to the mark to say that if we choose hermeneutics as a mode of understanding, then we also must rule out the idea of a single method. Gadamer makes it clear that the hermeneutic approach is distinguished by the fact that it is method-free; truth is not contingent on method but, rather, truth and method complement one another. Barratt's critique seems to assume that the task of interpretation is primarily one of uncovering, that listening is always carried out within a vertical mode. As soon as we consider the horizontal approach, then it would seem as if we can listen to the material on a variety of different levels, using a wide range of transformations. Each new reading of the Dora case or Freud's botanical monograph dream will find something new to say; this is a necessary consequence of the fact that understanding always takes place within a certain context, subject to a certain tradition, and that what strikes each reader as new and therefore worthy of comment will necessarily vary as a function of experience and training. And having compared Freud to Henry James and Sherlock Holmes would not seem to limit, in any way, the comparisons to come; we can confidently expect attempts to find points in common with culture heroes yet unborn.

In a similar way, an attempt to find a particular pattern in a patient's life and uncover a particular theme and variations does not exhaust (or even reduce) the truth of the clinical material, leaving less around for the next interpreter. We do not "account for" the truth in the clinical material in the same way as we account for the variance in a set of data by a coefficient of correlation. It is partly for this reason that questions of method seem out of place and why it is important to appreciate the fact that competent analytic work implies much more than merely decoding a text. If only decoding were involved, then it would be entirely proper to speak of true and false accounts – but this is not the case. There is clearly something more.

How can we extract and preserve the wisdom of the "something more"? It is here that concern with method and criteria most get in the way. Level II smoothing has the effect of turning a hermeneutic adventure into a staid, pseudoscientific account which gives the impression that all interpretations are overdetermined, that all surprise has been accounted for (if it ever existed), and that the received theory is entirely correct. Level II smoothing manages to eliminate alternative readings of the material and makes it impossible for the curious reader to participate in the encounter; it thus diminishes the reader's ability to contribute to the final understanding. Level II smoothing presents us with a finished product; it fails to open up the text for any kind of shared discovery.

THE CONTEXT OF DISCOVERY

In their zeal to prove Freud right in matters of fact and find every possible way of validating his theory in the clinical material, his heirs have produced a literature that says next to nothing about the process of discovery. Gray tells us that perhaps the most important element in the study of technique "lies in identifying, *in more than usual detail*, the manner or choice of the analyst's *forms of attention* during the conduct of the analysis" (1982, p. 621; first italics mine). We have seen how certain kinds of narrative smoothing tend to swallow up these details and present us with case reports that are largely predictable in their findings – and significantly mysterious as to how these findings were discovered. And although popular fiction (as noted) has attempted to rush into this vacuum with its own Gothic fabrication, we are still left in the dark as to how analysts really listen and what they do with what they hear.

The answer to Gray's plea for more detail must come from the analyst. It cannot be supplied by the transcript, which is mute with respect to the inner process of paying attention, and it cannot be supplied by Freud's classic cases, no matter how slavishly they are copied. Part of the reluctance to unpack the session more fully may come, as Gray suggests, from the fact that analysts often choose to protect themselves from too detailed an awareness of how they function – in part for narcissistic reasons. Part of the reluctance may stem from lack of practice (as Freud suggested in another context; see Gray, 1982, p. 651) and part from what Gray calls an "inner tendency to maintain a natural or at least a maturely typical state of virtual ignorance of those functions of the ego that potentially enable it to observe itself" (p. 651). And part may stem from the fact that we have not yet arrived at a model of clinical listening which does justice to the intricacies of the process and which would guide us in the study of the context of discovery.

Such a model, it would seem, must begin at the point where the analyst first "opens himself to the text" (in Gadamer's words) and begins to make distinctions between what has never been said before, what is being repeated, and what is repeated but slightly changed. The model must take into account both horizontal and vertical modes of listening and the conditions under which they occur. A careful study of process might, for example, reveal that an attempt to decode the target utterance (that is, to listen vertically) may take place when the utterance does not arouse any kind of historical interest or resonate with earlier fragments of the treatment. Conversely, attempts to listen horizontally may take place when clear parallels appear between different parts of the treatment (as may happen, for example, during the termination phase of treatment when earlier symptoms are revived).

But defining the newness of the material is never an easy judgment; it clearly depends on the context brought to bear at that particular time and place, and the model must find some way of defining this context and integrating it into the listening process. First, it must be unpacked in such a way that the outside reader comes closer to understanding the privileged competence of the treating analysts (see Spence, 1982) and their reasons for hearing the material in just the way they do.

A faithful account of the listening process and a full description of the context of discovery will very likely have the appearance of a disconnected series of insights, strung together by time. Surprise, bewilderment, and faint glimmers of understanding probably all circle one another during the average hour in much the same way that they appear during a dream state, and here we come to the greatest danger of narrative smoothing. The seamless account of the clinical detective cannot do justice to the way in which the patient's responses are first vaguely apprehended, then recombined with remembered fragments of earlier sessions or with pieces of theory to arrive at some partial understanding which often proves completely wrong and misdirected. An honest account must document these failures and begin to tell us when an hour ended in complete dismay, when an interpretation was misunderstood and intensified the resistance, and when – because this also happens – associations were properly decoded and the simple meaning of a dream or symptom stood out clearly for the first time. Current narrative accounts tend to focus only on successes and misrepresent the number of false hypotheses which must be discarded or the number of times the treating analyst was just plain wrong. No wonder that Gray warns us of narcissistic injury.

We begin to appreciate how narrative smoothing – particularly Level II – can be compared to secondary revision during dreaming. Such revision has the aim of processing the chaotic dream as experienced and turning it into something more followable and which conforms more closely to the narrative shapes we like to hear. A similar process seems to overtake our clinical experience and make it more palatable for outside consumption. But the stereotype has dulled our appreciation of the excitement, wonder, and surprise contained in the actual event, and the stereotype will teach us nothing worth knowing. The true discoveries lie ahead.

REFERENCES

Barratt, B. (1977). Freud's psychology as interpretation. In T. Shapiro (Ed.), *Psychoanalysis and Contemporary Science* (Vol. 5). New York: International Universities Press.

Brooks, P. (1984). *Reading for the plot*. New York: Knopf.

Bruner, J. (1984). Narrative and paradigmatic modes of thought. Invited address to the American Psychological Association, Toronto.

Dahl, H., Teller, V., Moss, D., and Trujillo, M. (1978). Countertransference examples of the syntactic expression of warded-off contents. *Psychoanalytic Quarterly*, 47, 339-363.

Edelson, M. (1983). Is testing psychoanalytic hypotheses in the psychoanalytic situation really impossible? *The Psychoanalytic Study of the Child*, 38, 61-109.

Eissler, K. (1963). Freud and the psychoanalysis of history. *Journal of the American Psychoanalytic Association*, 11, 675-703.

Freud, A. (1937). *The ego and the mechanisms of defence*. London: Hogarth Press.

Freud, S. (1953). Fragment of an analysis of a case of hysteria. *Standard Edition* (Vol. 7), 3-122. London: Hogarth Press. (Original work published in 1905).

Gadamer, H-G. (1984). *Truth and method*. New York: Crossroad.

Gill, M. and Hoffman, I. (1982). *Analysis of transference* (Vol. 2). New York: International Universities Press.

Gray, P. (1973). Psychoanalytic technique and the ego's capacity for viewing intrapsychic activity. *Journal of the American Psychoanalytic Association*, 21, 474-494.

Gray, P. (1982). "Developmental lag" in the evolution of technique for psychoanalysis of neurotic conflict. *Journal of the American Psychoanalytic Association*, 30, 621-655.

Grünbaum, A. (1984). *The foundations of psychoanalysis*. Berkeley: University of California Press.

Hartmann, H. (1964). Technical implications of ego psychology. In *Essays on ego psychology* (pp. 142-254). New York: International Universities Press. (Original essay published in 1951).

Hertz, N. (1983, Spring). Dora's secrets, Freud's techniques. *Diacritics*, 65-83.

Malcolm, J. (1984). The patient is always right. [Review of M. Gill and I. Hoffman's *Analysis of transference*]. *New York Reivew of Books*, 31 (20), 13-18.

Ricoeur, P. (1970). *Freud and philosophy*. New Haven: Yale University Press.

Rorty, A. (1979). *Philosophy and the mirror of nature*. Princeton, NJ: Princeton University Press.

Spence, D. (1982). *Narrative truth and historical truth*. New York: Norton.

Spence, D. (in press). When interpretation masquerades as explanation. *Journal of the American Psychoanalytic Association*.

Sterba, R. (1953). Clinical and therapeutic aspects of character resistance. *Psychoanalytic Quarterly*, 22, 1-20.

Weber, S. (1982). *The legend of Freud*. Minneapolis: University of Minnesota Press.

12

The Analysis of
Interview-Narratives

Elliot G. Mishler

Interviewing is a central research method in the social sciences. Much that we claim to know about individuals' attitudes, beliefs, and values is based on their responses to questions we ask them in our studies. No significant aspect of life has been beyond the pale of inquisitive interviewers. Respondents are routinely asked about their sexual and political preferences as well as their preferred detergents, deodorants, and beers; about their views of marriage and divorce and their reasons for having or not having children; about their fears of a nuclear war and their experiences of personal stress and illness. Unfortunately, this unbounded diversity of topics has not been matched by the development of interviewing methods that are appropriate and adequate to the tasks of eliciting and analyzing meaningful responses.

Essentially, the mainstream tradition has focused almost exclusively on problems of standardization, that is, on how to ask all respondents the same question and how to analyze their responses with standardized coding systems. This line of inquiry has been accompanied by almost total neglect of the intertwined problems of language, meaning, and context – problems that are critical to understanding how interviews work. In this paper, from an alternative perspective on interviews as a discourse between speakers, these problems are brought forward and made central topics for interview research. This is done by treating respondents' answers to questions as stories or narratives, and by applying methods of narrative analysis.[1]

I shall focus on one "text," the extended response of one respondent to one question in an interview, and I shall approach it from several different perspectives. Through this exercise, I hope to demonstrate the feasibility of treating responses as stories, suggest types of findings that result, and clarify some problematic features of narrative analysis. Among the questions discussed are the following: What forms do narratives take in respondents' accounts and under what conditions do they appear? What do narratives mean, and what different meanings emerge from alternative narrative-analytic models and methods? How does narrative interpretation differ from interpretations based on standardized coding procedures? What are the implications for theory and for research practice, both in the conduct and analysis of interviews?

INTERVIEWING PRACTICES AND RESPONDENT NARRATIVES

During an interview[2] with a husband-respondent about significant events in his marriage and family history, I asked: "You wouldn't call those times though troubling times? Uh, low points in that sense?" The question came about 22minutes into the interview. Its immediate context was a structured question asking him to review a time chart, beginning with the date of marriage, to select those years he would consider "high" and "low" points; after this screening question, he was to be asked about what "was going on" at each of these times. The respondent had been having difficulty making this determination between high and low points, and was talking about recurrent periods of financial distress when I asked this question.

The full response, before I attempted again to get a specific answer to what he would count as high point or low point years, ran somewhat over seven minutes; the typescript is included as an appendix to this chapter. In preliminary work on this interview, this response was recognized intuitively as a "story." At the same time, it was viewed as irrelevant in the sense that it did not appear to answer the question;

viewed this way, it was actually deleted from the transcript initially prepared for analysis and interpretation. I do not think my deletion was atypical of what researchers do when they focus on those aspects of a response that are relevant to the specific aim of a question. Further, the selecting-deleting activity occurs, as well, at earlier points, for example, during the interview when interviewers interrupt respondents who digress from the point of a question and record only those portions of a response they consider relevant.

The general point of these comments is that standard research practices preclude a firm answer to such questions as: how pervasive are stories in interviews and under what conditions are they more or less likely to occur? There is a cumulative suppression of stories through the several stages of a typical study: interviewers cut off accounts that might develop into stories, they do not record them when they appear, and analysts either discard them as too difficult to interpret or select pieces that will fit their coding systems. It has become evident to me from my own and others' experiences in a variety of studies, that stories are a recurrent and prominent feature of respondents' accounts in all types of interviews. Although they are more likely in relatively unstructured interviews, they also appear in response to moderately structured questions, as in the present example. The form and content of a particular question appears to be less important in whether or not a story will be elicited than the general stance of an interviewer as an attentive listener and how the interviewer responds to a response. That is, if we allow respondents to continue in their own way until they indicate they have finished their answer, we are likely to find stories; if we cut them off with our next questions, if we do not appear to be listening to their stories, or if we record a check mark or a few words on our schedules after they have talked at length, then we are unlikely to find stories. But this is a function of our research procedures and reveals nothing about a general tendency to tell stories, that is, to construct our understanding of our experiences in narrative terms.

SOCIAL ACTION AND THE STRUCTURE OF NARRATIVES

One model for analyzing interview-narratives has been proposed by the sociolinguist, William Labov (1972; 1982; Labov & Waletzky, 1967). He defines several components of a complete narrative, distinguishes between narrative and nonnarrative accounts, provides a theoretical framework relating language, meaning, and action, and presents detailed analyses of "narratives of personal experience." For all these reasons, his work is a major resource for this type of investigation and it serves as a point of departure and of reference for the particular analysis undertaken here.

From the full response I have extracted the core narrative, or skeleton plot; Chart 1 is the record of this reduced version of the original story. Labov defines narrative as a recapitulation of experience that maintains the strict temporal ordering of events as they occurred in the real world.[3] His definition is precisely grounded in temporal connections among successive clauses; flashbacks, comments that suspend the action, and descriptions of character and setting are all excluded from the core narrative itself. They are not, however, excluded from the full story where they serve other functions: orientation of the reader as to place, time, character; an abstract summarizing the story and its points; evaluative comments on events; resolution of the story or the conflict; a coda bringing the narrator and listener back to the present. The narrative sequence is referred to as the complicating action. Labov's categories are used in Chart 1; to maintain the focus on the core narrative, evaluative and other types of clauses have been deleted.

This reduction of the full response to the core narrative is quite radical. In this case, about 15 percent of the full response is included in the complicating action; adding the orientation and abstract bring the total to about 25 percent. I shall return later to what has been excluded. However, since this reduction is a suggestive and powerful analytic tool that offers, for example, guidelines for comparative analysis of collections of narratives from many respondents, I wish first to discuss what may be learned from an analysis of the core narrative.

The first question is: What is this story about? The point of the story is one answer to this question, albeit the most minimal one. My interpretation of the story's point, that is, what I think the narrator intended to communicate as the meaning of the account, is given as the chart title and is taken directly from the abstract: "Yet we always *did* what we had to do / some*how* we did it." It is important to recognize that determining *the* point of a story is an investigative problem. It is not simply stated by the narrator, who may not say explicitly: "This is the point." In this sense, it is not an observable piece of behavior and requires inference and interpretation on the analyst's part. Nor can it always be expressed in the narrator's own words, as it is here. My

CHART 1

The Core Narrative: "Yet we always *did* what we had to do some*how* we did it."

Orientation	004	They weren't troubles in the sense of real troubles no,
	005	but they were en- en- enforced *lean* times
Abstract	013	Yet we always *did* what we had to do
	014	some*how* we did it.
	015	We got through it.
	016	Ah, Danny got severely burned
	017	and uh, had to have skins- a skin graft
	018	and uh, surgery
	019	and was in the hospital for 45 days
	020	and it was expensive
Complicating Action	043	his clothing caught fire
	044	and he lost all of the skin up here, (I: uhm) from the top of his ankle all up t'here.
	048	And they did a graft from here down t'here.
	051	The whole bill came to fifteen hundred dollars. Everything.
	062	Anyhow he called me up one day,
	069	And he said "Jim, would it help you at all if I considered – If I-" he said "If I reduced my bill."
	070	Well I almost fell on the floor.
	077	And when he said that to me I- I almost- I think I did get a little bit dewy around the eyes,
	081	And I said "No, I wouldn't consider it," his reducing this bill at all.
	082	I said "I was about to call you up and here you are calling me up on the telephone."
	083	And I said "Believe it or not, you're next up at bat."
	086	'n I said "Bill, if you can just hang in there I'll get your- I'll mail a check in about three or four days
	087	and that will start a run on this thing
	088	and we'll *stamp* the *life* out of it."
Resolution	089	And that's what we did.

Note: This core narrative is drawn from the full response included in the Appendix; the numbering of clause/idea units follows that in the complete typescript. The labeling of sections as Orientation, etc. follows Labov's model of narrative analysis.

interpretation depends on a reading and assessment of the full response from which the core narrative was extracted.

Further, there is a dialectical relationship between the inferred point and the core narrative that serves empirically to exemplify it. That is, the narrative text in Chart 1 fits closely to the general point; the narrative is a concrete example through which the point is made in detail, the same point that is prefigured and partially expressed in the talk that surrounds *the* story. But this close fit has been constructed through the analytic work itself. For example, there are other temporally ordered sequences of clauses that have not been specified as core narratives, such as the description of a blood clot in his wife's leg and the consequent surgery (026-030), or the effects on the physician of his son's death (093-103).

This interpretive problem is not peculiar to the narrative analytic approach, but is integral to interviewing as a method. A mainstream researcher, reading the above paragraph, might be tempted to assert that this approach is unscientific and that it shows why standardization is necessary. But this is illusory. Standardization involves an analogous process of deletion-selection-interpretation from the complex discourse of the interview. Further, these steps tend to be hidden by the methods used so that we can never retrieve the actual discourse and therefore cannot evaluate the adequacy of any particular investigator's mode of standardization. Here, with the data available for any investigator, an assessment can be made as to whether the interpretation offered is plausible, not a definitive criterion, but certainly not inconsequential.

To return to the question of what the story is about, an answer may also be provided in the form of a paraphrase or summary of what takes place. For example, in the general context of "enforced lean times" where the narrator and his family "somehow" always manage to get "through it," they are faced with a heavy medical expense for treatment of a son's "terrible burn." The physician's offer to reduce the bill is refused. Instead, the narrator succeeds in paying the whole bill in installments. The general point of the story, stated in the abstract, is restated concretely as the resolution: "And that's what we did."

The question of what the story is about may be addressed at a more abstract level, a level of more generalized social meaning and social action. Labov's (1982) recent analysis of narratives of unexpected violence is a significant contribution to this mode of analysis and provides a prototype for this approach. Labov is interested in understanding the social meaning of a course of actions and reactions through an analysis of the sequence of narrative clauses. This requires a second-stage and equally radical reduction of the original story. His central concept, borrowed from Goffman, is that of a "move," that is, an act directed to affirming or changing the social status relationships between actors-speakers. He argues that his stories are instances of requests and the responses to them. Thus, he transforms and reduces the concrete particulars of act sequences in different stories to the following general structure: a request by one actor-speaker; a response by a second actor denying the legitimacy of the request and hence the speaker's claim for a level of social status that would entitle her/him to make the request; a violent response by the first speaker to this denial. The underlying social dynamic is that denial of the legitimacy of a request threatens the social status of the requester, does not allow for other more acceptable grounds for negotiating a response to the request, and therefore leads to violence.

Our story has a different structure. Rather than a request denial-violence plot, it is an offer-refusal-counteroffer plot. Nonetheless, Labov's analysis of the dynamics involved is directly applicable and the two plots can be seen as parallels. Thus, individuals making requests place themselves in an at-risk situation with respect to their social status relationship with the other person. If the request is accepted or if it is denied on reasonable grounds, then the status of the requester is affirmed; but if the legitimacy of the request is denied, then the requester's social status claim is threatened or placed in question.

Offers also raise social status questions, but there is a reversal of roles. Individuals receiving offers have their social status placed at risk. The recipient of an offer is placed in a potentially subordinate position vis-à-vis the person making the offer. The underlying presupposition of an offer is that the recipient has a need, an unsatisfied wish or desire, that the offerer is in a position to satisfy. An additional and more speculative inference is that an offer presupposes an implicit and unspoken request. That is, an offerer may assume that in the circumstances as they are understood the other person could be expected to make a request and would be entitled to make it, but for some reason has not done so. This suggests further that offers are unlikely to be made unless there is an expectation that they will be accepted. Otherwise, in the event of a refusal of the offer, the offerer's social status may be placed at risk: motives for the offer may be impugned, assumptions about the other's position as a potential requester may be questioned or denied, or the social status relationship that legitimizes the right to make an offer may be denied.[4]

Making and responding to offers is clearly a complex and fragile social enterprise. From the point of view of offer recipients, accepting the offer confirms the presumed status relationship with themselves in a subordinate position and validates the presuppositions about their need and implicit role as requesters. To refuse an offer deflects, defuses, and perhaps totally disarms this threat to their social status. However, there must be reasonable grounds for a refusal, otherwise it serves as a counterchallenge to the offerers' social status – implicitly impugning motives, questioning the accuracy of their perception of the situation, and so on. By providing reasonable grounds for a refusal, the status relationship is realigned but in a way that does not involve such a direct challenge to the other person.

In our story, the refusal takes the form of a counteroffer, namely, a promise to pay the unpaid bill in installments. The grounds for this refusal have already been prefigured by the respondent in earlier remarks to the interviewer, namely, by his assertions that he is a responsible man who always paid his debts despite financial stress: "we always got through it." The specific presupposition of the offer, that he may have been making an implicit request for relief of some kind by nonpayment, is also denied. Rather, he had been "saving this big *monster*" to do a "*front*al assault on it . . . when it came time to pay it" (066-067). As further evidence of his nonrequester role, he asserts (to the interviewer) that "believe it or not" other bills had been "*all cleared* out of the way" (064-065), and to the physician-offerer that "believe it or not, you're next up at bat" (083).

Let me summarize what has been learned so far from this approach. Labov's analysis of a request-request denied-violent reaction episode and my application of his model to an offer-offer refusal-counteroffer episode have been interpreted in terms of efforts by speaker-actors to reduce threats to their social status.[5] The analysis has been applied to a radically reduced version of the full response: first, the core narrative includes less than 20 percent of the full response to the initiating question; second, this plot has been reduced to three "moves," providing a highly abstract representation of what the story "means."

The claim that may be made from such an analysis is that we have learned something about the structure of social relationships, about the rules governing how social status is affirmed, challenged, and negotiated, and about the ways in which the meanings of events and actions are expressed in language. These are strong claims, but I would like to add one more, which is that theorizing about the structure, forms, and rules of social action requires either this type of narrative analysis, or an equivalent, that preserves the complex ordering of actions and reactions that constitute social reality. The interpretation of offers, requests, and their ensuing responses depends on models of analysis that include their connectedness to each other. This cannot be done through standard approaches where each step in the naturally ordered sequence is isolated from its context, coded within the framework of a standard code-category system, and then aggregated across populations of respondents and subjected to statistical analysis. This is the signal contribution of methods of narrative analysis: the story contains the sequence of socially meaningful acts without which it would not be a story; its analysis therefore provides the basis for a direct interpretation of a complex unit of social interaction, in comparison to the standard approach where such inferences are based on decontextualized bits and pieces (Mishler, 1979).

NARRATIVE THEMES, CULTURAL MEANINGS, AND PERSONAL IDENTITY

The description of social status relationships that emerges from the Labov model of narrative analysis is formal and abstract. The offer-refusal-counteroffer sequence of moves is a structure that may be filled with any type of content. For example, in an earlier study of first-grade classrooms, I reported children's offers and counteroffers of cookies and popcorn (Mishler, 1975), and it is easy to think of the great variety of institutional contexts, in which bargaining and negotiation through offers and counteroffers are prominent features, where such structures are likely to be found. The power of this form of analysis lies in its generalizability.

We may, however, be interested in other questions that require more attention to the particular content of offers and requests. This would be another meaning of the question: what is the story about? For example, we may wish to examine how cultural values are expressed in narratives, as well as how such values may structure and integrate individual experiences. Another model of narrative analysis that addresses such questions is proposed by Agar and Hobbs (1982). The focus on the problem of coherence, that is, on the ways in which parts of an account are connected together to make a unified, meaningful story. They describe three levels of coherence: local, where each successive utterance is tied to prior ones by syntactic, temporal, or causal relations; global, where utterances exemplify or move forward the overall intent or point of the story; and themal, where utterances express general cultural themes or values. For present purposes, to extend the analysis to questions of cultural values and personal identity, I will examine how this story shows global and themal coherence.

The general point of the story that directed and framed the earlier structural analysis again provides the point of departure. I have suggested that the respondent's account, that is, his response to the initial question, made one general point in a variety of ways: in a context of "enforced lean times," faced with recurrent medical expenses, he asserts that "we always *did* what we had to do some*how* we did it. We got through it" (013-015). Global coherence is achieved through repetition of examples making this same general point. Thus, the general circumstances of financial difficulty are stated several times, often framing a particular instance of an especially heavy bill. The first mention of enforced lean times is followed by a complaint about not being able to buy a boat he wanted to own "in the worst way" (007-009). His list of medical expenses, that will thread through his account, begins with Danny's burn and goes on through increasing childbirth expenses, and his wife's surgery for a blood clot that occurred at "a particularly bad time" (025-027). This extra medical expense "that, uh, took a year to pay that off" was met by "religiously . . . whacking away thirty dollars every week or every two weeks or something" (030-031). Later we learn about the persistent expenses of his wife's chronic illness, the "other doctors' bills from – Nancy used to support about five doctors, for about ten years" (053).

The "*mon*ster" bill for Danny's skin graft comes at another bad time, when there are bills for his wife's illness and a second mortgage on the house. Having "cleared out of the way" (065) all these other bills, he is ready to turn his attention to a "*front*al" assault on this big bill, prior to the physician's offer to reduce it. In this particular context, of the offer and his refusal and counteroffer, he reasserts the general "point" of the story, accenting his own attributes of responsibility and self-reliance: "Nobody had ever offered to do that for me as long as I ever lived" (071). And, "I had a very responsible job and I- I come into a lot of money every- everyday and I- I worked for people who absolutely crucify you if you made a mistake. And ah- I was hum- strung up all the time, really strung right out" (073-076).

Where does his story end? One prime candidate for an ending is what I referred to in the structural analysis as the resolution of the offer-refusal-counteroffer plot, namely, his success in paying off the "*mon*ster" bill. Having promised to "start a run on this thing" and to "stamp the life out of it," he concluded "and that's what we did" (087-089). However, he then continued without acknowledgment or response from the interviewer, although with false starts and a transitional comment that signified his position as one who would know the doctor's story since he "got very close to him" (090), with an episode that is a story in itself with its own point. The "enlightened" doctor's son was brutally killed in Vietnam. The doctor "never got over it," "moved out of Northgate," "sold a magnificent home," and "took his family up to Vermont," where he now practices. It "took the starch right out of him" (092-103). Earlier, we had heard of this doctor as a man of exceptional qualities who is highly regarded by the narrator. He had "imparted massive confidence" (035) to him, was a "rugged" and "athletic" man (039), had done "a terrific job on this kid. Everything came out beautiful" (079-080), and had made an offer to the narrator that "nobody" else had ever done "for as long as I ever lived" (071).

Within the Labov structural analysis, where a sharp distinction is made between narrative and nonnarrative clauses, this episode has a separate structure from the offer-refusal-counteroffer story. Agar and Hobbs do not make this narrative-nonnarrative distinction. Following their approach, we may ask how this episode is related to the general story, that is, in what ways is it globally and thematically coherent with the rest of the account. This leads to another version of our recurrent question of what the story is about, (one that directs us) to issues of personal identity and cultural values.

Two important assumptions underly such an analysis, the same assumptions underlying any interpretation of a personal account or telling about one's self in both clinical and nonclinical contexts: first, whatever else the story is about it is also a form of self-presentation, that is, a particular personal-social identity is being claimed; second, everything said functions to express, confirm, and validate this claimed identity. The first assumption directs us to the content of the identity, to the ways it is expressed through various particulars of the account, and to the ways it represents cultural themes and values. The second supports our search for identity-relevant material throughout the account, in this instance in the episode about the tragic turn in the doctor's life.

The image of self presented by the narrator, that is, the personal identity to which he is laying a claim through his account of repeated trials overcome through his own efforts, including his refusal and counteroffer to the doctor's offer to reduce his bill, may be summarized as follows: he is a responsible, self-reliant man who may have to forego his own personal desires (to own a boat, for example) because of difficult financial circumstances, but who always meets his obligations and pays his debts, debts that result from others' problems, namely his wife's and children's medical expenses. Against these odds, he systematically and "religiously" clears recurrent debts out of the way, mounts a "frontal" assault on a particularly heavy one, and "somehow" always succeeds in doing what has to be done. The doctor-son episode underscores this identity claim by contrast. That is, in contrast to the doctor who "never got over it," the narrator has always stood fast in the face of adversity, has always done what he had to do, and has not let the "starch" be taken out of him. I am suggesting that at this level of analysis, of identity and cultural values, that this extra story appended to the main plot has both global and themal coherence.[6]

In my more general discussion of narrative-analytic approaches (1986), I suggested that a cultural interpretation of stories, that is, an interpretation of how they express and reflect broader cultural frameworks of meaning, requires introduction of more general knowledge of the culture than is contained in the text itself. This is one variant of a methodological procedure Labov and Fanshel (1977) refer to as "expansion," where we bring into the analysis what else we know about the speakers and their local and general circumstances. Essentially, we introduce explicitly what we think must be presupposed by the narrator and listener in order for them to understand each other. These same presuppositions are required by analysts in order for them to understand what is being said.

I am not proposing that this narrator-respondent can provide an analysis of cultural values in terms that might be used by anthropologists. Rather, I am suggesting that for this story to make sense as an identity-claiming story, the narrator must presuppose that he and the interviewer share a view of what constitutes a valued identity in this culture. In this instance, he assumes that they both value responsibility and self-reliance, have high regard for a man who pays his debts, does not come apart in the face of adversity, and works out rational strategies to meet his obligations on his own terms. Further, he does not accept offers of help that might place him in a subordinate position vis-à-vis another person and that might perhaps place him in a situation where he is obligated to the other. These are, of course, well-recognized features of masculine character in the United States. The narrator has aligned himself with this cultural ideal. In Agar and Hobbs's terms, the doctor-son story is a companion to the others which serve as its local context, and it is, therefore, themally coherent with the full account.

NARRATIVE AND THE INTERVIEW CONTEXT

With few exceptions, effects on the form and content of a respondent's story of the research interview as the context in which it is told have received little attention. (See Mishler, 1986, for discussion of this problem.) The narrator is also a research subject and an interviewee who has entered into a limited relationship with a researcher-interviewer who is also the "listener" to the story (Bell, 1983). Typically, the aim of an interview is defined by the interviewer who also controls its shape and flow as well as the form and intent of specific questions. Within the complex of rules and norms that regulate this type of speech event (Hymes, 1967; 1972; also Mishler, 1986), the interviewee's primary obligation is to answer the questions that are asked. This is, of course, a very different context than those that produce the texts that narrative analysts have usually been concerned with, such as fictional narratives or historical accounts.

In the full response under examination here, the interviewer's overt participation was minimal; between the two questions bracketing the response, he inserted three comments (022, 038, 104) and four attention-markers (hm, uhm). Nonetheless, the interviewer was omnipresent in his dual role as researcher and listener. I have already referred to the interviewee-narrator's story as directed to the presentation of a particular image of himself – as an independent, self-reliant man who overcomes adversity and always pays his debts – and his presuppositions about shared cultural values that allow his story to take on the meaning he intends. Certain problems in the analysis and interpretation of interview-narratives may be brought forward by looking at some specific features of this interview within the context of the more general inquiry of which it was a part.

Paget (1983) discusses how her reflections during the course of an interview on the possible similarity between her own and her interviewee's life experiences influenced questions she asked and entered into her understanding and interpretation of the story she was being told. She also points out that her approach, which gave control of the interview process to the interviewee, and her hesitant and searching way of asking questions, encouraged searching, reflective, and extended responses. In a sense, she is describing an interview situation where solidarity was established between herself and her interviewee; they were engaged together in the same task of trying to understand important life experiences. My relationship to this respondent had a quite different quality; it would not be too far off the mark to say that we had an adversary relationship in that we were struggling for control of the interview.

It was a struggle that I lost. I was aware during the interview that I had lost control of what was happening. The respondent successfully evaded direct answers to my questions. He digressed from the specific topic and intent of questions, occasionally complained that they were unclear and difficult to answer, and told many stories. These observations would be inappropriate if this had been an in-depth, unstructured interview of the type that Paget describes where the interviewee was given control; in such an approach, nothing said could be considered digressive and there would be no specific questions about which to complain. But this interview was relatively well structured with a schedule of questions to be asked in the sequence in which they had been arranged; although the questions were often open-ended, each question was designed to elicit an answer relevant to a particular topic.

At the end, I did not think that this was a "good" interview. I had much detailed information about my respondent's life from more than an hour and a half of talk, but I did not have the sense that I had answers to my questions. I felt I had been "conned" or taken for a ride by an artful storyteller who, while entertaining me with a variety of amusing anecdotes, had successfully evaded telling me what I wanted to know.

At the same time I was interviewing him, my wife and collaborator, Anita L. Mishler, was interviewing his wife using the same interview schedule. These separate interviews followed, by about a week, a joint interview when we had interviewed the couple together, using an open and unstructured approach, asking them to talk with us about significant events in their marriage and family history. When Anita and I left the house together, after the follow-up individual interviews, her first comment to me was: "Did he tell you he was an alcoholic?"

It turned out that a significant and central topic in her interview with the wife was the husband's history of alcoholism and its impact on their marriage and family. The wife reported his erratic job history and attendant family financial problems, recurrent marital conflicts and crises including a time when she seriously considered separation and divorce, her decision that she had to be independent and able to earn an income that led to her return to school for further training and entry into a full-time job.

This problem, with all of its ramifying consequences and the ways in which it structured and conditioned their lives, had not been mentioned in the earlier joint interview. It was not mentioned or alluded to in any way in my interview with the husband.

In the light of this new knowledge, acquired outside the boundary of the interview but still within the boundaries of the study, the evasiveness that I experienced took on a more particular meaning. It appeared to represent an effort on his part – a successful effort – to prevent me from learning about this aspect of his life. Although he violated what I as a researcher would consider an essential presupposition of interviews, that is, the basic rule to answer my questions, he maintained its form by continuing to talk to me for the allotted time and keeping me interested through his stories, while keeping me from what really mattered to him. Furthermore, the image he presented of himself as responsive, self-reliant, and independent was made problematic by these additional facts of his personal history. If they had been part of our shared knowledge, the interview might have taken a quite different course. But his self-protective stance was itself a result of the status/power differential between us that is a central feature of standard interviewing procedure and the consequent struggle for control I noted earlier. If I had adopted a different approach, for example, giving him control of the interview as Paget did in her study or offering to "empower" him by enlisting his participation and collaboration in the work (see Mishler, 1986), then he might have told a different story.

This discovery, this new fact learned fortuitously, raises more questions than it answers.[7] The problem is not peculiar to narrative-analytical approaches, nor to interviewing in particular, but is present in all research. We are always making inferences on the basis of partial information. Further, we do not know whether and how the missing information may be relevant to our interpretations. For the type of analysis I have been recommending, this example directs us to the interview situation itself as another context that we must take into consideration in trying to answer the question of what the story is about. In addition to what we have learned from analyses of this respondent's story as a text about normative structures of social action, about the negotiation of status relationships in request-and-offer-sequences, about the narrative expression of cultural values and the ways personal identity claims are aligned with these values, we have also learned that a response serves a purpose, that is, has a function within the social-interpersonal context of the interview itself; in this instance, a self-protective and status-maintaining function vis-à-vis the interviewer. Another type of interview with a less power-centered relationship between interviewee and interviewer would have a different dynamic. The lesson to be learned is not that interviewing is a flawed and faulted method, but that we must include analysis of the interview situation and process in order to arrive at a fuller and more adequate interpretation of respondents' answers to our questions.

DISCUSSION

This is a brief chapter for its intended burdens. One general aim of this analysis of one interview-narrative is to interest other investigators and to encourage them to undertake similar inquiries. What has been learned, I believe, is the following: first, narratives are a naturally-occurring feature of respondents' accounts and, under some interviewing conditions, may be ubiquitous; second, a variety of methods are available for their systematic analysis; third, different methods may be particularly appropriate to questions central to different disciplines, for example, the sociological study of normative structures of social action, anthropological study of cultural values, and psychological study of personal identity; fourth, there are general problems of interviewing and specific problems in the analysis of interview-narratives that require further investigation.

There are two general implications, one for theory and one for research practice, that I wish to highlight in these closing remarks. First, the distinctive feature of narratives is that they refer to meaningful and coherent courses of action, with beginnings, middles, and ends. This makes their analysis especially significant and appropriate for theory construction in the social sciences. That is, a central aim of our work is the description and theoretical explanation of social process, of complex relationships that change through time. But theories of the dynamics of social life rest, in large part, on findings of relationships between static states or attributes, often in the form of an association between two variables. Narrative constructions display the dynamic ordering of events. As we learn how to analyze them in systematic ways, we can begin to develop empirically grounded, more comprehensive, and more adequate dynamic theories.

Second, I have already remarked the ways that standard research practices suppress narrative accounts in interviews. Further, narratives are context-sensitive, their form and content responsive to the aims and conditions of an interview situation. The asymmetric power relationship between interviewee and interviewer that is the key feature of typical research interviews, where the interviewer controls the aims, structure, flow, and eventual use of interview data, is a particularly significant influence on whether and what kinds of narratives appear. If we wish to hear respondents' stories then we must invite them into our work as collaborators, sharing control with them, so that together we try to understand what their stories are about.

APPENDIX

Typescript of an Interview-Narrative

001 I: You wouldn't call those times though troubling times?
002   Uh, low points in that sense?
003 R: Well they were- they were troubling times no,
004   THEY WEREN'T TROUBLES IN THE SENSE OF REAL TROUBLES NO,
005   BUT THEY WERE EN- EN ENFORCED *LEAN* TIMES
006   (I: Hm hm) where I can remember when the kids were young,
007   I wanted to own a boat in the worst way.
008   I didn't care if it cost a hundred dollars
009   I wanted a boat.
010   (. . .) I was into (. . .) things to do with (. . .)
011   I think that one of the single things held me back more than anything else, the feeling of financial s- security.
012   It always seemed to be absent. (P)
013   YET WE ALWAYS *DID* WHAT WE HAD TO DO
014   SOME*HOW* WE DID IT.
015   WE GOT THROUGH IT.
016   AH, DANNY GOT SEVERELY BURNED
017   AND UH, HAD TO HAVE SKINS- A SKIN GRAFT
018   AND UH, SURGERY
019   AND WAS IN THE HOSPITAL FOR FORTY-FIVE DAYS
020   AND IT WAS EXPENSIVE
021   and the uh, expense of the- of the children and childbirth and so forth went from I think with Suzy the first one something like six dollars up into a couple of *thou*sand dollars.
022 I: (heh heh) Six dollars sounds incredible.

023 R: (. . .) The Blue Cross Blue Shield covered everything for her except six dollars, (I: hh) at Maintown Hospital.

024   They were all born at Maintown.

025   And uh, when Richard was admitted (P) ah, that would be ah (P) (. . .) that was a- that was a- that was a particularly bad time.

026   When Richard was uh- When Nancy was admitted to the hospital with Richard,

027   they discovered she had a blood clot in her legs, in her vein,

028   did surgery on her at 29 so I guess (. . .) that probably saved her life.

029   (I: Hm hm) They did a ligation

030   and (P) and that uh, took a year to pay that off.

031   It was one of these things where you religiously had to whack away 30 dollars every week or every two weeks or something.

032   I remember one time when Danny was severely burned.

033   (P) We had a doctor here by the name of- of William Turner affiliated with Northgate Hospital to do the skin graft on the boy

034   'n he lives right up the street here.

035   And I- somehow or other, he- he imparted *mass*ive confidence to me.

036   I would put myself in his care *any* day, *any* day. (I: uh)

037   Whatever that man said it- he seemed to come down *right on* the *right* place.

038 I: They take special courses in that in medical school, (R: Do you?) doctor's presence. (R: uh huh) (I: heh heh)

039 R: Well he was a- a very rugged 'n short uh, extremely uh, athletic man uh, uh, wavy blond hair and he hadda uh-

040   He wrestled and did gymnastics and like he- he- built like a flying wedge.

041   And he was- he was rather short.

042   And Danny got a- this terrible burn,

043   HIS CLOTHING CAUGHT FIRE

044   AND HE LOST ALL THE SKIN UP HERE, (I; uhm) FROM THE TOP OF HIS ANKLE ALL UP T'HERE.

045   Danny's somewhere upstairs in bed,

046   he's got the flu.

047   He came in early today.

048   AND THEY DID A GRAFT FROM HERE DOWN T'HERE.
049   And I remember being so concerned about it,
050   but anyhow I think Bill Turner-
051   THE WHOLE BILL CAME TO FIFTEEN HUNDRED DOLLARS. EVERYTHING.
052   (P) (. . .) and it came in at a time when we were just taking on a second mortgage on the house for some reason.
053   And it cum in at a time when the other doctors' bills from- Nancy used to support about five doctors, for about ten years.
054   She's been very ill over- she's very ill now by the way.
055   She has Meniere's Disease
056   and she fell over backwards in school (P) last Friday- Thursday or Friday last week.
057 I: You mean the inner ear (. . .)?
058 R: Inner ear yeah.
059   And she took a- just her- her feet gave out from underneath
060   and she's been in- in bed since- since then.
061   Today's the first day- (. . .)
062   ANYHOW HE CALLED ME UP ONE DAY,
063   (P) because I hadn't paid the bill.
064   And believe it or not when he *called* every other bill that had gotten *in the way of his getting paid had been paid*
065   and they're *all cleared* out of the way
066   but I was saving this big *mon*ster, the biggest one of all, up
067   so I could do a *fron*tal assault on it when it- when it came time to pay it.
068   And I was sitting right where you are we had the phone here then.
069   AND HE SAID "JIM, WOULD IT HELP YOU AT ALL IF I CONSIDERED- IF I-" HE SAID "IF I REDUCED MY BILL."
070   WELL I ALMOST FELL ON THE FLOOR.
071   Nobody had ever offered to do that for me as long as I ever lived.
072   (P) And I was so over*whelmed* that I- I was (P) beset by-
073   I had a very responsible job
074   and I- I come into a lot of money every- every day
075   and I- I worked for people who absolutely crucify you if you made a mistake.
076   And ah- I was hum- strung up all the time, really strung right out.

077 AND WHEN HE SAID THAT TO ME I- I ALMOST- I THINK I DID GET A LITTLE BIT DEWY AROUND THE EYES,

078 to think that *any*body would have that much consideration

079 who had, in *par*ticular, just done *such* a *terr*ific job on this kid.

080 Everything came out beautiful.

081 AND I SAID "NO, I WOULDN'T CONSIDER IT," HIS REDUCING THIS BILL AT ALL.

082 I SAID "I WAS ABOUT TO CALL YOU UP AND HERE YOU ARE CALLING ME UP ON THE TELEPHONE."

083 AND I SAID "BELIEVE IT OR NOT, YOU'RE NEXT UP AT BAT."

084 And I said "I- you don't even know it, but-"

085 'n I- I think I had kept him waiting about four months to pay the bill.

086 'N I SAID "BILL, IF YOU CAN JUST HANG IN THERE I'LL GET YOUR- I'LL MAIL A CHECK IN ABOUT THREE OR FOUR DAYS

087 AND THAT WILL START A RUN ON THIS THING

088 AND WE'LL *STAMP* THE *LIFE* OUT OF IT."

089 AND THAT'S WHAT WE DID.

090 But uh- uh- that- I got very close to him

091 and uh- He had three or four children

092 and was very much a- uh- an enlightened man

093 and his son was in the Marines in Vietnam

094 and his hands were tied behind his back

095 and he was forced to kneel on the ground

096 and they shot him through the head.

097 And he never got over it.

098 He moved out of Northgate.

099 He *sold* a *magnif*icent home over in the Adam's Pond area

100 and took his family up to Vermont.

101 He is a great skier

102 and he does all his fracture work with the skiers up there now in Vermont

103 and it just- took the starch right out of him.

104 I: it's a terrible thing.

105 (P) But I take it- Part of the question is what- what would you count as a high point or low point years

106 and what's the meaning of (. . .)?

107 R: Well that would be a low point.

Notes on Typescript Notation. The typescript is arranged to display the narrative aspects of the response as clearly as possible: each line represents an "idea unit" (see Chafe, 1980; also Paget, 1983) and the units/clauses of the core narrative discussed in the text are capitalized. Italics mark extra stress, (P) indicates a pause, (. . .) unintelligible words. For discussion of transcription as a problem and different approaches, see Mishler (1984).

NOTES

1.   These assertions about the mainstream tradition are based on an extended critical analysis of current research practices that may be found in my recent monograph (Mishler, 1986). Limitations of space preclude representation of that detailed argument. The analysis of an interview narrative in this paper depends on, and carries one step further, an alternative approach to interviewing developed and proposed there.

2.   The interview used in these analyses comes from an unpublished study of marital relationships at mid-life (Mishler & Mishler, 1976).

3.   The question of whether temporal ordering is a necessary and/or sufficient condition for narratives is discussed in Mishler (1986) with reference to other models of narrative analysis.

4.   Requests and offers are among the prominent types of illocutionary acts discussed by speech act theorists. Searle (1975) refers to them as instances of the more general classes, respectively, of directives and commissives. On the whole, this tradition of linguistic-philosophic analysis has focused primarily on the presuppositions and implicit rules under which a statement will be understood as having a particular illocutionary meaning. There has been little attention to the problem addressed by Labov and the present analysis of the actions and reactions that follow a statement and of the complex social status dynamics involved. For further discussion of speech act theory, see Austin, 1962; Searle, 1969, 1975; also the review by Fraser, 1974.

5.   This discussion of the status implications of offers and requests assumes relationships as defined within a commodity-exchange culture. Hyde's (1983) analysis of the difference between such a culture and one where the "circulation of gifts" has a significant place, suggests that offers might have different meanings in different cultural contexts.

6.   The multilayered meanings of this, or any, story may be illustrated by Dr. Roberta Isberg's response to my analysis. She reported no difficulty in understanding how the tag-episode about the doctor and his son was related to the "other" story, that is, coherence was not problematic for her, since she had viewed the full response as all being about fathers and sons.

7.   Garfinkel (1967) reports a striking instance of a post-study revelation and raises but does not pursue in detail how it might affect his original analysis. Eight years after a sex-change operation, when a penis was replaced with an artificial vagina,

the individual who had undergone the operation reported a fact that "she" had concealed from both physician and researcher, despite 35 hours of tape-recorded interviews with each of them over a period of three years. This fact was a history of taking female hormones from adolescence onwards; knowledge of this would have radically altered the medical understanding of the patient's condition and would have led to a refusal to perform the operation. It also has significant implications for the investigator's interpretation. (See Chapter 5 and the postscript Appendix.)

REFERENCES

Agar, M. and Hobbs, J. R. (1982). Interpreting discourse: Coherence and the analysis of ethnographic interviews. *Discourse Processes, 5,* 1-32.

Austin, J. L. (1962). *How to do things with words.* Oxford: Oxford University Press.

Bell, S. (1983). *Narratives of health and illness I: DES daughters tell stories.* Unpublished manuscript.

Chafe, W. L. (1980). The deployment of consciousness in the production of a narrative. In W. L. Chafe (Ed.). *The pear stories: Cognitive, cultural, and linguistic aspects of narrative production* (pp. 9-50). Norwood, NJ: Ablex.

Fraser, B. (1974). [Review of J. Searle's *Speech acts*]. *Foundations of Language, II:* 433-446.

Garfinkel, H. (1967). *Studies in ethnomethodology.* Englewood Cliffs, NJ: Prentice-Hall.

Hyde, L. (1983). *The gift: Imagination and the erotic life of property.* New York: Vintage Books.

Hymes, D. (1967). Models of the interaction of language and social setting. *Journal of Social Issues, 23* (2), 8-28.

Hymes, D. (1972). Models of the interaction of language and social life. In J. J. Gumperz and D. Hymes (Eds.). *Directions in sociolinguistics.* New York: Holt, Rinehart, and Winston.

Labov, W. (1972). The transformation of experience in narrative syntax. In W. Labov (Ed.). *Language in the inner city: Studies in the black vernacular.* Philadelphia, PA: University of Pennsylvania Press.

Labov, W. (1982). Speech actions and reactions in personal narrative. In D. Tannen (Ed.). *Analyzing discourse: Text and talk.* Washington, DC: Georgetown University Press.

Labov, W. and Fanshel, D. (1977). *Therapeutic discourse: Psychotherapy as conversation.* New York: Academic Press.

Labov, W. and Waletzky, J. (1967). Narrative analysis: Oral versions of personal experience. In J. Helms (Ed.). *Essays on the verbal and visual arts.* Seattle, WA: University of Washington Press.

Mishler, E. G. (1975). "Wou' you trade cookies with the popcorn?": Talk of trades among six year olds. In O. K. Garnica and M. L. King (Eds.). *Language, children and society.* New York: Pergamon.

Mishler, E. G. (1979). Meaning in context: Is there any other kind? *Harvard Educational Review, 49* (1), 1-19.

Mishler, E. G. (1984). *The discourse of medicine: Dialectics of medical interviews.* Norwood, NJ: Ablex.

Mishler, E. G. (1986). *Research Interviewing: Context and Narrative* Cambridge, MA: Harvard University Press, in press

Mishler, E. G. and Mishler, A. L. (1976). Marital relationships at midlife. Unpublished study proposal and interview schedule.

Paget, M. A. (1983). Experience and knowledge. *Human Studies,* 6 (2), 67-90.

Searle, J. R. (1969). *Speech acts: An essay in the philosophy of language.* Cambridge: Cambridge University Press.

Searle, J. R. (1975). Indirect Speech Acts. In P. Cole and J. L. Morgan (Eds.). *Syntax and semantics* (Vol. 3). New York: Academic Press.

13

Deconstructing Histories: Toward a Systematic Criticism of Psychological Narratives

Robert S. Steele

"Watch out when they swears they's telling the truth"
(old wives wisdom)

Narratives which purport that they are true – like case studies, biographies, histories, or certain kinds of theories – have a marginal position in American psychology which has purposely limited its domain to what can be ascertained by experimental or empirical research conforming to a peculiar mixture of methodological criteria imported from logical empiricism, natural science, engineering, horticultural statistics, and the "show me" common sense of Missouri farmers. While productive of findings about everything from the visual system of the squid to the behavior of college students pretending to be prison guards, this psychology has had little success in dealing with narrative psychologies, like psychoanalysis, which claim to be scientific and produce elaborate accounts that describe how the psyche works, trace the diachronic and synchronic dimensions of human development, and plot the interactions between the person and the environment responsible for producing both the idiosyncracies of the individual and the commonalities of human character.

Science conceived of on the American plan cannot deal with the complexities of such narrative psychologies. At best it extracts hypotheses from them, like quotes out of context, to be tested in the laboratory on some randomly coerced group of subjects. Some studies validate a hypothesis, some disconfirm it. Debate about a theory's validity soon moves from the ideas to quibbles over methodological rigor. Meanwhile, case studies which are the primary evidence for most varieties of narrative theories, and especially for psychoanalysis, are ignored. Why prefer the experiment to the case study? Fisher and Greenberg in their massive review, *The Scientific Credibility of Freud's Theories and Therapy,* provide the typical experimentalist's answer. They say that in citing evidence for or against a Freudian hypothesis they did not "rule out studies that had defects in their experimental designs or that were based on oversimplistic notions concerning Freud's model" (1977, p. 15). They assure us that they cite only information gained from "procedures which are repeatable and in which one can check on the objectivity of the reporting observer" (p. 15). In opting for the two sacred requirements of experimentalism – repeatability and objectivity – Fisher and Greenberg are willing to excuse stupidity. However, they rejected all case studies. While they allow that such work may contain interesting and important information, they assert that "there is no way to separate the good from the bad" (p. 15). Of course they accepted both good and bad experimental work, but that has the advantage of appearing scientific.

I submit that there are ways of judging the quality of psychological narratives and evaluating the evidence they present, but that because of scientism, like that displayed by Fisher and Greenberg, American psychology has failed to explore, debate, or use methods of textual criticism.

A META-METHODOLOGICAL RATIONALE FOR TEXTUAL CRITICISM

Evaluating psychological narratives, which are a subset of the literature of fact, can be conceived of as a broadening of Popper's criterion of falsifiability for solving the problem of demarcation between the scientific and unscientific. The falsification criterion holds that "statements or systems of statements, in order to be ranked as scientific, must be capable of conflicting with possible or conceivable observations" (Popper, 1963, p. 39). Science, according to Popper, does not advance by verification, but by falsification – by testing conjectures in an attempt to refute them. Although Popper maintains that psychoanalytic theories are unscientific because they are "simply non-testable, irrefutable," and that there "is no conceivable human behavior which could contradict them," (pp. 37-38) this is not true. While psychoanalytic hypotheses, and propositions of other narrative psychologies, may be difficult to test either by experiment or field observation, they are not – as Popper says – irrefutable. This is because it can be shown – in the spirit of falsification – that many psychoanalytic statements conflict with observations. For if the range of empiricism is extended to include close textual reading then narrative works are testable and refutable on a variety of grounds. These include: internal inconsistencies in the formulation of theory, ideology and not observation forming the bases of theory, the failure of case studies to support theoretical conjectures, and the omission of relevant data when reporting findings. Put succinctly, whenever a psychological narrative claims to be true, then it can be evaluated by the falsification criterion because one can decide if what it says is false.

While Popper limits his critical methodology to the scientific testing of hypotheses, Collingwood elaborates a similar approach for the evaluation of histories. Collingwood accepts no authorities or authorial truth claims. He says, "the scientific historian does not treat statements as statements but as evidence: not as true or false accounts of the facts which they profess to be accounts," but as data which can be continually re-sorted into differing narrative accounts (1956, p. 275). The history, for him, is like the novel in that both stand on their own account and are to be judged by the coherence of the picture they create. In addition both the history and the novel can be judged by whether or not they make sense to the imagination and the necessity they create for events to be arranged in precisely the way the narrative orders them. Where novelist and historian part company is in the fact that "the historian's picture is meant to be true." He or she must "construct a picture of things as they really were and of events as they really happened" (Collingwood, 1956, p. 245-246). These criteria for writing history can of course be used in evaluating psychological narratives.

Collingwood's approach to history, and to a limited extent Popper's to science, are hermeneutic in that they recognize and explore the role that interpretation plays in human constructions of reality (Radnitzky, 1973). While positivism has always maintained the existence of the fact as a near sacrosanct unit of information unadulterated by human interests and secured by objectivity, hermeneutics does not seek a grounding in fact. It maintains that a fact is a construction, a part of a whole. The fact both gives to and takes meaning from the context of explanation in which it is situated. Hermeneutics, which is the art or science of interpretation, has since its inception been concerned with the interpretation of texts and contexts; that is, explication and exegetics (Palmer, 1969). For over a century it has been a study central to the arts and humanities. Recently its domain has been expanded to the study of psychoanalysis (Ricoeur, 1970; Steele, 1979).

At base hermeneutics is dialogue; the engagement between text and reader, client and therapist, other and self in coming to mutual understanding or in clarifying disagreement. Grounded as they are in conversations between analyst and analysand, psychoanalytic psychologies share with hermeneutics a fundamental commitment to making sense of human communication. Unlike natural science, hermeneutics thus provides a meta-theoretical framework for the evaluation of psychoanalytic narratives which is in harmony with the daily practices of analysts themselves. Just as engagement, care, and critical distance are essential in good clinical work, so too are they vital in hermeneutics. The interpreter must become intimate with the texts s/he is reading and must immerse her or himself in the wordly worlds texts create. S/he must also care for the text, trying to insure that s/he does not do violence to the meaning or intent of the work. The text must be cultivated, that is its sense of the world must be brought to fruition by the intepreter. But despite her or his care and engagement the reader must claim her or his independence as a subject not allowing her or himself to be subjugated by the text. To understand, not to worship, is the goal of hermeneutics. So much psychoanalytic writing has failed at this last point because having conceived of themselves as followers of Freud, Jung, or Adler many authors have sacrificed their subjectivity and judgment in order to maintain the founder's legend and to advance his paradigm.

Through the use of five different interpretive strategies I will, after briefly outlining what deconstruction is, show by means of example how the meta-methodological framework established above can be used in reading the works of both Freud and Jung. Like science, hermeneutics progresses by the slow accumulation of evidence or readings which are not devoted to saving the appearances but to clearing away idols which stand between us and our engagement with existence. When present in a narrative which insists on its truth, inconsistency, tailored evidence, omissions, mythic accounts, and unexamined biases of perspective all serve to disguise truth, which from an idealist deconstructive point-of-view is what is left when all distortions have been analyzed.

DECONSTRUCTING THE LITERATURE OF FACT

Deconstruction is the literary activity of taking apart a text. When dealing with fictions such critical readings examine the ways in which plot, character, time, situation and authorial perspective articulate in building a story. Applied to factions – narratives which claim to be true and in which facts are the narremes of the discourse – deconstruction extends its domain to the epistemological. When an author claims that her or his story is true or that the theory s/he is proposing is based on observational fact then textual deconstruction becomes critical scientific reading examining how a text or *oeuvre* invalidates itself.

The tools for performing such "taking aparts" are numerous, ranging from Marxist criticisms of science to Lacanian interpretations of painting. Herein, however, my reading will be oriented by three modes of textual deconstruction: psychoanalysis, structuralism, and feminism. Interpretation is at the heart of psychoanalysis which, according to Laplanche and Pontalis, can be defined as "the bringing out of the latent meaning of given material" (1973, p. 222). Given a dream, symptom, joke, or recollection of some event Freud rarely accepted the manifest account as anything but a text which required interpretation in order to uncover its significance or latent meaning. Distortion motivated by denial was to be undone by interpretation which by considering associations, condensations, displacements, narrativization, and symbolism would right the wrongs of a story produced by a consciousness wishing to hide sexual secrets from itself and others. Reading Freud is an education in interpretation not only because he is a master hermeneut, but also because his accounts of his life and theories are themselves distorted.

At a microtextual level in terms of examining tropes, word play, allusions, misbegotten sentences, or factual misrepresentation psychoanalytically guided textual analysis is useful, but at a macrotextual level in terms of identifying the forms to which a narrative accommodates itself psychoanalysis is too limiting because it reduces each work to a replay of a sexual tragedy peopled by the archetypes of mother, father, and child. To be able to see the form to which a narrative tends is important because the type will shape how situations, evidence, character, and time are coordinated within a text (Frye, 1957; White, 1973). When real events are given the form of a story then not only are questions of their veracity important, but the ways in which they have been narrativized must also be examined (Boswell, in press).

Continually reproducing the structure of its central drama, the Oedipus myth, Freud's case studies along with his formulations about how the psyche functions are tragic and ironic, while Jung's continual replotting of the journey of the hero makes his cases and theory romantic. The tropological structures of Freud's and Jung's writings also differ. Consonant with his romantic emplotment Jung's work turns around synecdoche; psyche and environment are related synchronistically, that is, in acausally meaningful ways wherein the microcosm of the soul finds symbolic resonance within the macrocosm of the world. While Lacan (1977) maintains that psychoanalytic discourse is governed by the tropes of metaphor and metonymy, the reductionistic thrust of Freud's interpretations wherein body parts, psychosexual developmental stages, or object relatedness are used to characterize the entirety of psychic life argue that metonymy (part for whole) is the major trope of his discourse. Another figure of speech, anacoluthon, plays a significant role in psychoanalysis. Anacolutha are contradictory speeches and these dominate analysands' accounts of their lives. As an interpretive strategy, psychoanalysis transforms contradictory speech into ordered discourse by representing experience in the limited terms of the meaning-filled psychosexual body.

Form is surrounded by genre which is embedded in a cultural-historical context. The genre I am here considering is the literature of fact or factions. These are histories, life stories, and theories which claim to be true and which if not written in an explicit story form use a variety of narrative devices in presenting themselves. Created in the wake of the scientific revolution this genre often assumes an objective perspective, but that assumption distorts factions in several ways. For example, those written by educated white men, who themselves founded objectivity, often display ethno and androcentrism as well as class, racial and religious prejudice. Feminism has been a powerful deconstructive force in uncovering the masculine bias of the literature of fact and in the following I shall demonstrate a few ways in which feminist criticism can be used to question both Freud's and Jung's objectivity.

A GUIDE TO IDENTIFYING TEXTUAL DISTORTIONS

Inconsistency is the most easily read sign of narrative distortion. A good writer often avoids the appearance of it by subtly tailoring accounts in order to disguise their flaws. Seeing how an author has constructed a passage in order to "make the pieces fit" requires not only a thorough familiarity with the author's style and thought, but also a suspicious eye. The third type of textual distortion I'll examine is the least obvious and yet the most powerful: all narratives leave out people, events, or ideas which if included would cast doubt on the truth of the theory being expounded or the story being told. Textual distortion by omission of relevant data is difficult to see when reading a work because there are often only obscure signs in the text that point to what is missing from it.

When one has ferreted out various instances where a text is inconsistent, where an author has strained the fabric of a narrative in order to make it fit together, and where vital information has been omitted one has simply collected the data and has at most shown that this or that author is mortal and like all humans tells lies, distorts the facts, and leaves out information which would defame her or him. To be of more than incidental interest this data must be systematized by the interpreter. S/he must show that these pieces form a pattern by constructing an argument or narrative about why and how these disparate distortions form a heretofore unseen unity which tells us something we have not known about the author or texts.

Textual deconstruction spreads beyond the work of one text or the *oeuvre* of an author. Every text and every author shares with others a worldview, a cultural-historical perspective on humankind, nature, and existence. Such background assumptions are, because we as readers often share them, difficult to see and yet they are the most pervasive and devastating forms of textual distortion because they are created by our collusion in a civilization. They are the common sense of culture which often hides both prejudice and misunderstanding.

I will illustrate how one reads for each of these five different types of textual distortion by drawing on analyses I have done in a more extensive study of the lives and works of Freud and Jung (Steele, 1982).

Inconsistency

Freud is utterly consistent in his insistence that his work before 1907 was completely rejected by his colleagues. For example he says his "writings were not reviewed in medical journals, or, if as an exception they were reviewed, they were dismissed with expressions of scornful or pitying superiority" (1914, pp. 22-23). Similar complaints are found in other places (Freud, 1900, p. xxv; Freud, 1925, p. 49), and almost all of Freud's psychoanalytic biographers repeat this story of the master's early rejection (Jones, 1953; Kris, 1954; Schur, 1972). But, how could a man whose first major study, *The Interpretation of Dreams,* published in 1900 have been so completely rejected if only nine years later he was honored by being invited to give a series of lectures on his work at a foreign university? This seeming inconsistency is perhaps the first that most people encounter when reading Freud, but we are so familiar with stories of great men being rejected in their own land and time that we fail to see that Freud never offers a single quote from reviews to substantiate his claim, or that of the three reviews his biographer Jones (1953, p. 252) cites as evidence of Freud's rejection two are actually positive!

Collingwood insists that a historical narrative must make sense, but how does one make sense of a man becoming famous and yet being rejected by his colleagues? Going back to the records of the time and reading the actual reviews is a way to check on the rejection story. This is what Bry and Rifkin (1962), Ellenberger (1970), and Decker (1977) did. They found that in professional journals and lay publications Freud's early works were widely reviewed and that all the reviews were respectful of his efforts and most were positive in their evaluation of his work.

Jung, too, is fond of the story of his rejection. He complains that his works received poor reviews and says about his years of service at Burghölzi, "I need scarcely mention that my concentration and self-imposed confinement alienated me from my colleagues" (1973, p. 113). This complaint is similar to one he makes about being an outcast during his college years, but simple research into his achievements and going back to letters written when he was at Burghölzi cast doubt on the lonely hero scenario. In college he was elected president of his fraternity, a job rarely held by social misfits. At Burghölzi within less than seven years of beginning work there he had risen to second in command, and his letters from this time are full of complaints about the administrative demands on his time (McGuire, 1974).

Stories of rejection told in the context of famous men's autobiographies are *prima facie* contradictory. There may be cases in which ostracism has occurred, but it is more likely that these men have shaped their histories to a popular narrative pattern among successful men of the modern era: the story of the outcast who perseveres despite disapproval to reveal a profound truth to a disbelieving world. Freud so believed in his rejection that the dismissal of his work by critics became for him essential to its validity. He postulated that given his patients' denials of infantile sexuality it was obvious that his readers would also want to deny such events and so they must reject his theories (Freud, 1914). That he was incapable of seeing the acceptance of his ideas is consistent with his self-portrait as the outsider, marginal Jew, and leader of a revolutionary movement. His stories of rejection served also to foster solidarity among his followers.

Jung repeatedly shows that in hero myths the protagonist is often cast-out from his own land to wander the world where he makes a great discovery with which he then returns to his people. The stories of both Freud's and Jung's self-analyses conform to this pattern. They left the normal terrain of consciousness on inward journeys of discovery where within the unconscious realm they grappled with the demons of human nature in order to return as enlightened souls to minister to humankind. Jung and Freud both knew the myth of the hero and the necessity of his being rejected. Each of them ennobled himself by accommodating his life story to its narrative pattern. Both men were extremely sensitive to criticisms because each felt he had discovered the greatest of truths. They therefore took their reviewers' lack of universal acclaim or studied indifference as rejection. We need not follow them in this mis-reading which lead them and their followers to produce the story of the rejected prophet for this tale is inconsistent with the actual reviews and the rapid acceptance of both men's ideas into the canon of Western thought.

Inconsistencies spread. Having seen one, then doubt is sensitized and they begin appearing everywhere. Notice, for example. Freud's statement that his collaborator in writing *Studies on Hysteria*, Josef Breuer, was not in favor of the hypothesis that hysteria has a sexual cause (1896c, p. 199), but a month earlier he wrote that he and Breuer both maintained that hysterical symptoms were the result of a psychic trauma originating in "the patient's sexual life" (1896b, p. 162). Breuer did write in *Studies* that the majority of severe neurosis in women "*have their origin in the marriage bed*" (1895, p. 246), but in 1925 Freud says, "It would have been difficult to guess from the *Studies on Hysteria* what importance sexuality has in the aetiology of neurosis" (p. 22). There is, however, no need to guess. Freud said it was the cause; Breuer that it was a factor.

There are several reasons for these inconsistencies in Freud's accounts of Breuer's support, or lack of it, for the hypothesis that hysteria is caused by sexual disturbances. Breuer did vacillate on this issue because he felt more evidence was needed to support the conjecture, however Freud demanded Breuer's absolute support and he was severely disappointed by Breuer's caution. Also, once Freud was completely committed to the sexual hypothesis he tried to make it his discovery alone by eliminating any references to Breuer's contributions, to those of Wilhelm Fliess, or to the work of another Viennese physician – Albert Moll – whose investigations of infantile sexuality and its aetiological significance in neurosis slightly predated Freud's work (Sulloway, 1979). Because scientific fame is often linked with being the first to make a discovery and Freud very much desired to be famous he and his followers in producing his reputation had to expunge from their historical records the fact that Freud had help in his researches and that other investigators had made similar discoveries before he did (Ellenberger, 1970).

Inconsistencies in Freud's accounts of the history of his work are disturbing because he insisted that as an analyst his job was to establish, often in opposition to his patients' denials, the actual but censored histories of their lives. He also insists that the analyst is the measuring instrument in psychoanalysis and therefore can tolerate no "distortions" in himself because these would inevitably warp his therapeutic investigations (1912). Unfortunately, Freud's historical accounts of his own life are riddled with inconsistencies. How then could he, by his own criterion, be a satisfactory analytic investigator? The answer is, if one refuses to accept contradictions, that he could not be one. The evidence for this is plentiful, but I will illustrate it with another example of textual inconsistency.

In three papers published in 1896 Freud set forth his first psychoanalytic formulation: the seduction theory. In each of these research reports he insists that adult hysteria is a delayed reaction to sexual abuse in childhood. However, he explicitly states that none of his adult patients ever told him actual stories of having been molested as children (1896a, p. 153; 1896b, pp. 165-166; 1896c, p. 204). He argues that the power of his new psychoanalytic methods are that they allow him to piece together these "seduction scenes" from his clients' fragmentary, distorted and denied recollections. His patients' denials of his reconstructions are taken as evidence by him that the sexual abuse actually occurred, but remains too traumatic for his analysands to avow.

Although the nature of the infantile sexual trauma would change as Freud's work evolved, the seduction theory provided the paradigm for psychoanalytic narrative explanation: infantile sexual events are traumatic causes in adult neurosis. Adults in treatment repress all knowledge of such events, but through the analyst's interpretive acumen, persistence, and construction of a convincing account of such events clients will eventually come to admit to these sexual catastrophies and probably be cured. Our belief in Freud's methods rests on our trust in him as a truthful narrator. If we are to accept that he uncovers what his patients deny then we must be able to believe that he can reconstruct historical truth.

This belief is severely shaken by inconsistencies in Freud's retelling of history. Just a decade after announcing the seduction theory, and now wishing to reject it, Freud tells us that he was taken in by his patients' stories of seduction and had unfortunately believed their accounts (1906). He repeats this excuse in 1914 and again in 1925. Finally about this early theory he says, "Almost all my women patients told me that they had been seduced by their fathers" (1933, p. 120).

Did Freud's patients tell him they were sexually molested as children or did they as his original 1896 papers maintain deny these events even when he insisted that seduction had taken place? There is no text unauthored by Freud to which we can return to establish the historical reality and Freud does not ever quote directly any of his patients' accounts. Given the prevalence of the sexual abuse of children today and its traumatic effects on some adults' lives it seems likely that some of Freud's clients must have been abused as children. The problem for us here, however, is not with the reality of childhood sexual abuse, but with Freud's reliability as a historian. From 1906 on he fails to recount accurately the recorded textual history in his 1896 papers of his own work on seduction. Such a textual inconsistency must cast grave doubts on our belief in him as a teller of the truth.

Making the Pieces Fit

Textual inconsistencies are instances in which an author has failed to construct a seamless narrative and they serve to heighten a reader's sensitivity to less glaring textual distortions. Theories organize narratives which in turn order facts into a coherent account. It is a commonplace misunderstanding of science that facts are rather miraculous units of information which stand free from any theoretical coloring. How this could be so can best be explained by a positivist, but for the hermeneutically trained reader a fact is an information unit, a narreme, in factive discourse or writing about what really happened.

If as Freud pictured it reconstructing a life history is like putting together a puzzle, then making the pieces fit is similar to filing off the corners of jigsaw puzzle pieces in order to force them together.

Freud's filing is always guided by his desire to prove a theory: infantile sexual events cause adult neurosis. It is difficult for him to prove this because he never did longitudinal studies, but depended on his interpretations of adult patients' reminiscences to establish the efficacy of childhood traumas. At best he could provide reasons, not causes: write history, not science.

At a microtextual level let us see how Freud manufactures the facts of a case. The Wolf Man case was written by Freud in order to refute Adler's and Jung's criticisms that psychoanalysis confuses adult recollections with actual childhood events. It is fitting, therefore, that the case should turn around an event that Freud asserts actually happened in the patient's infancy, but which is in large part his own reconstruction. The Wolf Man recollected from a time when he was two-and-a-half "a scene, incomplete but, so far as it was preserved, definite. Grusha [a servant] was kneeling on the floor, and beside her a pail and a short broom made of a bundle of twigs; he was also there, and she was teasing him or scolding him" (Freud, 1918, p. 91). Taking two pieces of information from other parts of the analysis, Wolf Man's compulsion as an adult for falling in love with servant girls and his boyish compassion for John Huss which Freud asserts is common in enuretics, Freud constructs his revised version of the Grusha scene: "When he saw the girl scrubbing the floor he had micturated in the room and she had rejoined, no doubt jokingly, with a threat of castration" (1918, p. 82). The phrase "no doubt jokingly" is a clever piece of writing because it distracts the reader from questioning the reality of the events focusing attention instead on whether or not Grusha was joking. This sleight of pen camouflages two additions Freud has made to Wolf Man's recollection: urination and the threat of castration. Wolf Man remembered neither of them; both of them, however, are facts necessitated by the narrative Freud is constructing. Later in the case Freud uses his constructed scene, not the Wolf Man's recollection, as an event which proves that even at the age of two-and-a-half children are capable of remembering earlier observations of adult intercourse, mimicked supposedly by the urination, and being traumatized by threats, joking or not, of castration.

Freud proves the existence of infantile sexuality by taking Wolf Man's recollection and making it fit his theories. The memory of a woman kneeling beside a pail and a broom, and teasing is proof of very little, but the scene Freud constructs of urination and threatened castration is a powerful piece of evidence. Throughout the rest of the case Freud uses his constructed scene as fact, as a foundation for other constructions, and as a refutation of criticisms that adult recollections do not provide evidence for the aetiological significance of sexual events in childhood causing later neuroses. With facts like these, who needs fictions?

Freud is a builder of narratives which he uses to make sense of people's lives. Guided by his theories he molds recollections into scenes which he then maintains are what really happened. He then uses these facts to prove his theories. However, such scenes cannot be judged to be either true or false because we will never be able to establish what really happened. The only records of the intimate events of a person's childhood are usually an individual's memories and this historical resource has been lost to us with the death of Freud's patients. The only extant record of what they told Freud is what he tells us they said. We can, however, show and be certain of the way in which Freud and others recast recollections into stories which they claim prove theories. But, narratives do not prove; they tell and retell stories which being true to experience, and not to some abstract scientific epistemology, are always a confabulation of the imaginary, the symbolic, and the real.

Omission

Omission is an extremely effective management technique for the construction of coherent stories because if there are events or people an author does not wish to have in his or her narrative s/he simply leaves them out. Omissions are difficult for the strict textual deconstructionist to analyze because if the leaving out is done well it leaves no traces of its disappearance.

In studying the works of Freud and Jung I could, having read someplace else about events in these men's lives, spot in their autobiographies and research papers where they had left out occurrences which would be damaging to both their self-portraits and their theories. Freud and his followers are by now famous for omitting any references to nonpsychoanalytic researchers who were conducting investigations into sexuality at the turn of the century. Both Ellenberger's (1970) and

Sulloway's (1979) books have helped to restore many of these names to the historical record which had been nearly erased by the success of psychoanalysis and its overexaggerated claims that Freud, alone and rejected, rediscovered sex at the turn of the century.

Jung's work provides several interesting instances in which knowing what has been omitted throws what is presented into richer relief. The most important of these is the omission of Antonia Wolff from his autobiography. Wolff was his mistress for over 30 years. Their relationship began in the years from 1912 to 1915 when Jung was severing his collaboration with Freud (Hannah, 1976). Jung's entire account of this difficult time is written in the form of a spiritual journey, his "Confrontations with the Unconscious" (1973). He is the hero of this narrative meeting a diverse group of figures in dreams, hallucinations, and fantasies all of whom challenge, guide, and instruct him in the mysteries of the unconscious and in the secrets of the archetypes.

Knowing that Wolff served as his therapist, confidant, *femme inspiratrice*, lover, and projection screen for his anima fantasies helps one to better understand why Jung's entire autobiography and perhaps a good deal of his psychological theory is inhabited by spiritual fantasy figures and not actual people. Jung kept his relations with Wolff out of the public eye, although his circle in Zurich knew about her and she, herself, was active in analytical psychology. To have revealed this relationship to unsympathetic readers might have thrown into doubt the whole spiritual thrust of Jung's psychologizing. Indeed knowing about Wolff makes obscure passages like the following written in 1916 far more understandable. Jung speculates that if a man's love "goes to a human being, and it is a true love, then it is the same as if the libido went direct to the unconscious, so very much is the other person a representative of the unconscious, though only if this other person is truly loved" (1970, p. 454). Once an interpreter knows about Wolff the obscurity here is made transparent: If Jung truly loved Wolff then she served as a transference figure for his unconscious fantasies and was therefore essential to his explorations of the unconscious.

Knowing about Wolff also makes an essay by Jung on modern women, "Woman in Europe" (1927), far more comprehensible. He writes about man's polygamous and woman's monogamous nature. Even though he simply repeats the conventional masculine double standard, the essay takes on a certain poignancy when one knows that Emma Jung, C. G.'s wife, long objected to his relationship with Wolff, but that he insisted on his need to have both a wife and a mistress.

Knowing how easy it is to leave out of one's work relevant details from one's life in an attempt to disguise personal self-interest as abstract argument, all people interested in life narratives should be aware that objectivity is often an easy excuse for omitting from the record of one's researches personal experiences which one should know are intricately entwined with one's findings as psychologist, biographer, historian, or scientist.

The Systematization of Distortion

The narrative frame is the typical story to which an idiosyncratic account of events tends to accommodate itself. As a story is repeated what is unusual in it is tamed by repetition and that which is typical and therefore fits the standard frame remains. Great men are stock figures in history. Whatever their personal histories might have been is often lost to the cultural necessity of portraying some men as extraordinary. To insure the unusualness of these men a stock narrative which celebrates their nobility, power, or genius and forgets their ordinariness, pettiness, and stupidity is used to write the historical factions of their lives. I can think of no more telling evidence for the tendentiousness of this process of narrative canonization than the fact that there are so few great women. In male dominated "great men" societies women are not allowed to be the subjects of such stories because their lives filled as they are by women's work cannot be fitted into this masculine frame of reference.

Freud and Jung are both great men. They themselves arranged, selected, and distorted the events of their lives in order to construct narratives of their greatness. Freud's frame is that of the earthy rebel; Jung's the spiritual prophet. The Freud story is of the rebellious young researcher whose daring findings are rejected by the fathers of German science. Forced into isolation by these tyrants, he worked relentlessly to prove himself by proving his theories. Because of his genius a loyal group of daring young men gathered around him, a band of brothers who with the fundamental discoveries of psychoanalysis as their pledge swore allegiance to his cause. There was discord within the ranks, the weak and cowardly defected. Freud persevered. As the father of his own movement he insisted on loyalty to the truth and accepted no challenges to his authority. He triumphed in the end as the psychoanalytic movement spread his name and theories throughout the world. If this tale sounds mythic that is because the events of Freud's life have been honed, filed, shaped, and joined to fit a mythic pattern by him and his biographers. Because this narrative resonates with other stories we have been told about great men it is easily remembered and rather resistant to criticism.

The Jung story is a complement to it. Cast out of society because of his other-worldly nature Jung loyally followed his spiritual calling. Although earthly entanglements almost ensnared him in the illusions of worldly riches his visions always called him back to the land of the soul. Fighting lonely noble battles with the powerful figures of the collective unconscious and mundane skirmishes with his critics he brought back to humankind the lost wisdom of the ages. Through his trials he achieved spiritual transcendence which was evident to all who followed him. In his later years he was a guide counseling a civilization that had lost contact with its soul. At his death there were miraculous signs.

Textual distortions facilitate the construction of such modern myths of greatness. The multiplicity and ambiguity of experience are simplified when they are narrated and each retelling of a story wears down the rough edges of complexity. If told often enough by unquestioning narrators the story is polished to mythic form with every fact a gem of belief to loyalists. (See for example Eissler's, 1951, insistence on the factual status of most of the mythic elements of Freud's biography and various biographies of Jung [Hannah, 1976; van der Post, 1975] which make him a modern day prophet.) Nothing would be wrong with any of this if it did not claim to be fact instead of fiction, or if we as readers could accept that the literature of fact is fiction written in the register of the real. However, as long as those working in the psychoanalytic tradition labor under the sign of science and insist that their narratives are true renditions of the facts then these texts must be deconstructed as factions so that their pretentions to truth can be evaluated.

The Power of Perspective

Revolutions in self-consciousness engender revisions in a person's life story and cultural revolutions require the rewriting of history. Colonized as we are by science we live in a civilization ordered by the power of the real; that is supposedly existent events, objects, and forces which interact in ways describable by objectively ascertainable laws. Both psychoanalysis and analytical psychology identify themselves as sciences within this tradition, although Freud's insistence on the natural scientific status of his work was always more vehement than was Jung's in defense of his more openly interpretive studies.

To show that research, a study, or a text is not objective and that a theory is no law but is instead a concatenation of biases has always been an effective challenge to a work's coveted scientific status. The most effective criticism of the objectivity of both Freud's and Jung's work, and in fact the objectivity of science itself, has come from feminist criticism. Neither Freud nor Jung wrote without bias, and seldom without derision, about women, and since the majority of their patients were women this challenges the truth of most of their findings. From his valorization of heterosexuality, to his penis envy fantasy, to his insistence in the case study of "Dora" that a teenage girl when attacked by an older man should feel lustful and not disgusted, Freud insists that women's lives be subjugated to the power of the phallus (Chodorow, 1978; Gallop, 1982). His paternal bias is also obvious when he says that "he cannot think of any need in childhood as strong as the need for a father's protection" (Freud, 1930, p. 72), while he denigrates maternal care by analogizing it to a hen tending her eggs claiming that the newborn is not in an intimate relationship with her or his mother/caretaker, but is autoerotic (Jacobsen & Steele, 1979; Kohn, 1984). The male from Freud's perspective is to be strived for, the female is taken for granted, despised, castrated.

This androcentric bias even shapes Freud's structural model (id, ego, superego) of the psyche. For example, his famous, "Where id was, there ego shall be. It is a work of culture . . ." (1933, p. 80), asserts that the telos of psychoanalysis and of Western civilization are the same: the natural "it" (id) shall be controlled and displaced by the conscious acculturated "I" (ego). Indeed the triumph of consciousness over instinct, of man over nature – often personified as a woman, and of man over woman – who is characterized by Freud as less cultured than men or as "a child of nature" – are the common misogynist dreams of both psychoanalysis and science (Griffin, 1978; Steele & Swinney, in press).

The continued propagation of this masculine perspective as an objective view of the world is insured by men controlling the writing of the literature of fact. A cultural evolution, the women's movement, has for centuries, however, challenged male hegemony and it is the revolution in the consciousnesses of many women and a few men that has facilitated a critical examination not only of psychoanalysis, but of science itself, as a masculine cultural enterprise controlling both women and nature (Merchant, 1980).

Even though he preached the necessity of a man integrating his feminine natural unconscious anima with his masculine cultural ego, counselled reconciliation of mankind with nature, and saw himself as being outside the dominant rationalistic materialist ethos of Western culture, Jung too spread the masculinism of his society. He decried women's colleges, he advised women to retain their intuitive, emotional gifts and avoid aping men's power of reason, he told women that their role was as man's helpmate and the bearer of his children, and he encouraged the women around him – his wife, his mistress, and a loyal coterie – to follow in his footsteps and take up his work (Steele, 1982).

Criticisms like these of the masculine bias of the works and lives of Freud and Jung can be passed off with the naive defense of *autres temps, autres moeurs* if one does not realize that there has always been a feminist movement in this century and that both Freud and Jung were vehemently antifeminist (Freud, 1931; Jung, 1948).

Feminism is a threat to male power and any woman who writes claims a privilege that has long been jealously guarded by men. Women's voices first began to be officially published in the early nineteenth century and by now, at least in fiction and essays, there is a women's perspective in letters. That the literature of fact, governed as it is by the scientific ethos, has more strenuously resisted women's encroachments and feminist attacks is understandable because factions are the sacred texts of the keepers of the real – the men of science. They insist that such works are fact, not fiction. However, deconstructions of these texts deflate them by revealing their pretences to truth, exposing their inconsistencies, showing how they make facts fit together, detailing how their distortions are systematized into well told tales, and by bringing to the foreground their embeddedness in cultural biases. As long as existence is bifurcated into the hard masculine world of the real and the soft imaginary realm of women and children, and the world of words is split into fact and fiction, then taking apart factions will be essential to the critical evaluation of literature which claims it is about what really happened, but which is often "just a story."

REFERENCES

Breuer, J. and Freud, S. Studies on hysteria. In J. Strachey (Ed. and Trans.), *The standard edition of the complete psychological works of Sigmund Freud* (Vol. 2). London: Hogarth. (Original work published in 1895).

Bry, I. and Rifkin, A. (1962). Freud and the history of ideas: Primary sources, 1886-1910. In J. Masserman (Ed.), *Psychoanalytic education*. New York: Grune & Stratton.

Boswell, D. (in press). *Human lives*. New York: Erlbaum.

Chodorow, N. (1978). *The reproduction of mothering: Family structure and feminine personality*. Berkeley: University of California Press.

Collingwood, R. G. (1956). *The idea of history*. New York: Oxford University Press.

Decker, H. (1977). *Freud in Germany: Revolution and reaction in science, 1893-1907*. *Psychological Issues*, Monograph 41. New York: International Universities Press.

Eissler, K. (1951). An unknown autobiographical letter by Freud and a short commentary. *International Journal of Psycho-analysis*, 32, 319-324.

Ellenberger, H. (1970). *The discovery of the unconscious*. New York: Basic.

Fisher, S. and Greenberg, R. (1977). *The scientific credibility of Freud's theories and therapy*. New York: Basic.

Freud, S. (1955). Heredity and the aetiology of neuroses. In Strachey, *S.E.* (3), pp. 143-153. (Original work published in 1896a).

Freud, S. (1955). Further remarks on the neuro-psychoses of defense. In Strachey, *S.E.* (3), pp. 221-225. (Original work published in 1896b).

Freud, S. (1955). The aetiology of hysteria. In Strachey, *S.E.* (3), pp. 191-199. (Original work published in 1896c).

Freud, S. (1955). The interpretation of dreams. *S.E.* (4-5). (Original work published in 1900).

Freud, S. (1957). My views on the part played by sexuality in the aetiology of the neurosis. *S.E.* (7), pp. 223-241. (Original work published in 1906).

Freud, S. (1958). Recommendations to physicians practicing psycho-analysis. *S.E.* (12), pp. 109-121. (Original work published in 1912).

Freud, S. (1957). On the history of the psycho-analytic movement. *S.E.* (14), pp. 7-66. (Original work published in 1914).

Freud, S. (1955). From the history of an infantile neurosis. *S.E.* (17), pp. 7-124. (Original work published in 1918).

Freud, S. (1959). An autobiographical study. *S.E.* (20), pp. 7-76. (Original work published in 1925).

Freud, S. (1962). Civilization and its discontents. *S.E.* (21), pp. 21-103. (Original work published in 1930).

Freud, S. (1962). Female sexuality. *S.E.* (21), pp. 120-190. (Original work published in 1931).

Freud, S. (1964). New introductory lectures on psycho-analysis. *S.E.* (22). (Original work published in 1933).

Frye, N. (1957). *Anatomy of criticism*. Princeton: Princeton University Press.

Gallop, J. (1982). *The daughter's seduction: Feminism and psychoanalysis*. Ithaca, NY: Cornell University Press.

Griffin, S. (1978). *Women and nature: The roaring inside her*. New York: Harper Colophon Books.

Hannah, B. (1976). *Jung: His life and work*. New York: G. P. Putnam's Sons.

Jacobsen, P. and Steele, R. (1979). From present to past: Freudian archaeology. *International Review of Psycho-analysis*, 6, 349-362.

Jones, E. (1953). *The life and work of Sigmund Freud* (Vol. 1). New York: Basic.

Jung, C. G. (1965). Woman in Europe. In R. F. C. Hull (Trans.), *The collected works of C. G. Jung* (Vol. 10), pp. 113-133. Princeton: Princeton University Press. (Original work published in 1927).

Jung, C. G. (1970). Foreword to Harding, *Woman's mysteries*. In R. F. C. Hull (Trans.) *C. W.* (18), pp. 518-520. (Original work published in 1948).

Jung, C. G. (1970). Adaptation, individuation, collectivity. In R.F.C. Hull (Trans.), *C. W.* (18), pp. 449-454. (Original work published in 1916).

Jung, C. G. (1973). *Memories, dreams, reflections.* A. Jaffe (Ed.), R. and C. Winston (Trans.), (rev. ed.). New York: Pantheon.

Kohn, A. (1984). *Infancy as ideology: A critique of object relations theory.* Unpublished undergraduate thesis, Wesleyan University, Middletown, CT.

Kris, E. (1954). Introduction. In M. Bonaparte, A. Freud, and E. Kris (Eds.), *Sigmund Freud: The origins of psycho-analysis: Letters to Wilhelm Fliess, drafts and notes.* New York: Basic.

Lacan, J. (1977). *Écrits: A selection.* New York: Norton.

Laplanche, J. and Pontalis, J-B. (1973). *The language of psychoanalysis.* New York: Norton.

McGuire, W. (Ed.) (1974). *The Freud/Jung letters: The correspondence between Sigmund Freud and C. G. Jung.* Princeton: Princeton University Press.

Merchant, C. (1980). *The death of nature: Women, ecology and the scientific revolution.* San Francisco: Harper & Row.

Palmer, R. (1969). *Hermeneutics: Interpretation theory in Schleiermacher, Dilthey, Heidegger, and Gadamer.* Evanston, IL: Northwestern University Press.

Popper, K. (1963). *Conjectures and refutations: The growth of scientific knowledge.* New York: Harper.

Post, L. van der (1975). *Jung and the story of our time.* New York: Pantheon.

Radnitzky, G. (1973). *Contemporary schools of metascience.* Chicago: Henry Regnery.

Ricoeur, P. (1970). *Freud and philosophy: An essay on interpretation.* New Haven, CT: Yale University Press.

Schur, M. (1972). *Freud: Living and dying.* New York: International Universities Press.

Steele, R. (1979). Psychoanalysis and hermeneutics. *International Review of Psychoanalysis,* 6, 389.

Steele, R. (1982). *Freud & Jung: Conflicts of interpretation.* With Consulting Editor S. V. Swinney. London: Routledge & Kegan Paul.

Steele, R. and Swinney, S. (in press). *Everyday interpretation.* New York: Guilford.

Sulloway, F. (1979). *Freud: Biologist of the mind.* New York: Basic.

White, H. (1973). *Metahistory.* Baltimore, MD: Johns Hopkins University Press.

14

Literary Pathfinding:
The Work of Popular
Life Constructors

Kevin Murray

Social actors often need a past to satisfy the requirements of many different dramatic situations. These situations can vary from the extraordinary – the television show "This Is Your Life" – to the mundane, such as getting to know an acquaintance. The way in which the biographical subjects and their audience construct this past is likely to vary according to the rhetorical demands that govern the situation in which this practice of life emplotment occurs. This context is likely to influence at least three dimensions of this process: the choice of events that are seen as relevant to the construction of the life, the themes that provide coherence between these events, and the degree and type of narrative closure to the life story.

The structures used by people as they construct lives – the language of self-reflection employed in this discourse – is an important new field of research (see Potter, Stringer, & Wetherell, 1984). Such an approach assumes that life construction is a discursive practice governed by the social settings which demand that a life history be presented. In the present chapter, I examine the form of the life manual, especially Gail Sheehy's *Passages*, in order to discover the sort of resources offered through this medium for the social construction of lives. In common with other theories of biography (see Kohli, 1981; and Runyan, 1980) this analysis assumes that more than one possible account can be construed from the events of a person's life, according to the perspective of the biographer. This chapter emphasizes, in addition, the role of narrative structures in the way an account is constituted, specifically those structures provided in the language of self-reflection employed in life manuals.

The language of self-reflection is most obvious in specialized forms of discourse such as works of autobiography and biography, but there are other social events and institutions which are partly designed for the construction of life narratives. Two common rituals which involve the telling of a story about a life are the speeches at testimonial dinners and weddings. These stories usually have contrasting emphases: wedding speeches emphasize human and everyday aspects of character, while retirement speeches highlight achievements that distinguish the subject from others.

The process of life construction is important in many social events designed to establish a moral character (see Gergen & Gergen, 1983, for a discussion of the social utility of this practice). This is highlighted in the statements of a character witness in the courtroom, though it is no less evident in the responses of an interviewee when asked to account in a research interview for certain actions. In the former, the witness attempts to construct a story about character which makes more sense of one interpretation of the accused's acts than another, less innocent one; and in the latter, the research question of the interviewer makes it imperative that the interviewee construct an account of past actions that is coherent and sensible (see Mishler, this volume).

In each case, the rhetorical demands of the situation require a relatively unambiguous reading of motive: the situation demands thematic generality over a disparate course of events. So, for example, a character witness might begin the testimony with, "When he was five he saved a kitten from drowning," in order to highlight how the theme of consideration for others marks the life events of the accused. For the account to have an easily read *point* (that is, the likely innocence of the defendant), the narrative must sift out those details that do not add to the coherence of the story.

Given the pervasiveness of the process of narrative construction of life events, one is naturally prompted to investigate its function. However, there is an obstacle to this investigation. One of the reasons

278 / NARRATIVE PSYCHOLOGY

why these processes have received relatively little study is the assumption that the function of telling stories about lives is mimetic and therefore unproblematic; that is, that life narratives are largely a transparent means of representing the truth. However, while it is necessary that these processes bear an ostensible relation to a commonly perceived reality, the success of an account is also likely to be judged by how well it fits certain rhetorical demands, including the set of conventions in language that govern the telling of stories.

The debate about the representational nature of narrative has occurred in other disciplines. History has been popularly conceived as concerned exclusively with the mimetic function of revealing the truth about the past. However, in an analysis of nineteenth-century historians, Hayden White (1973) demonstrates the importance of other factors in writing history such as ideology, world view, and what he terms "explanation by emplotment," which is presenting a description of the past that convinces by its success as a story; specifically, how well it conforms to the conventions of comedy, romance, tragedy, and satire. Although White would agree with other relativists, such as Runyan, on the plurality of narratives for the construction of life events, he would differ in the emphasis placed on *language* as a system that imposes form on reality. For Runyan, relativism extends only to the ideological and theoretical perspective of the biographer, whereas for White, the narrative account of the past is determined by the preconscious linguistic structures (tropes) imposed on reality by the constructor – the choice of structure is determined by aesthetic and moral reasons.

The nonrepresentational factors which figure in this *professional* sense-making are also likely to apply to everyday constructions of the past. The criterion of truth is certainly not dominant in informal social activities such as gossip, when the members of a group exchange "interesting" stories about people not present, and popular culture, especially in magazines concerned with media personalities whose lives are regularly encapsulated in touching, shocking, and amusing stories.

Given the prevalence of narrative structures in constructions of the past, it is difficult to argue for life stories as a transparent means of representing truth. A qualified case for this mimetic view may, however, be cast in information-processing terms. These stories may be seen as attempts at information reduction, in which the large variety of life events is reduced to a set of narratives so that it may be cognitively processed more efficiently. The function, therefore, remains representational, though this is by means of an information-simplifying structure rather than by a mirror of reality. However, this ignores the pleasure with which apparently useless additional information is sought about people who have no practical relation to one's life. Who should care if Elizabeth Taylor marries again? It would be difficult to see a story of Elizabeth Taylor's remarriage being used as an aid in the cognitive organization of the social environment. The moral function of such a story seems more evident than the information-processing function; the remarriage may continue a story about a prominent public figure whose actions have relevance as standards of conduct in everyday life; the happy or sad outcome of the story indicates whether the course of action is correct or misguided. For Hayden White, one purpose of narrative is moral:

> Narrativity, certainly in factual storytelling and probably in fictional storytelling as well, is intimately related to, if not a function of, the impulse to moralize reality, that is, to identify it with the social system, that is the source of any morality that we can imagine. (1980, p. 18)

If one looks again at the process of gossip (Sabini & Silver, 1982), one finds emphasis on the embodiment of codes of conduct on the elaboration of moral rules in concrete examples. The gossipy stories in the popular media seem to instantiate the moral order, thus exercising it and ensuring that it is able to organize the events of everyday life.

Besides the moral function of this process, life construction is also likely to be an attempt to find a narrative structure by means of which life can be granted meaning. This is what Frank Kermode describes as an explanatory fiction: "In 'making sense' of the world we still feel a need, harder than ever to satisfy because of the accumulated scepticism, to experience that concordance of beginning, middle, and end, which is the essence of our explanatory fictions" (1967, pp. 35-36). This sense of beginning, middle, and end, in terms of a life path, is provided by a set of conventionalized narrative forms. Jerome Bruner, in his essay "Myth and identity" (1962), describes this set as the "controlling myths of community," which provide a "library of scripts" that give recognition to certain life paths. This library of scripts is an abstraction of the narratives that are evident in the ways the biography of an individual is presented in public. The aim of this chapter is to demonstrate, in popular psychology at least, that these life constructions are determined as much by the moral and narrative conventions contained in the hypothetical library of scripts as they are by the facts of life.

GAIL SHEEHY

The popular book *Passages* (1977), by Gail Sheehy, presents a revealing document for studying these socially recognized life paths. First, it explicitly sets out to provide a prescribed route through life events, and tells many stories about people as examples of a general theory. Second, Sheehy is a popular writer (her books reach the top of bestseller lists), and her books are more likely to be consumed as myths than books directed to an academic audience. Given these factors, Sheehy's works are likely to indicate ways in which lives can be constructed as resources that can be used by members of society in the choosing of a life path.

Sheehy's work is examined here with an emphasis on the manner in which she constructs life narratives and on the theory from which she draws to support her constructions. The relativity of her constructions can be established by two sets of contrasts: first, by a comparison with two of her contemporaries: Daniel Levinson and Roger Gould; and second, because many of the assumptions Sheehy makes may seem at first to be self-evident to participants of the same culture. I cite a theorist from a different time: the Victorian moralist and biographer, Samuel Smiles. Smiles, like Sheehy, achieved great popularity while telling stories about how people should live their lives.

Because our interest is partly in the consumption of Sheehy's book it is useful to approach it initially from the perspective of the ordinary reader. It is likely that the prospective reader goes to this book as a guide to ways in which one deals with problems in life. This seems to be the ostensible purpose of the book. As the reader inspects it in the bookstore he or she sees the blurb on the cover reinforce this expectation:

'A revolutionary way of looking at adult life'
– THE SUNDAY *TIMES*, LONDON

Brilliant new insights on the predictable crises of adult life.

However, if at this point the reader decides to gauge Sheehy's style by examining the first page of the main text, the expectation of a serious academic work is soon put in doubt. Chapter One of *Passages*, entitled "Madness and Method," immediately immerses the reader in the excitement of Sheehy's adventure in Northern Ireland. There is no conceptual argument; it begins much more like a novel than an academic tract.

If the reader had looked at the cover notes in a little more detail the expectation would not have been of a serious theoretical work. The notes on the inside of the cover are more representative of the style of the introductory chapter:

'A lively, passionate and readable message . . .'

– Margaret Mead

'Provokes the same recognition that we experience in a good novel . . .'
– New York *Times* Book Review

'Extraordinarily good reading . . .'

– *Publishers Weekly*

The readableness of Sheehy's book is evident in the clever literary style she adopts throughout. This style partly consists of tropes, such as, "Killing time is a suicidal act. The time she is killing is all she has left to live." This emphasis on the literary style may seem irrelevant to the purpose of this chapter, but it is important to recognize the context in which Sheehy's theory is cast – the medium which contains the message. The decision in adopting this particular style may be related to what she is trying to say, and the way in which she wants her message to be consumed.

The rest of the statements used to package *Passages* emphasize the involvement of the reader in the text.

PASSAGES IS YOUR LIFE STORY.
You'll recognize yourself,
your friends, and your lovers.

'Passages shakes you up, shakes you out, and leaves you shaking hands with yourself.'

– Shana Alexander

These statements stress the prospect of the reader being changed by the text – either in the acts performed in life or the process of self-reflection. (For a discussion of the influence of reading on everyday life, see Sarbin, 1982.) The impression of *Passages* gained from this bookshop browse is likely to be of an entertaining text which has the power to recast one's own life story.

At this point we will leave the impressions of the prospective reader and turn to the actual theory which Gail Sheehy offers to account for life events. According to Sheehy, adult life consists of a negotiation between two powerful forces within the psyche, and the outside world. The primary force is essentially good, Sheehy calls it the "dream." The dream has its origins in the fantasies of childhood. Adult ambitions, such as vocational success, establishing a secure family, and becoming famous, are attempts to realize this dream. Opposed to the dream is the "inner custodian." This is a negative psychic force, similar to the superego,[1] which has its origin in the demands that parents make of the child. The inner custodian, which Sheehy calls a "nasty tyrant," demands that one live up to these ideals or be nothing. It is a critical annihilating force that engenders a feeling of helplessness.

The conflict between these forces comes to a head in midlife. In this "passage" there is usually a threatening event which triggers a crisis, usually a *memento mori* such as the death of one's parents, or a heart attack affecting oneself or a friend. Sheehy's book begins with the event which triggered her own crisis: the sense of futility in life resulting from her experience of a Northern Ireland massacre. For Sheehy this is a particularly dramatic event in the lives of everyone: "There is a moment – an immense and precarious moment – of stark terror." This crisis engenders a period of depression and inactivity – a sense of hopelessness in coping with the threat.

Sheehy advises people at this point in their lives to act bravely, to face the conflict squarely and be hopeful of the future. The hope which Sheehy offers is a romantic one; there is an optimistic commitment to the self as the only force of authority in one's world. This becomes clear when her statements about the crisis are examined:

> For whether we know it or not, and usually we don't, it is this dictator guardian from whom we all are struggling at last to be free. In midlife, all the old wars with the inner custodian flare up again. And eventually, if we let it happen, they will culminate in a final, decisive battle. The object of that battle is to overtake the last of the ground held by the other and end up with the authority for ourselves in our own command. (1977, p. 436)

Given Sheehy's literary style, it is not surprising that she employs a metaphor to describe this conflict. It is, rather, her *choice* of metaphor which is interesting. By using a metaphor of *battle* she is encapsulating the event of midlife crisis in terms which make it compatible with the literary structure of a romance.

Indeed, Sheehy's theory readily allows for a romance narrative. There is already the notion of a dream, which can be seen in terms of a romantic quest, and the inner custodian, which can be easily viewed as the elemental foe opposed to the realization of the quest. Given these initial terms, the equation of romance is completed by Sheehy's view of life as a perilous journey consisting in a series of adventures leading up to a crucial struggle in the midlife crisis. This is clearly indicated by Sheehy's statement of romantic hope:

> To reach the clearing beyond, we must stay with the weightless journey through uncertainty. Whatever counterfeit safety we hold from overinvestments in people and institutions must be given up. The inner custodian must be unseated from the controls. No foreign power can direct our journey from now on. It is for each of us to find a course that is valid by our own reckoning. And for each of us there is the opportunity to emerge reborn, *authentically* unique, with an enlarged capacity to love ourselves and embrace others. (1977, p. 364)

Sheehy aims to *inspire* the reader with a sense of hope in life by constructing personal development in terms of a romance. And given the nature of the crucial struggle in romance – that it allows for the rebirth and rejuvenation of the hero – it structures a difficult period in life in a way which allows for the possibility of an optimistic outcome. If she had chosen to structure life according to alternative forms, such as a tragedy in which childhood hopes are destroyed by the cruel realities of adult life, or a satire where the idealistic dreams of childhood are disillusioned by the ironies and complexities of adulthood, the effect would be to engender despair.

The purpose of using a literary style can thus be seen as allowing Sheehy the license to use literary forms to construct lives. In effect, Sheehy is teaching the readers to read their own lives in terms of romance so that they may share in this hope: "the capacity for renewal in each human spirit is nothing short of amazing." The message on the cover saying "*Passages* is your life story" now can be translated as "You too may emplot your life as a romantic adventure."

There is further evidence for this point in *Pathfinders* (1982), the sequel to *Passages*. Here Sheehy presents heroes of her system. The heroes must pass three tests:

1. To confront crossroads.
2. To cause a minimum of human damage.
3. To seek a purpose outside oneself.

What is significant about these three tests is that, according to critics of the romantic literary form (see Frye, 1957), the heroes of classic forms of romance must also face three tests, and the nature of these tests roughly corresponds to Sheehy's. The first test (*agon*) involves conflict between the hero and the evil force. The second test (*pathos*) is the final death struggle between the combatants. Sheehy's second test is compatible with this; it assumes that the person has tried to resolve the conflict by re-assessing commitments such as an unchallenging job or a sour marriage. She is specifying that the outcome of this test should not merely be the annihilation of previous commitments – persons should salvage some of their pasts from this crucial struggle. The third test (*anagnorisis*) is the discovery of a transcendent meaning or truth as part of the process of renewal after the struggle. Sheehy similarly specifies that the pathfinder should discover a meaning beyond the pursuit of pleasure or self-gratification. It is understandable that if Sheehy invests in the mythos of romance as a source of optimism, then she also buys the baggage of the romantic conventions.

In *Passages* Sheehy refers to the work of two other researchers as promoting her own interest in human development: Daniel Levinson and Roger Gould. Levinson's book, *The Seasons of Man's Life* (1978), is seen by some as an academically respectable work from which Sheehy draws her theory. Certainly, the Dream concept figures as strongly in Levinson as it does in Sheehy, but, unlike *Passages*, *Seasons* constructs a force opposed to the Dream which is not an object with whom one can engage in battle – it is not like Sheehy's inner custodian ("nasty tyrant"); rather it is a tragic flaw within the character, something over which one has no control. Levinson's scenario for midlife does not provide the reader with the same sense of adventure as Sheehy because the enemy or frustrating force is part of oneself – it cannot be easily externalized as a foe: "The tragic sense derives from the realization that great misfortunes and failures are not merely imposed upon us from without, but are largely the result of our own tragic flaws" (1978, p. 225). Given the absence of clear opposition between good and bad, the metaphor for the process of growth cannot be battle; Levinson chooses instead to compare development in midlife to a geographical study, in which basic faults are *revealed* to the explorer. The aim then is discovery, rather than the victory which Sheehy envisages.

Gould is another theorist who refers to the Dream as a primary force in human development, but he provides a different metaphor for the process of growth. The negative force for Gould rests with the "angry demons" of childhood, which remain fostered in the illusions carried into adulthood: "To enjoy full access to our innermost self, we can no longer deny the ugly, demonic side of life, which our immature mind tried to protect against by enslaving itself to false illusions that absolute safety was possible" (1978, p. 218). Midlife thus becomes a period for facing up to reality. The metaphor Gould employs is breaking a wild horse; evil cannot be defeated in battle, it must simply be exposed to reality and, through experience, tamed. Gould holds an existentialist position toward life – he sees it as a process of demystification: "Time . . . strips away our last remaining illusion of safety and makes existentialists of us all." The breaking down of illusions through *experience* is the goal presented by Gould, contrasting with Levinson's *discovery* of tragic flaws and Sheehy's *victory* over the inner custodian. The goals typify the myths of satire, tragedy, and romance, respectively.[2] The fact that these authors examine the same issue, with similar materials, yet construct their theories in such contrasting ways, demonstrates the relativity of narrative constructions, and especially highlights that Sheehy's view of life is as much a product of the structures of narrative emplotment and their associated assumptions about human nature as it is of representation.

SAMUEL SMILES

Samuel Smiles is a writer whose success in the Victorian era is compatible with Sheehy's success in our own time. Smiles authored many life manuals, the most popular being *Self-Help* (1925, originally published, 1854). The impact of *Self-Help* on Victorian culture can be gauged by the fact that it sold more copies than any of the great nineteenth century novels. The purpose of the comparison between Smiles and Sheehy is not to analyze historically the changes in sensibilities concerning life constructions, but simply to highlight more distinctive features of Sheehy's approach.

Looking at the cover notes of *Self-Help*, the reader is less encouraged to find a literary masterpiece within. Smiles' style is praised as being "clear and attractive," but the emphasis is largely on the inspirational nature of his works:

> [*Self-Help* will] help to inspire the rising generation with ennobling sentiments.
>
> – *Builder*

There are few departments of public life in which this book may not inspire to higher self-devotion. . . .

— Liverpool *Mercury*

Smiles' style is less colorful than Sheehy's, and more precise.

The force which drives personality in Smiles' system is *character*. Character is made up of various elements or moral qualities of personality. These are energy, duty, reverence, will, courage, self-control, cheerfulness, and manners. The general theme of these qualities is a positive desire to do right by society. According to Smiles, character is determined by social milieu. Thus the greatest formative influence on personality is family, followed by teachers, peers, spouse, patrons, books, and society's heroes.

Many of Smiles' books display the means by which character can become manifest to others, especially as it is evident in the lives of heroes of Victorian society; their story is usually of boys from modest and devout backgrounds who through application are able to raise themselves and do good in society. Their character is made evident in two ways. First, it can be seen in the daily contributions to society that eventually amount to a character-building set of good works: "Indeed, character consists in little acts, well and honourably performed; daily life being the quarry from which we build it up, and rough-hew the habits which we form" (1925, p. 468). Alternatively, character may become manifest by means of a dramatic gesture: "When Stephen of Colonna fell into the hands of his base assailants, and they asked him in derision, 'Where is now your fortress?' 'Here', was the bold reply, placing his hand upon his heart" (1925, p. 453). In this way character becomes something which is easily read by others, in terms of one's history of good works (moral career) or through self-presentation strategies.

Compared to Sheehy, the essence of Smiles lies on the surface. Smiles' lives are flat and undynamic – there is no struggle within the self to arrive at a self-determined meaning. In the language of self-reflection discussed by Potter et al., Smiles holds an "honest soul" theory of character, one which sees self as consisting of a stable set of traits, whereas Sheehy sees self as something that must be strived for, the romantic self.

For Smiles, the meaning which determines one's life comes necessarily from outside oneself; there is an objective moral order, the same for all, by which one's personal worth is judged. This may sound restrictive and uninviting, but Smiles does offer a bonus. Because the example of others acts as an independent force which permeates our moral capabilities, our own actions are granted a significance outside ourselves as they become part of the moral fabric of society which in turn controls the behavior of others. Smiles' theory of character thus implies a secular immortality:

> The spirits of men do not die: they still live and walk abroad among us. . . .
> Thus, every act we do or word we utter, as well as every act we witness or word we hear, carries with it an influence which extends over, and gives a colour, not only to the whole of our future life, but makes itself felt upon the whole frame of society. (1925, p. 428)

According to Sheehy the worth of an individual is in the ability to face reality by finding a balance betwen seeking and merging, independence and intimacy. In contrast, Smiles simply believes that people operate like a Marxist economic system; that the value of a product is directly related to the labor involved in its creation, thus there is no honor without struggle. The value for Smiles is labor, whereas for Sheehy it is authenticity. A comparison of the moral orders of Islam and St. Thomas of Aquinas by Rom Harré (1984) reveals a similar difference. While the Islamic concept of *quaadar* prescribes a universal life path for all that is achieved by faith and determination, Aquinas refers to the necessity of making decisions in the life-course.

So far, Sheehy and Smiles have been contrasted in their theories of how lives are constructed. To gain knowledge of their *method*, attention should be paid to the many case histories included in their books. Both writers use cases very much as exemplary lives which not only demonstrate their theories about human nature and conform to the narrative patterns seen as typical in life, but also provide models of how the readers should live their own lives.

THE CASE OF DWIGHT

In *Passages* (1977, pp. 256-271), Sheehy uses the case of Dwight to illustrate the rebirth of a person who avoided experimentation in early life. It begins as an example of the hazards involved in a lack of risk taking when young, and ends as a celebration of the potential to overcome a bad start by taking on adventures later in life.

Dwight is presented as a person whose early development was stamped with the traditionalism of his established New England family.

Sheehy exploits the rhythm of language to highlight his lack of experimentation. After Dwight gains a large inheritance from his grandfather:

> He safed it all away in blue chip stocks. Lock!

> He wasted not a moment between finishing basic training and starting married life with Vanessa. Lock!

And she describes his becoming a teacher despite his father's objections:

> With almost no experimentation Dwight had found his one true course in life. Lock!

Slowly becoming aware that his life had been too restricted to allow the realization of any authentic sense of self, Dwight begins to break out. He leaves his wife and starts experimenting with one of Sheehy's stock figures, the "Testimonial Woman." When she leaves him Dwight is devastated, but this leads him to realize that: "a change of mates was not the key. A change in *him* was." Following this revelation Dwight sets out on the romantic quest to find himself, and he begins to grow: "As he began to assume the authority for his own support, Dwight stretched on all levels." In keeping with the romantic mythos, Sheehy even has Dwight disappearing into the sunset: "On the brow of 40, brimming with vitality and more daring than he had ever before displayed, Dwight whisked off with his new wife to the last wilderness in the West to make a documentary: in his field, using her medium."

There is, however, another story embedded in the case of Dwight that Sheehy chooses to deny by her use of poetic license. Dwight's previous life may be alternatively represented as a series of rebellions. First, he turned against his father's expectations of him to become an executive and chose to become a teacher instead. This, according to Sheehy, happened with no experimentation, but "experimentation" seems to be something which serves the narrative structure of the case rather than the "facts" of Dwight's life. Second, he entered the political arena by working for a year as an administrative aide to a congressman; but this was, "For want of excitement. . . . It tickled him to make contacts with celebrities." After this change of style he went back to teaching. By employing metaphor, Sheehy again uses poetic license to make one interpretation seem more obvious than another: "At 30, the outlines of his life in the academic world seemed to fall into place as clearly as the stone geometry of an old land-grant college." The metaphorical neatness of Sheehy's image allows her interpretation to slip in without being subject to a serious critical scrutiny.

Sheehy's romantic story of Dwight's life is not the only one that can be constructed. One could construct it as a satire, in which a good and honest man is influenced by the romantic ideal of selfhood and destroys his family and personal future in the misguided belief that he would achieve greater authenticity. Instead, Sheehy chooses the romance mythos which generates an altogether more inspiring and optimistic scenario. Her choice is not guided solely by the match between this mythos and reality; also at play are Sheehy's moral and aesthetic visions of life.

THE CASE OF DOCTOR LEE

A typical case from the works of Samuel Smiles reveals a different force driving personality. The case of Dr. Samuel Lee (1925, pp. 413-415) typifies the story of the man who through the force of character hauls himself up from modest beginnings to outstanding achievements. "One of the dullest boys" at school, Dr. Lee began life as a carpenter, reading books with Latin quotations in his leisure. Becoming more interested he mastered Latin, and went on to study ancient Greek, followed by the Chaldee, Syriac, and Samaritan dialects. All this was without support from any academy. However, the strain of reading began to tell on his eyes and he had to forego his study until a fire destroyed his carpentry tools and he was forced to take up teaching language for his livelihood. Through the patronage of Dr. Scott, a neighboring clergyman, Dr. Lee expanded the languages under his command and eventually became a professor of Arabic and Hebrew at Queen's College, Cambridge. According to Smiles, the point of this story is to reveal "the power of perseverance in self-culture," though it could just as easily be to demonstrate the unpredictable and impressive nature of a natural gift for languages.

Absent from Smiles' narrative is any discovery within Dr. Lee of a goal which has personal relevance, which would have marked Sheehy's version of the same story. The catalyst for Dr. Lee's rise was not self-discovery, but the patronage of Dr. Scott and the recognition from others of Dr. Lee's "unaffected, simple, and beautiful character." The story of Dr. Lee's life can be viewed as an epic narrative in which the hero undergoes adventures that do not interact with his relatively static and simple character. Scholes and Kellog (1966) contrast the epic with the romantic form, especially the modern romance involving a psychological search for identity, where the adventures dynamically affect the character of the hero. The form of character emplotment used by Sheehy typifies the themes of modern romance.

Despite these differences in their chosen forms of life emplotment, Sheehy and Smiles have in common a moral framework upon which their constructions are based. In this framework the hero is understood to be an exemplar of certain virtues – for Sheehy it is authenticity, and for Smiles it is commitment. An alternative framework for constructing character is suggested by Hunter's (1983) study of the practice of "reading" character in drama criticism. Sheehy and Smiles typify a practice of reading character in which the worth and workings of a person are formed by moral qualities. An alternative means of reading character was practiced in the eighteenth century. This involves viewing character as a rhetorical object, whose plausibility and quality is determined by the dramaturgical rules of everyday life. This practice is evident in the typification of characters into such categories as the "eccentric" and the "conformist." What such characters lack is a temporal dimension which would give their lives a stronger narrative underpinning, and thus a greater moral relevance. By providing definite narrative frameworks for life, Sheehy and Smiles enable character to be read morally.

CONCLUSION

Gail Sheehy's books can be seen as attempts to construct life in terms of the narrative conventions of romance, of a struggle between good and evil which sets the stage for a discovery of inner truth. The outcome of this construction is to create adventure in personal conflict and thus allow the possibility of hope in a period of potential despair; it gives personal crisis a meaning by encapsulating it in narrative terms. Compared to Sheehy, Smiles' narratives grant the individual much less authority in resolving the issues of selfhood, and offer the less individually-determined Stoic path of moral goodness as a guarantee of happiness. Smiles' books demonstrate that the conventions used by Sheehy are relative. What is found in the works of two of Sheehy's contemporaries, Levinson and Gould, are the life manuals which *do* grant the individual this authority, but their metaphors for selfhood lack the spirited adventure with an externalized foe that characterizes Sheehy's vision. Certainly there are enough materials in any life for the construction of a romance, but whether romance is chosen before other narrative structures such as tragedy and irony will depend on the aesthetic and moral will of the constructor.

All of these life constructions serve a basic need to provide a narrative concordance in human development, but they obviously differ in the values they attach to the individual and society, the limits of human freedom, and the resulting degree of hope, despair, resignation, or pragmatism that is appropriate in life's progress. The first step has been to recognize the process of life construction at work in the popular life manual, the next stage is to determine its aesthetic, moral, psychological, social, cultural, and historical contexts.

NOTES

1.   For an analysis of Gail Sheehy's relationship to popular psychoanalysis see Murray, K. (1984). *Romanticizing psychoanalysis.* Unpublished manuscript, University of Melbourne, Australia.
2.   For a description of these myths see N. Frye, 1957; and for a statement of their theoretical relevance in the social sciences see K. Murray, in press.

REFERENCES

Bruner, J. S. (1962). *On knowing: Essays for the left hand.* Cambridge, MA: Harvard University Press.
Frye, N. (1957). *Anatomy of criticism.* Princeton, NJ: Princeton University Press.
Gergen, K. J. and Gergen, M. (1983). Narratives of the self. In T. R. Sarbin and R. E. Scheibe (Eds.). *Studies in social identity.* New York: Praeger.
Gould, R. (1978). *Transformations: Growth and change in adult life.* New York: Simon & Shuster.
Harré, R. (1984). Psychological variety. In P. Heelas and A. Lock (Eds.), *Indigenous psychologies.* London: Routledge & Kegan Paul.
Hunger, I. (1983). Reading character. *Southern Review,* 16, 226-243.
Kermode, F. (1967). *The sense of an ending.* Oxford: Oxford University Press.
Kohli, M. (1981). Biography: Account, text, method. In D. Bertaux (Ed.), *Biography and society.* California: Sage.
Levinson, D. (1978). *The seasons of man's life.* New York: Ballantine Books.
Murray, K. (in press). Life as fiction: Proposing the marriage of dramaturgical model and literary criticism. *Journal for the Theory of Social Behavior.*

Potter, J., Stringer, P., and Wetherell, M. (1984). *Social texts and context: Literature and social psychology*. London: Routledge and Kegan Paul.

Runyan, W. M. (1980). Alternative accounts of lives: an argument for epistemological relativism. *Biography*, 3, 209-224.

Sabini, J. and Silver, M. (1982). *Moralities of everyday life*. Oxford: Oxford University Press.

Sarbin, T. R. (1982). The Quixotic principle: A Belletristic approach to the psychological study of meanings and imaginings. In V. L. Allen and K. E. Scheibe (Eds.), *The social context of conduct: Psychological writings of Theodore Sarbin*. New York: Praeger.

Scholes, R. and Kellog, R. (1966). *The nature of narrative*. London: Oxford University Press.

Sheehy, G. (1977). *Passages: Predictable crises in adult life*. New York: Bantam.

Sheehy, G. (1982). *Pathfinders*. New York: Bantam.

Smiles, S. (1925). *Self-help: With illustrations of conduct and perseverance*. London: John Murray. (Originally published in 1854).

White, H. (1973). *Metahistory*. Baltimore, MD: Johns Hopkins University Press.

White, H. (1980). The value of narrativity in the representation of reality. *Critical Inquiry*, 7, 5-28.

Author Index

Subject Index

About the Editor
and Contributors

Stephen Crites has been a member of the department of religion at Wesleyan University since 1961. He is currently the Hedding Professor of Moral Science. He has held visiting professorships in the departments of philosophy at the Berkeley and San Diego campuses of the University of California and in the religion department at the University of Virginia. He received the Ph.D. from Yale University in 1961. His scholarly interests center on nineteenth century continental philosophy and religious thought. He has published many articles and some books related to Hegel and Kierkegaard in particular, and is presently completing a book treating the transformation of Christian themes in the development of Hegel's thought. He has also written a number of articles on the aesthetic formation of experience with special emphasis on narrative forms, and is currently at work on a book treating this theme.

Kenneth J. Gergen is Professor of Psychology at Swarthmore College. He received his Ph.D. at Duke University and taught at Harvard University for five years before coming to Swarthmore. His major research interests have been widespread, and have included such domains as the self, altruism, social explanation, and social construction. His persistent concerns with problems of historical change, concepts of mind, and foundationalist philosophy have also been manifest in a number of writings in metapsychology. Many of these concerns are represented in his book, *Toward Transformation in Social Knowledge* (1982). He works closely with his wife, Mary M. Gergen, on many projects. Together they have authored a textbook on social psychology and edited a volume on historical social psychology.

Mary M. Gergen is Assistant Professor of Psychology at Pennsylvania State University, Delaware County Campus. She received B.S. and M.S. degrees at the University of Minnesota, and the Ph.D. at Temple University in Philadelphia. Her interests currently involve issues in women's studies using narrative analysis within a social constructionist paradigm. Previous research work has focused on social explanation and reactions to aid. She has collaborated with her husband, Kenneth J. Gergen, at Harvard University and Swarthmore College. They are co-authors of *Social Psychology* (1983) and co-editors of

Historical Social Psychology (1984). She is currently involved in developing emancipatory research methods, and serves as a consultant in human resources for business and professional agencies.

Linda Hawpe is Visiting Assistant Professor of Psychology at the University of Louisville where she earned the Ph.D. in 1983 in cognitive psychology. Her dissertation centered on the nature of children's developing internal representation of grammatical categories. She has co-authored papers dealing with language processes, among them, "Defining man through language" (*International Journal of Pavlovian Science*, 1979) and "Space, time, and the acquisition of spatio-temporal terms" (*Journal of Experimental Child Psychology*, 1981). Her current research interests include the development of narrative skills for problem solving.

Ernest Keen has been at Bucknell University since 1964 where he is Professor of Psychology. During sabbaticals he has done clinical work in various settings. He was a National Humanities Institute Fellow at Yale, 1976-77. In recent years his interests have turned to the teaching of interdisciplinary social science and, more recently, humanities, and other general education courses. He is convinced that undergraduate curricula are too specialized and fragmented and is committed to finding a way to make them better. His major publications include *Three Faces of Being: Toward an Existential Clinical Psychology* (1970), *Psychology and the New Consciousness* (1972), *Primer in Phenomenological Psychology* (1975), and *Emotion* (with Candland, Fell, Leshner, Plutchik, and Tarpy) (1977).

Misia Landau is Assistant Professor of Anthropology at Boston University. After completing her undergraduate studies in anthropology at the State University of New York at Buffalo (1974), she studied human biology at Oxford University (Diploma, 1975) and anthropology at Yale University (Ph.D., 1981). Among her essays on the narrative aspects of science are "Human evolution as narrative" (1984); "The Baron in the trees: The rule of language in the study of human evolution" (1985); and "Paradise lost: The theme of terrestriality in human evolution" (1985). She is currently writing a book on early twentieth century theories of human evolution with the working title, *Altars to Unknown Gods: Story and Meaning in Science*.

James C. Mancuso is Professor of Psychology and Associate Dean of the School of Social and Behavioral Sciences at the State University of New York at Albany. He received his Ph.D. in 1958 at the University of Rochester. His writings have been focused on elaborating a constructivist theory of personality. His research efforts have been directed toward analyzing cognitive organizations of people as they process information about deviant conduct, reprimand, and parenting practices. His research and scholarly work have led him to the conclusion that a person's processing systems are subordinate to his or her construction of a narrative framework into which every encountered event may be fit. Among his recent books are *The Construing Person* (co-edited with Jack Adams-Webber) (1983), *Schizophrenia: Medical Diagnosis or Moral Verdict* (with Theodore R. Sarbin) (1980). A book on computer assisted assessment of cognitive systems is in progress (Mildred L. B. Shaw, co-editor).

Elliot G. Mishler is Professor of Social Psychology in the Department of Psychiatry at the Harvard Medical School, Chief Psychologist at the Massachusetts Mental Health Center, and Director of the post-doctoral Research Training Program in the Social and Behavioral Sciences. Methodological and theoretical issues in the study of discourse are central topics in his work. He has published many reports of his research on language and communication in families, classrooms, and clinical practice, and is senior author of *Interaction in Families: An Experimental Study of Family Processes and Schizophrenia* (1968) and *Social Contexts of Health, Illness, and Patient Care* (1981). His recent work on interviews and the analysis of narrative accounts is reported in his *The Discourse of Medicine: Dialectics of Medical Interviews* (1984) and in the forthcoming *Context and Discourse in Research Interviews: Perspectives on Practice.*

Kevin Murray has received a bachelor's and a master's degree in psychology from the University of Melbourne. His interest in narratives arose out of a study of middle-aged people who had decided to participate in a marathon for the first time "to say they've done it." This led him to consider the possibility of combining literary criticism and the dramaturgical model in an approach to understanding biography ("Life as fiction," *Journal for the Theory of Social Behavior* (1985). This path currently leads to the nature of comedy in the ritual construction of identity, the cultural relativity of "tragic" biography, and the place of travel in Australian life construction. The latter interest is allied to his involvement in the Melbourne Campanilismo Group the activities of which concern the problems and assets of regionalism in various disciplines.

John A. Robinson is Professor of Psychology at the University of Louisville. He received his Ph.D. at Pennsylvania State University in clinical psychology. He joined the faculty of the University of Louisville in 1964, introducing courses on cognition and the psychology of language. In recent years, he has focused his research on autobiographical memory ("Sampling autobiographical memory," *Cognitive Psychology* (1976); "Temporal reference systems in autobiographical memory," in Rubin, D. (Ed.) *Autobiographical memory* [in press]). His interest in narrative is an outgrowth of reflections on the roles of memory and discourse in the construction of personal histories.

Theodore R. Sarbin is Professor Emeritus of Psychology and Criminology at the University of California, Santa Cruz. He received his Ph.D. in 1941 at the Ohio State University. He served on the faculty of the University of California, Berkeley, from 1949 to 1969. He was a Fulbright Fellow in 1962 (University of Oxford), a Guggenheim Fellow in 1965-66, and several times a Fellow of the Center for the Humanities at Wesleyan University. He was president of Division 30 (Psychological Hypnosis) of the American Psychological Association. He is the author, co-author, or editor of over 175 publications. His current work is in the psychology of self deception, metaphor, social identity, dramatism and dramaturgy, and the narrative. His recent writings include *Studies in Social Identity* (co-edited with Karl E. Scheibe) (1983), *Schizophrenia: Medical Diagnosis or Moral Verdict* (with James C. Mancuso) (1980) and a chapter "Emotions as Situated Actions" in a volume edited by Seymour Wapner (in press).

Karl E. Scheibe is Professor of Psychology at Wesleyan University. He received his B.S. degree from Trinity College in 1959 and his Ph.D. from the University of California, Berkeley, in 1963. He has twice been a Fulbright Fellow to Brazil, teaching at the Catholic University of São Paulo. His publications include the books *Beliefs and Values* (1970) and *Mirrors, Masks, Lies, and Secrets* (1979) as well as the edited volumes *The Social Context of Conduct: Psychological Writings of Theodore Sarbin* (with Vernon L. Allen) (1982) and *Studies in Social Identity* (with Theodore R. Sarbin) (1984). His current research and writing concerns the psychology of human identity.

Donald P. Spence is Professor of Psychiatry at Rutgers Medical School, University of Medicine and Dentistry of New Jersey. He earned his B.A. at Harvard University and his Ph.D. at Columbia. He is a certified practicing psychoanalyst, trained at the New York Psychoanalytic Institute. Before coming to Rutgers, he was professor of psychology at New York University and attached to the Research Center for Mental Health. He is the author of *Narrative Truth and Historical Truth* (1982).

Robert S. Steele is Associate Professor of Psychology and Women's Studies at Wesleyan University. He completed his doctoral studies in psychology at Harvard University in 1973. He has published a number of papers on psychoanalysis and hermeneutics. He is the author of *Freud and Jung: Conflicts of Interpretation* (1982). He has recently co-authored, with Susan Swinney, *Everyday Interpretation* (1985), a feminist critique of academics and popular culture.

Brian Sutton-Smith is Professor of Education at the University of Pennsylvania. He heads the program in Interdisciplinary Studies in Human Development. He also has a joint professorship in the Faculty of Arts and Sciences in the Department of Folklore. He received the Ph.D. in educational psychology from the University of New Zealand in 1954. He has been president of Division 10 of the American Psychological Association (Psychology and the Arts) and president of the Association for the Anthropological Study of Play. His interests are primarily in children's play and games, in children's expressive development in the arts, and more generally in their social development. He is the author, co-author or editor of 20 books and 200 articles. Recent books include *Toys as Culture* (1985), *The Masks of Play* (with D. Kelly-Byrne) (1984), *A History of Children's Play* (1981), and *The Folkstories of Children* (1981).

Frederick Wyatt received his Ph.D. in 1936 from the University of Vienna. He teaches at the Universität Freiburg (West Germany) where he is professor (Honoris Causa), and he has a psychoanalytic practice. He is also professor emeritus of the University of Michigan, having served as Professor and Director of the Psychological Clinic from 1952 to 1974. He has done research and has published on the structure and clinical use of fantasy, psychoanalytic theory of personality, the use of psychoanalysis in literary criticism and history, and theory and technique in psychoanalysis.